APR '98

W9-DHU-848

428.007 M225c

ENTERED SEP - 2 1997

Mainstreaming ESL

Multilingual Matters

The Age Factor in Second Language Acquistion
    D. SINGLETON and Z. LENGYEL (eds)
Approaches to Second Language Acquisition
    R. TOWELL and R. HAWKINS
Asian Teachers in British Schools
    PAUL A.S. GHUMAN
Building Bridges
    MULTILINGUAL RESOURCES FOR CHILDREN PROJECT
Coping with Two Cultures
    PAUL A.S. GHUMAN
Curriculum Related Assessment: Cummins and Bilingual Children
    TONY CLINE and NORAH FREDERICKSON (eds)
Foundations of Bilingual Education and Bilingualism
    COLIN BAKER
Language, Minority Education and Gender
    DAVID CORSON
Language Minority Students in the Mainstream Classroom
    ANGELA L. CARRASQUILLO and VIVIAN RODRIGUEZ
Making Multicultural Education Work
    STEPHEN MAY
Multicultural Child Care
    P. VEDDER, E. BOUWER and T. PELS
A Parents' and Teachers' Guide to Bilingualism
    COLIN BAKER
Teaching Science to Language Minority Students
    JUDITH W. ROSENTHAL
The World in a Classroom
    V. EDWARDS and A. REDFERN
Working with Bilingual Children
    M.K. VERMA, K.P. CORRIGAN and S. FIRTH (eds)

Please contact us for the latest book information:
Multilingual Matters Ltd, Frankfurt Lodge, Clevedon Hall,
Victoria Road, Clevedon BS21 7SJ, UK

Mainstreaming ESL

Case Studies in Integrating ESL Students
into the Mainstream Curriculum

Edited by
John Clegg

MULTILINGUAL MATTERS LTD
Clevedon • Philadelphia • Adelaide •Toronto • Johannesburg

COLUMBIA COLLEGE LIBRARY
600 S. MICHIGAN AVENUE
CHICAGO, IL 60605

428.007 M225c

Mainstreaming ESL

Library of Congress Cataloging in Publication Data

Mainstreaming ESL: Case Studies in Integrating ESL Students into the
Mainstream Curriculum/Edited by John Clegg
1. English language–Study and teaching–Foreign speakers–Case studies.
2. English language–Study and teaching–United States–Case studies.
3. Mainstreaming in education–United States–Case studies. I. Clegg, John.
PE1128.A2M315   1996
428'.007–dc20   96-11904

British Library Cataloguing in Publication Data

A CIP catalogue record for this book is available from the British Library.

ISBN 1-85359-349-4 (hbk)
ISBN 1-85359-348-6 (pbk)

Multilingual Matters Ltd

UK: Frankfurt Lodge, Clevedon Hall, Victoria Road, Clevedon BS21 7SJ.
USA: 1900 Frost Road, Suite 101, Bristol, PA 19007, USA.
Canada: OISE, 712 Gordon Baker Road, Toronto, Ontario, Canada M2H 3RT.
Australia: P.O. Box 6025, 95 Gilles Street, Adelaide, SA 5000, Australia.
South Africa: PO Box 1080, Northcliffe 2115, Johannesburg, South Africa.

Copyright © 1996 John Clegg and the authors of individual chapters.

All rights reserved. No part of this work may be reproduced in any form or by
any means without permission in writing from the publisher.

Typeset by Bookcraft, Stroud, Glos.
Printed and bound in Great Britain by WBC Book Manufacturers Ltd.

Contents

Preface

In the spring of 1992, seven of the authors of this book met at the TESOL Convention in Vancouver to present a colloquium on teaching ESL students in the mainstream curriculum. There were two teachers, one primary and one secondary, from Australia, Canada and the UK, and myself as convenor. I had wanted for a long time to get teachers from different parts of the world to talk at TESOL about their work in mainstreaming ESL. With help from Chris Davison of Melbourne University and Joyce Rogers, Coordinator for ESL/ESD at the Toronto School Board, we assembled our Vancouver panel. When it came to the idea of publication, we felt the lack of representatives from the USA, and were helped by Keith Buchanan, Jean Handscombe and Katharine Davies Samway to make contact with our two American contributors. Finally, we felt that it would not be right to publish a book on language and content without a contribution from the Vancouver School Board, where such influential work has been done: hence our tenth author.

I would like to acknowledge the generous support of the British Council and Multilingual Matters. I am also very grateful to Cressida Jupp, Constant Leung and Manny Vazquez for their comments on the introduction.

John Clegg

Contributors

Sharon Bergquist-Moody is an elementary teacher in Portland, Oregon. She received her BA from North Park College in Chicago, Illinois. She has taught for 12 years, the last nine in a school with many second-language learners. She is married and has two grown children.

John Clegg is a Principal Lecturer at the School of English Language Teaching, Thames Valley University, London, England. He has worked there for 20 years, specialising in teacher-education for both ESL contexts in UK schools and in English-medium education systems in Africa.

Ruth Evans has had extensive teaching experience in Australia and overseas both at the post-primary and tertiary levels. Her work on the Topic Approach to ESL was done whilst teaching at an intensive English Language Centre in Melbourne, Australia. At present she is lecturing in English for Academic Purposes in an undergraduate programme at the Royal Melbourne Institute of Technology. She is well known for her work on Content Based Language Instruction and is the co-author of a series of ESL Topic Books in science and social sciences.

Anne Filson came to English-as-a-Second-Language teaching via a Bachelor degree in geology and a Master degree in library science. While working as a librarian, she began to specialise in geography and cultural studies and, wanting her 'own' students, sought certification in ESL. She teaches high school ESL happily in Virginia.

Hugh R. Hooper is responsible for the development and coordination of ESL Programmes K-12 for the Vancouver School Board. Hugh has been involved in the field of ESL as a teacher, department head, consultant, sessional lecturer, author and administrator over the past 18 years. His areas of interest include teacher development and learning organisations.

Cressida Jupp has worked with pupils learning English as an additional language in West London primary schools for most of her teaching career. She is currently a member of the London Borough of Hounslow Language Service. As well as teaching, she is also involved in in-service training, and is particularly interested in the writing development of pupils who are learning to write in their second language.

Nancy Kitegawa has taught for 23 years with the Toronto Board of Education and teaches at present at Rose Avenue Junior School. The works of James Britton and Myra Barrs have profoundly influenced her teaching. Later the studies of Jim Cummins shaped her thinking as an ESL teacher. Over the years she has given many presentations of her experience in working collaboratively with classroom teachers to support ESL students within the mainstream.

Ross McKean has been a teacher with the Toronto Board of Education for the past 14 years. During that time he has taught English and History to ESL and native Canadian students at Jarvis Collegiate Institute and City Adult Learning Centre.

Elina Raso's teaching experience has been as a classroom teacher, a LOTE teacher (Italian), an ESL teacher in mainstream classrooms and as a new arrivals teacher. She is co-author of *About Teaching Languages*, a professional development package for teachers. Her current responsibilities at the Catholic Education Office, Melbourne, include the coordination of ESL provision and support services to Catholic schools.

Julie Reid is currently a vice-principal with the Toronto Board of Education and an instructional leader in York University's 'Becoming a Leader in ESL' programme for teachers. Her doctoral studies which focused on the role of the school principal in teachers' on-the-job learning coincided with and strongly influenced her work at Rose Avenue school in helping to make ESL an integral part of every teacher's programme.

Manny Vazquez has worked as an English Language development teacher alongside mainstream colleagues for 16 years. Most of his work and publications have been in the area of language/content integration in mainstream science classrooms. He is currently Deputy Head of Service (Secondary) of the Language Team in the London Borough of Hounslow, with main responsibility for in-service training.

L. Westbrook has worked with language minority children for 10 years as a Spanish-English bilingual classroom teacher and as an ESL specialist. She is currently an elementary teacher in Portland, Oregon. She has an MAT in ESL from the School for International Training in Brattleboro, Vermont.

Introduction

JOHN CLEGG

This book is about educating the children of ethnolinguistic minorities in four countries of the industrialised world. It documents how the schooling of young developing bilinguals is shifting its location from somewhere beyond the bounds of regular school into the mainstream of classroom and curriculum.

The shift in location is a surface manifestation of a fundamental change in philosophy and policy. To carry it through may not be an easy thing for a school to do. As the education of ESL learners merges increasingly with mainstream education, both ESL and mainstream teachers need guidance in accommodating the language needs of pupils who do not have fluent command of the medium of instruction, and in giving them the fullest possible access to the curriculum. The purpose of the book is to provide such guidance through the narratives of practising teachers. In doing so, we will pay close attention to pedagogical detail. Without an interest in classroom practice, mainstreaming policy tends to remain purely exhortative. When applied, it fails to work, becomes discredited and ESL pupils suffer. In addition, teaching ESL learners in mainstream classes is not something which comes naturally to many teachers, especially in upper primary and secondary classrooms: it requires a set of specific adjustments to mainstream practice, and teachers who want to make it work need support of a fairly exact kind in order to do so.

1. Different Countries, Different Contexts

The contexts described in this book differ considerably from one another in many respects. There are variations both between and within countries. Australia, Canada, the USA and the UK are all linguistically and culturally diverse societies, but the diversity is differently constituted. It may comprehend indigenous groups, powerful ethnic (often colonising) majorities, and more recent immigrant communities. The current language minority groups taught by the authors are mainly recent or second- and

1

third-generation immigrants. They come from a wide variety of countries, have differing reasons for immigration, speak a range of languages, wield greater or lesser societal influence, represent varying social classes and educational backgrounds (from the highly educated to the illiterate), and are present in schools in numbers varying from very small to very large. The UK authors, for example, teach in communities into which immigration, much of it from former colonies in the Indian subcontinent, was at its highest in the 1950s and 1960s, but has now greatly slowed down. Children may speak a minority language at home, but quickly learn English as they move through pre-school education into the primary school. Thus in a classroom where the large majority may be bilingual, an ESL teacher may be supporting a relatively small number of children with marked English language needs. In the context of the Canadian contributors, by contrast, recent and current levels of immigration may be extremely high, resulting in classrooms where the proportion of children who are insufficiently fluent in English is at 60% or above. Cummins (1994) reports predicted minority enrolments for the year 2001 in parts of the United States school system at between 70 to 96%.

What these contexts have in common is what forms the focus of the book: children who speak a home or community language which is different from the medium of school instruction. For them, coming to school means entering a new culture, learning a new language and – most significantly – learning to use it for the purposes of cognitive and academic as well as social development. It may also mean learning to face prejudice and experience powerlessness, and perhaps embarking on the process of losing fluency in the language of the home.

In all four countries, it has historically been customary to teach such children in forms of educational provision which are separate from mainstream schooling. These forms of provision can be roughly characterised as follows: ESL learners are separated from their English native-speaking classmates and taught outside the mainstream classroom in 'withdrawal' or 'pull-out' classes or in on- or off-site centres. Such classes also tend to separate language from content in that learners follow a mainly (English) language-led curriculum. This provision either precedes mainstream schooling, in that students delay joining the mainstream classroom until they are considered fluent enough to do so; or (as in most cases) it runs concurrently with mainstream education, providing students with a part-separate, part-integrated timetable until they are considered ready to be fully mainstreamed.

Originally teaching in these separate classes was based on a structural model of language and an audiolingual model of teaching relying much on controlled input and practice; later, a communicative and curriculum-related model developed. Separate provision – in either full- or part-time form – can last for a matter of weeks or even years. Teachers are often ESL specialists with a greater or lesser degree of specialist training and their status, along with that of their pupils, has tended to be lower than that of their mainstream colleagues. It has often been commented that the underlying premise of such teaching is that the child's lack of fluency in English is a deficiency which must be remedied before she is allowed to play her full part in the school. The child must change to suit the school, not vice versa.

2. The Objectives of Minority Education

This approach to the education of language minority students has often been a diminishing experience, not only for the students themselves and for their academic and social development, but also for the way in which the educational establishment has come to conceptualise ESL learners as a whole. Because ESL students have specialised language needs which majority students may not share, we have come, by this bizarre process of reductionism, to regard these needs as paramount. What should be seen as an educational enterprise has been reduced to a merely linguistic one. By this token, minority children are often seen to be the responsibility not of the whole school, but only of language teachers; similarly, language, culture and race are not issues to be faced by the school as a community, but problems to be contained within the confines of specialist classrooms. When we define objectives, we talk not about academic achievement, but only about communicative competence.

The authors in this book want to avoid this 'reductionist' tendency. The idea of mainstreaming recognises the broader educational purpose of school: language minority learners are in school for the same reasons as all other learners. The main point of their learning English as an additional language is so that they can use it for their cognitive, academic and curricular development. Personal and social needs are also clearly vital; but if we over-emphasise the social domain at the expense of the academic, we are in danger of devaluing our work (Harklau, 1994), and of shortchanging our students (Saville-Troike, 1988).

This is not to obscure the real distinctions between language minority and language majority students. ESL learners do indeed suffer more from discrimination and have the double burden of learning both curricular contents and the medium of instruction. What it does mean is that we must cease to confine responsibility for policy and practice in minority education to a small corner of the educational establishment.

One consequence of this is that we will need to re-examine our traditional view of objectives for ESL learners. Our descriptions of competence must look different (Leung, 1995). True, they must contain statements of communicative ability on models such as those which Canale and Swain (1980), for example, have provided. But they must also show the cognitive and academic uses to which this ability is put. We will then be able to use these objectives to monitor not only a child's language development, but also her learning progress across the curriculum, and hopefully they will compel us to recognise our responsibility for the latter as well as the former. Competence descriptions of this kind are thin on the ground, but there is compelling academic work which links communicative and academic competence (Collier, 1994); there are ESL-mainstream bridging programmes which highlight cognitive development (Chamot & O'Malley, 1989) and we have seen the emergence in Australia (Curriculum Corporation, 1994, Leung, 1995) of scales of communicative and academic attainment which can be used to cross-reference ESL practice to the conventional curriculum.

The 'reductionist' tendency has a further consequence of which we in the ESL community are guilty: in classifying ESL learners as having primarily linguistic needs, we tend to treat them as if they were all the same. Our experience, of course, as well as educational and second language acquisition (SLA) theory (Skehan, 1986), tells us that like all other human beings they vary along several dimensions.

ESL learners, especially recent immigrants, differ, for instance, in the prior experience of school-based learning which they bring to second language-medium education. Some are literate in their mother-tongue; others are not. Some have experience of the types of activity and discourse which are peculiar to schooling; others find this alien. Some will have considerable experience of parts of the school curriculum; for others this will be new. ESL learners also vary in confidence and self-esteem. This may happen because they are unable, for instance, to use the language of the environment, or because the school may give no recognition to their own linguistic and cultural identity, or if they suffer from outright racist abuse.

Some differences are important in SLA terms. One such dimension is the learner's enthusiasm for social interaction. Children differ in their social orientation: some love talking to each other; some prefer to listen and analyse. Wong Fillmore (1979) proposes that this may be partly culturally determined. The learning preferences of girls as opposed to boys are also reflected in the SLA literature as a tendency in mixed-sex non-native-speaker groups for males to generate more comprehensible output and for females to generate more comprehensible input (Gass & Varonis, 1986). Another key variable is the learner's ability to develop her second language skills by using cognitive capacities, such as attending to pattern in input, or to use deductive and inductive reasoning in the search for meaning (Skehan, 1986), and metacognitive skills such as the planning, monitoring and evaluation of learning (Rubin, 1987).

We may draw two conclusions from this variability. Firstly, differences between ESL learners are considerable and complex, and a school cannot make blanket decisions about them; it must decide on a case-by-case basis. Secondly, what distinguishes students within the 'ESL' category is often greater than what distinguishes them from 'native-speakers'. Further evidence, therefore, for the chief message of this book, which is that we should see ESL learners as full members of the school community, who have specific learning needs, rather than as a separate group who must prove themselves linguistically before they can claim their full entitlement.

3. The Rationale Behind Mainstreaming

The shift towards mainstreaming has been motivated by our contemporary understanding of the sociopolitical, psychological, academic and pedagogical needs of language minority pupils. When we look at these needs carefully, the argument that they can only be fulfilled through mainstream education becomes compelling. In the following section I will list these needs. For each category of need, I will outline the case for mainstreaming. I will not enter in detail into the debate which may surround these issues. For this, the interested reader is referred to key sources.

Two things should be said in advance about this list of needs: firstly, it is longer than the needs descriptions which we normally use in ESL; secondly, its categories are very similar to a needs description which one might draw up for the education of native-speakers of English. In other words, it reflects the view that we should see ESL learners as less 'different'.

Equal opportunity needs

Language minority children need equality of educational opportunity. This means that they need to share the same rights within the school, which language majority children and their parents take for granted. These include:

- the right to study the full curriculum;
- the right to achieve a high level of proficiency in English;
- the right to fairness of treatment in assessment and in any streaming/banding arrangements;
- the right to use the mother-tongue in learning;
- the right to learn in a context which accepts and reflects the home culture;
- the right to protection from discrimination;
- the right to play a full role in the life of the school.

The main 'equity' argument for mainstreaming is that separate provision, it is claimed, is discriminatory in effect if not in intent. As McKay and Freedman (1990) note, this political perspective has driven mainstreaming more powerfully in some countries than in others: indeed in the history of ESL in the USA the pursuit of equal treatment in education led rather to the establishment and maintenance of separate provision than to its demise. In the UK, by contrast, mainstreaming policies spread rapidly through education authorities in the 1980s once the Commission for Racial Equality had declared separate provision in one education authority discriminatory (CRE, 1986) and a government report endorsed this (DES, 1985). Arguments in support of this latter view include the following:

(a) Separate provision does not offer to ESL learners the breadth of curriculum to which they are legally entitled.

(b) It can split ESL learners off from their English-fluent peers, affect their sense of belonging within the school and prevent them from taking their rightful place in mainstream school life.

(c) It may stigmatise the education of ethnic minorities.

(d) It works against the mission of the school to challenge racism through whole-school policy; indeed it may reinforce divisions which exist in the wider society.

(e) It can delay the education of ESL learners to a degree which constitutes an injustice.

Community needs

What parents want for their children is a powerful determinant of those children's educational success. Parents in minority language communities need to benefit from the same kinds of influence over the school as those in majority communities.

They need:

- to enjoy the full range of channels of communication with the school in a language they understand;
- normal access to positions of influence in the school such as parent-teacher associations and governing bodies;
- to feel that the school is responsive to the particular needs of their children.

Although schools need strong links with the minority communities which they serve, it is not clear whether separate provision encourages or constrains this cooperation. It is often, for example, the dedicated ESL teacher in a withdrawal class, taking upon herself the responsibility of making contact with parents, who finds the energy to build contacts with the minority community. On the other hand, it is probable that in such cases it is not the whole school, but only the withdrawal class which is showing responsiveness. A school which integrates its ESL learners is more likely to gain a pervasive institutional understanding of its responsibilities to minority communities.

Academic needs

Here, we are concerned with what is perhaps the most fundamental need of ESL learners, which is to get a school education. For the language majority, as we have already seen, cognitive and academic needs are what we often assume school to be about. For ESL children, however, these needs tend to be concealed by the overemphasis of language requirements. They include:

- access to the full curriculum (mentioned above);
- teaching which is cognitively challenging;
- teaching which takes into account learners' prior academic and cognitive achievements;
- teaching which aims at developing their facility in 'language for learning' or what Cummins (1984) calls 'cognitive academic language proficiency' (CALP).

ESL learners share with English-fluent learners the need to develop cognitively and academically, and the need to deploy a special cognitive/academic variety of language in order to do so. ESL learners differ only in that they need to develop this facility in their second language. Learning curricular contents and learning the language which is the vehicle for this, are, it is claimed, best done concurrently and in the mainstream classroom. I set out four related arguments in support of this proposition.

(a) One cannot separate language from learning. In this respect the mainstream teacher with a language-impoverished teaching style is as pedagogically limited as the ESL teacher cut off from the mainstream curriculum. In a withdrawal class or in forms of bridging provision, an ESL learner can be *prepared* for studying a subject. But ultimately the only way in which a student can learn to meet the cognitive and linguistic demands which a subject makes is by studying it in the mainstream classroom.

(b) Separate provision tends to be thought of as an easy option. Although this is often unjustified, even the most curriculum-orientated withdrawal classroom will not be able to provide the same intellectual challenge as a hands-on encounter with a curricular subject. Many ESL teachers are aware of this and many ESL students complain about it (Harklau, 1994).

(c) Separate provision cannot easily take into account the prior learning of ESL students. It may properly claim to do this for those with low levels of English, L1 literacy and curricular content knowledge; but it often fails the student who has limited English proficiency, but considerable prior academic achievements (which may be unrecorded and over-looked). For her, the ESL class can be especially undemanding.

(d) It takes a long time for ESL learners to catch up with their English-fluent peers (Collier, 1994; Cummins, 1984). Both research and practical experience tell us that a long-term commitment (of 5–7 years) is needed. Thus even if we argue for delaying a child's entry to mainstream education in the short-term at the start of this period, much of her ESL development will take place in integrated contexts. Although much of our formal provision tends to focus understandably on early and acute needs, we have to take a longer view if ESL learners are to achieve their full potential. The longer view of necessity means supporting ESL learners in the mainstream curriculum.

Personal and social needs

These needs derive partly but not wholly from the student's status with respect to the distribution of power and rights within the school. If, for instance, an ESL learner is denied rights, or suffers racist abuse, or is made to feel bad about her ethnolinguistic identity, this can have a major impact on her personal and social development. Like the English native-speaker, she needs to feel that the school:

- recognises her cultural and linguistic identity;
- is committed to to her emotional and social development;
- has the highest possible expectations of her.

There is plenty of evidence which shows that language minority children can suffer from personal and institutional racism in school; that their linguistic and cultural identities can be undermined; that teachers can harbour low expectations of them (Wright, 1985); that cultural incongruity in patterns of interaction and social behaviour between home and school can disadvantage them (Erickson, 1984); and that these injuries can cause damage to their personal and social development and to their academic success. To see how these things happen, we must look at individual circumstances; but that they do happen is well attested (Trueba, 1989).

Whether mainstream or separate provision fosters or counters such influences is unclear; it is also a question which can only be answered by studying particular cases. There is good evidence, for example, for the view of the withdrawal class as 'haven': the place in the school which acts as a buffer to culture-shock, refuge from racist abuse, and comprehensible language environment; and the ESL teacher as preserver of cultural and linguistic identities, support for self-esteem, and source of high expectations. In this view, it is in the mainstream school where damage can be done. Much must be said in many schools for the value of such a withdrawal facility on a temporary basis. On the other hand, as we have said, a child's personal, cultural and linguistic identity is a whole-school responsibility and the longer ESL teachers cling to their protective roles, the longer they may delay the institution as a whole from accepting it. If, in addition, the school ethos stigmatises separate provision, which even the most progressive institutions may subtly do, then separation must be seen as damaging to a child's identity. In the matter of the child's social development, it is undoubtedly true that separate provision may prevent a child from mixing socially with language majority children and that this may not only affect her personal development, but also severely constrain her second language learning (Cummins, 1994).

Language-learning needs

The main need which sets ESL learners apart from their language majority peers in school is that they have two jobs where their peers may only have one: they are learning not only the curriculum, but also the medium of instruction. Thus they need a school environment which enables them:

- to develop communicative and academic competence in the medium of instruction;
- to allow this competence to develop interactively and concurrently with the acquisition of academic knowledge and skills.

Much of the support for mainstreaming derives from claims that separate provision is not the best environment in which to learn a second language. Here again, several related and persuasive arguments are deployed.

(a) What ESL learners are entitled to is the best available environment for language and cognitive development. Given the language-rich, child-centred quality of kindergarten and primary practice in all the countries represented in this book, there is little doubt that in the early years of schooling, the mainstream classroom forms the best basis for this. Upper primary and secondary classrooms (see Section 5) may be much less obviously facilitative of language development and considerable support for the ESL learner and adjustments to mainstream practice may be required.

(b) Language is learned best at the point of communicative need and in the service of other learning. The study of mainstream curricular subjects is an obvious source of such communicative needs and its potential for language development should be fully exploited.

(c) Separate provision presents a paradox. On the one hand it splits the ESL learner off from the mainstream curriculum because she does not speak the medium of instruction well enough to study it. On the other, as most contemporary programmes see their role as preparation for mainstream learning, separation uses the sheltered language context of the withdrawal class to recreate a version of mainstream contents and thus bring learner and curriculum back together again. While good reasons can be found to justify this, it presents a central contradiction which often strains the credibility of the practice: why go to the trouble of artificially recreating the mainstream classroom when the real thing is available next door? As with all forms of 'service' teaching, there is a limit to how far we can go to meet a learner's mainstream language needs outside the mainstream.

(d) Most withdrawal classes are basically language classes. There are exceptions, such as sheltered subject classes and pre-mainstream content classes, both of which feature in this book. In the main, however, even ESL specialists who orientate their withdrawal language work as far as they can to the mainstream curriculum know that there is a limit to the level of detail they can achieve in subject study. Outside sheltered and pre-mainstream classes, most ESL teachers conduct their curriculum-orientated work at a low-to-middle level of subject-specificity; the limits of their own subject expertise and the language-development priorities of the ESL class determine this. In addition, certain significant chunks of school language are subject-specific. This 'content-obligatory' language (Snow *et al.*, 1989) is difficult to teach in separate provision.

(e) Although ESL teachers quite properly set out to teach the social as well as the academic uses of language, students' social fluency usually develops, as we have noted, through interaction with English-fluent peers, often without teacher intervention. Mainstream provision maintains this socially and linguistically important contact; separate provision can cut it off. The other side of this coin is the argument that the peer-input of learner-English which an ESL learner gets in an ESL class may not be best suited to her target language development.

(f) Finally, telling new research is claiming that, measured against its own language-learning objectives, separate provision does not work – at least not as well as it should. Collier (1994) reports that in a comparison between the academic achievements of students in 'ESL-only', 'early exit bilingual', 'late-exit bilingual' and 'two-way bilingual' programmes in the USA, 'ESL-only' or withdrawal programmes score worst. While we should be wary of applying this finding to the vast multiplicity of separate ESL provision in the countries represented in this book, it is nevertheless one which will ring a bell with a lot of ESL teachers.

So far we have derived our arguments for mainstreaming from a consideration of the needs of ESL learners. It would be wrong, however, to make the case solely on this basis. It is important also to argue the benefits to the school as a whole. In this view, separate provision impoverishes mainstream schooling. Monocultural schools, in other words, which find it difficult, as Cummins (1994) puts it, to 'amplify' the linguistic and cultural experiences which minority children bring with them, are likely ultimately to be the losers. The main arguments in favour of this view are as follows:

(a) Schools in the multicultural, multilingual societies represented in this book need to ensure that all children, not just the dominant group, find their language and culture reflected in the curriculum and in their physical surroundings. The business of school is to *add* English language and culture to a minority child's world, not to *subtract* her home language and culture. Separate provision may reinforce monoculturalism.

(b) Separate provision removes from the mainstream teacher the responsibility for the education of a group of learners for whom the school is not adequately equipped. The school is charged with the duty to take account of the linguistic, cultural needs of all its pupils, as well as securing their freedom from discrimination. To discharge this duty is a whole-school responsibility to be shared by all staff. To recognise this and undertake the institutional changes which it may require, is ultimately rewarding but initially difficult. Many teachers will prefer to preserve the *status quo* and separate provision may help them to do that.

(c) It is by now a commonplace in ESL work that the language-rich diet of an ESL group can turn out to be nourishing for the whole mainstream class. It can help all the children use language for learning in ways which were not previously available to them. Mainstream teachers who enter into a framework of language support are often quick to recognise this. In this sense, ESL work is recognisable as only part of a wider reorientation to the role of language in the curriculum which is visible in the theory and practice of schooling generally in all our four contexts (Corson, 1990).

On the face of it, these seem to be telling points. Their chief weakness is that they often say what is wrong with separate provision rather than what is right about mainstreaming. In this sense they deal in issues of principle, rather than the lived reality of classroom experience: they address what could and should happen to ESL learners in mainstream classrooms, rather than what actually does. In reality we all know that many mainstream classrooms can be harsh places for second language learners: many education authorities may indeed not permit ESL students to be 'submerged' in them. We need, therefore, to look closely at the real mainstream environment and assess the extent to which it needs adapting if ESL learners are to flourish in it. Before dealing in reality, however, it will be useful to consult our ideals: ESL teachers know how they would *like* mainstream classrooms to be in order to to facilitate the education of ESL learners. In the following section, we will look at what our experience of practice and our knowledge of theory tell us about this ideal 'facilitating environment'.

4. Second-Language Learners and the Facilitating Environment

We can nowadays call on plenty of evidence from professional good practice and from research about what constitutes an environment which facilitates academic development and second language acquisition in second language learners. We should be able to agree that this idealised 'facilitating environment' has certain key features. A list of these features would help us to measure the appropriateness of any given form of provision for ESL learners. In what follows I propose some of the core features of such a list; note that we are not talking solely about what helps a child learn a second language, but about what helps her use it for school learning – to develop cognitively, academically, personally and socially. We will look first at the wider school environment, focusing on matters of school policy, community links, mother-tongue use and cross-curricular language development. We will then turn to classroom processes and draw considerably on second language-learning theory and practice.

(a) The wider school environment

School policy

We should emphasise at the outset that the 'facilitating environment' is greater than the classroom. If we restrict discussion to the classroom, we are again in danger of subscribing to the 'reductionist' tendency. In practice, it does not help an ESL child if good minority education stops at the ESL classroom door. ESL learners, as we have already noted, spend most of their school careers outside any form of special ESL provision and their needs pervade the curriculum, especially in schools with majorities of ESL users. L2-medium learning is thus a whole-school matter.

The same is even more true of multicultural and anti-racist education. Good minority education is built on multicultural and anti-racist foundations. A good school recognises that racism and cultural exclusiveness can operate across the institution both through interpersonal behaviour and institutional practices, and the school works hard to counteract them. Thus our facilitating environment is one in which the school acknowledges that language, culture and racial justice may raise serious issues which are difficult to deal with, but that they are matters which the school as a community must have the courage to face.

In addition, these issues raise a practical question of the management of change. Changing people's minds about language, race and culture means affecting deep-seated attitudes and ingrained habits. There is no short cut to this goal: we are involved in a long march through the institutions. We therefore have to pay special attention to top-down, institution-wide, policy-led processes. These are management functions, to be exercised within a consensual framework. However important it is to act locally in the classroom, our efforts may be fruitless if we do not also act institutionally (Bourne, 1989).

Community

To continue the theme of the larger picture, the educational environment goes not only beyond the classroom door, but beyond the school gate. Whether an ESL student flourishes in school depends very much on the relation the school maintains with her parents and their community. We have been aware for several decades that parental aspiration is a key indicator of educational achievement. More recently, we have become persuaded that partnerships of different kinds between school and parents can also exert a powerful influence on how well a child learns. There is evidence for this especially in the area of reading development (Tizard *et al.*, 1982). For similar reasons, we know that cooperation with parents in the language minority community benefits the education of ESL learners (Pease-Alvarez & Vasquez, 1994). Equally, we know that unless efforts are made to build up this cooperation, such parents may find communicating with the school difficult; their confidence in dealing with teachers may be low, and they may feel unable to take full advantage of statutory powers to influence the school. Thus a school which values and strengthens its roots in the minority community is one in which minority children have a chance to achieve.

L1 use and status

While dominant language groups take it as axiomatic that their first language is fundamental to their children's education, ethnolinguistic minorities often have to fight for this to be recognised. In the communities with which this book is concerned, they do not always find ready allies amongst ESL professionals, who are apt to forget that their learners' first language is one of the main aspects of a facilitating school environment for ESL users. Research supports practical experience in suggesting that a student's L1 is a vehicle not only for personal and social identity and experience of the speech community, but also for early cognitive development (Cummins, 1994), later academic achievement (Collier, 1994) and later SLA capacity (Cummins & Swain, 1986).

The debate about the place of L1 in the education of minority children is large and complex. Proponents of L1 in minority education take any of a spectrum of policy positions on the issue, ranging from strong views of bilingual education to weak views of minor support for the mother-tongue as an aid to the transition to English fluency in the classroom. There is a rich body of practice available for any of these positions. The contributors to this book represent countries in which fully-fledged bilingual programmes are common (such as the USA), as well as those which are extremely reluctant to countenance them (such as the UK). They also represent local contexts in which there are large concentrations of speakers of one mother-tongue, as well as those in which the number of languages is too large to make bilingual education an easy option. The whole issue has wide-ranging implications for the organisation of minority education, and there is room in this book only to hint at it; suffice it to say that L1-use must be a basis for ESL policy rather than simply an adjunct to it.

Support for academic and cognitive development

Language is a primary vehicle for cognitive development. Teachers (especially in the secondary school) are often reluctant to acknowledge this: they see themselves as teaching 'contents', thus attempting to split off language from learning and leave it to a more competent colleague. 'Constructivist' educational theory, on the other hand (Mercer, 1995; Wells & Chang-Wells, 1992), as well as a good deal of practical classroom experience, suggests that it is useful to look at the learning of a particular subject from the viewpoint of the linguistic and cognitive processes which constitute it.

Linking language and content is even more important for the education of second language learners. From the viewpoint of academic development, an ESL learner needs to develop the capacity to use the second language for learning; that is, she needs to be fluent in cognitive academic language proficiency. Similarly, from the language-learning viewpoint it is a good thing (Met, 1994) to harness acquisition to the primary message of communication – which in school is the curriculum. Thus, the facilitating environment in this sense is one in which the curriculum is the hook on which to hang language development and vice versa.

This has implications for both the management and pedagogy of provision for ESL learners. Managerially, it means that the school needs to find ways of bringing together the second-language and the academic development of ESL learners under one roof. Pedagogically, it means that teachers need to find ways of linking language and academic work which are successful and user-friendly.

(b) The classroom environment

Ethos and atmosphere

Students work better in a warm, encouraging atmosphere, in which teachers respond to them supportively within firm pedagogical boundaries. This is hardly peculiar to ESL learners, but within the minority education debate it takes on additional significance, in that a school in which minority groups flourish, recognises and values linguistic and cultural diversity and challenges racism (Cummins, 1988). This will be visible both in the declared policy of the school and in the finer detail of classroom relationships, materials and display. In narrower SLA terms, the question of atmosphere emerges in Krashen's (1981) concept of the 'affective filter' which proposes that learners absorb and process comprehensible language input better when they are in circumstances in which they feel comfortable.

Language input characteristics

A good environment for ESL learners provides language input of the kind that helps students to learn the language. An important source of this input is in teacher-talk which is roughly-tuned to learners' needs and which manifests the kinds of modifications which make it comprehensible (Ellis, 1985). Experiential evidence from ESL teachers (Mouneimne, 1988) highlights in particular the usefulness to learners of teacher-talk which displays normal redundancy features such as repetitions, explanations, examples and clear boundary markers, and which is also interactive and visually supported. SLA research also points to features of teacher-talk such as careful questioning and corrective feedback, a degree of pattern within natural language use (Wong Fillmore, 1985) and the encouragement of pupils' extended utterances (Ellis, 1992).

English-fluent peers are an equally – if not more – important source of language input. Interaction with them is a most powerful influence on ESL students' social fluency (Cummins, 1994). This makes normal social interaction between ESL learners and fluent users of English both inside and outside the classroom a key ingredient in the facilitating environment. Within the classroom such interaction can be encouraged by the teacher. Within the school as a whole, school policy should do its best to engineer it.

Interactional forms

Facilitative teacher-talk needs to be balanced by facilitative small-group talk. Small-group talk can have particular, measurable SLA benefits. Interactional modifications to discourse, made by interlocutors as they negotiate meaning (Long, 1983), are said to be useful to second language development; and these are claimed to be more readily generated in small groups than in the canonical discourse patterns of the teacher-controlled classroom (Long & Porter, 1985). Swain (1985) suggests that small group talk encourages language learners to extend their interlanguage boundaries. This accords with the thinking of language-in-education theorists (Barnes, 1975; Wells & Chang-Wells, 1992) that exploratory small-group talk can be particularly valuable to the development of concepts and curricular knowledge. Studies both in second language task-based learning (Skehan, 1992) and in L1-medium education (Barnes & Todd, 1977) warn us, however, that these benefits are only available through careful structuring of the task.

'Embeddedness' in discourse

Most ESL practitioners also know that they need to pay attention to the 'embeddedness' of communication. This concept refers to the range of ways in which the meaning of an utterance can be supported by its context. Early L2 learners rely on retrieving meaning from other sources than solely the utterance: the more the meaning is distributed across visual and other contextual sources, the more mental processing capacity is available to focus on the unfamiliar target language. As they become more proficient, learners rely less and less on contextual props and more and more on the elements of the utterance itself. Thus the facilitating environment for ESL users manifests a variety of forms of contextual embeddedness: a focus on real objects in the here-and-now; the use of visual support of all kinds; involvement in manipulative activity; the full range of gestural and paralinguistic cues available in face-to-face interaction; known concepts and, especially with ESL learners, contents which are culturally familiar. Cummins (1984), in particular, uses the dimensions of context-embeddedness and cognitive involvement to show how ESL learners need to move from a relatively painlessly acquired ability to function in context-embedded situations, to much more demanding proficiency in the context-reduced and cognitively demanding situations characteristic of schooling, especially at the secondary level.

Task and task sequence

At the heart of the facilitating environment is the task. This is where we need to look to see whether a child is or is not learning. In L1-medium schooling, with our minds more on content and outcome, we tend to neglect the fine detail of tasks: we simply ask pupils to do them without looking at the language and learning skills they might require. Faced with the extra complexity of an ESL learner's job, it is necessary to pay extra attention to task design. Thus ESL teachers sift carefully through their repertoires of language support activities to find one which fits the language demands of the task, meets the conceptual requirements of the subject matter, gives pupils access to the task at their level of language ability and makes clear for them what they have to do. Teachers also need to compose groups not only to get some constructive, purposeful engagement, but to ensure that ESL learners can get support from their peers and, where possible, take initiatives. The ESL task repertoire constitutes a body of very practical achievements. It is reinforced by SLA thinking: Wong Fillmore (1985), for instance, stresses the importance of clarity and consistency in task sequence; and task-based learning emphasises the need for pupils to be able to check and adjust their language in meaningful interaction, and to force the pace of interlanguage development (Skehan, 1992).

Support for language skills development

School learning tasks make complex language demands on pupils. When we analyse these we see that to perform the simplest of activities, a child must not only attend to complex conceptual contents, but also deploy an array of language skills – grammatical, lexical, phonological, functional, discourse, stylistic and so on – in order to process those contents. Pupils who are learning a second language cannot do all this without support. Language support tasks are of course the bread and butter of the language teacher. Their function is to supply to the learner a lot of the language data necessary to carry out a communicative task, thus freeing mental capacity to permit her to concentrate on making a few selected language choices for herself. Language teachers have a regular repertoire of support tasks for listening, speaking, reading and writing. In the facilitating ESL environment, this repertoire is extended to apply across the curriculum, to be appropriate to specific subjects, and to encompass information and study skills. Importantly for the message of this book, some ESL teachers maintain that there are areas of language skill for which many ESL learners will always need specialist support, such as grammatical development (Davison, 1995).

What we have here is a picture of what teachers and researchers might agree to be the main ingredients of an environment which would best foster the linguistic and academic development of ESL learners. It is obviously an ideal picture. It is also looks like a tall order. Schools which wish to do the right thing by their ESL learners should, it seems, pursue language, multicultural and anti-racist policies; strengthen their community ties; foster L1-medium learning; link language with the curriculum; value linguistic and cultural diversity; pay attention to teacher-talk; encourage small-group interaction; provide contextual support for learning; be careful in the choice of tasks and consciously foster language skills. On the other hand, when we look at the list again, we might acknowledge that we know quite a lot of good schools with ESL populations which are attempting something like this. We might also very properly comment that few of these measures are peculiar to ESL; with this many ESL teachers would agree, and it is an issue to which we will return. What the authors of this book propose is that a policy consisting of this cluster of measures can only be pursued by educating ESL learners in close association with the mainstream curriculum. This is, as we have noted, an ideal position. In the next section, we will look at the reality of mainstream classrooms and attempt an assessment of what ESL students do actually encounter when working in them.

5. The Mainstream Classroom as a Language-learning Environment

To what extent will second-language learners flourish in mainstream classrooms? In what follows, we assess the extent to which such classrooms might fulfil some of the conditions of the ideal 'facilitating' environment set out in the previous section. Because classrooms vary enormously, both within and across the four countries which we are dealing with, we will look separately at the primary and secondary sectors and take into account further variables such as teaching style and subject-matter.

Primary sector

Although styles in primary education vary, the influence of child-centred education – also associated with schools of practice such as 'whole language' and 'active learning' – is widespread in our four countries. This kind of classroom supplies many of the characteristics we would look for in a facilitating environment for ESL learners (Enright & McCloskey, 1988). It provides a good deal of varied and concurrent small-group activities interspersed with teacher-led sequences; forms of interaction thus vary from small-group work to one-to-one teacher-pupil exchanges to whole-class groups. Teacher-talk, especially in visually supported and highly motivating contexts such as story-telling, is likely to manifest the kinds of input modification (see Section 4) which are useful in SLA terms; Small-group work may supply a forum for generating comprehensible input and output. Tasks are likely to be richly embedded in context through the use of visual support in the form of objects and pictures, reference to here-and-now activity and to familiar concepts, and through face-to-face, one-to-one interaction. Primary training enables teachers to provide good support for basic language skills and tends to dissuade them from divorcing language from content, thus helping their ESL learners to link their linguistic and academic development. Most of these features are even more prevalent in early years education in nursery and kindergarten, where multilingual classrooms may benefit from the additional advantage of bilingual teachers.

Not all child-centred classrooms will share these advantages. In this connection it is worth noting that recent research in the UK into L1-medium schooling (Gipps, 1994) shows that in many such classrooms, teacher-child interactions tend to be insufficiently sustained, challenging and extended and thus not cognitively useful enough to the child. Similarly, many small-group interactions may be 'parallel' rather than truly interactional (Galton & Simon, 1980). We should also note Wong Fillmore's (1979) finding that children have varying 'social style characteristics': those who are quieter and more dependent on teacher-talk for their language input may learn language more slowly, the less whole-class teacher-talk there is. In addition, poorly run 'open' classrooms can verge on the chaotic: tasks can lose clarity, purpose and consistency, and teacher-talk can lack coherence.

In more traditional teacher-centred classrooms, there may be less groupwork and thus less pupil-pupil interaction, and fewer opportunities to take initiatives and risks with the language. However, this may be made up for in the quality and quantity of available facilitative teacher-talk, which is particularly useful to the quieter child.

Secondary sector

It is fair to generalise that as we proceed up the school and through the secondary sector a 'constructivist' approach often gives way to a 'transmission' approach to teaching (Barnes, 1975). As the compartmentalised subject curriculum dominates, teaching looks less like the cultivation of new concepts within the child and more like the passing of information from one person to another.

Many secondary teachers do of course think carefully about a variety of interactional forms and the design and contextualisation of tasks. Moreover, teachers who run a teacher-centred regime may nevertheless adopt a style of talk which is clear, visually supported and stimulating. In the main, however, secondary teachers are not well prepared by virtue either of their training or their view of their job to support language development; and they tend to see what goes on in classrooms in terms of subject-matter rather than process. It can thus happen that in this kind of environment, language in the form of teacher-centred, information-dense and formal academic discourse in large public groups, is the main channel for learning. This is difficult enough for fluent users of the medium of instruction. For ESL learners, mastering this variety of discourse, struggling with it as a second language, and using it to deal with unfamiliar curricular concepts, is often an impossible task.

Curricular subjects make a difference. They often present different teaching environments, either because of pedagogical tradition or because of something inherent in the way they constitute knowledge-building. Some subjects provide a lot of contextual support: they involve visuals and artefacts, require learners to engage in manipulative or physical tasks, or lend themselves naturally to small-group task-focused activity. As such they are good candidates for 'sheltered' subject teaching, that is, waystage classes between separate ESL provision and full integration into the mainstream, which ease ESL-only groups into mainstream work. Sheltered subjects may be graded for ease of accessibility by teaching first the subjects with high contextual support, such as geography or science, and later those which tend to be more language-dependent, such as history or social studies.

Individual teachers and school policies also make a difference that is usually tangible on entering a school or a classroom. The atmosphere may be welcoming or bleak; racist behaviour may be challenged or overlooked; linguistic and cultural diversity may be celebrated or ignored.

6.   Forms of Mainstream Language Support

What, then, does this diversity of mainstream provision mean for the ESL learner? We may draw three conclusions at this point. The first and fundamental message is that many mainstream classrooms will not give the ESL learner what she needs. *Some* early ESL learners will certainly flourish without support in *some* classrooms, probably in the early grades. A decision to place a child will depend on several factors including characteristics of the individual (see Section 2), of teaching style and of subject, and need to be made on a case-by-case basis. By and large, however, adjustments, small or large, will have to be made. It may be a small matter of a mainstream teacher learning, for example, to use more visuals; or it may mean that she enters into a fully collaborative and perhaps radically innovative partnership with an ESL specialist.

The second conclusion is that a school may always have need of a withdrawal facility. Within integrated provision, ESL learners may have needs which cannot be supplied in the mainstream classroom: brief intensive courses, 'culture-shock' problems, literacy support, grammatical development, or simply quiet, are examples. For many children, we should remember, a structured language programme of limited duration may be necessary. For these purposes, it will often be useful for a school to retain the option of the withdrawal class. Such arrangements do, however, need to be protected from the stigma which might attach to traditional low-status separate ESL teaching. This can be secured through regulations, laid down by a whole-school language policy, which preserve the status of any withdrawal work as a time-limited exception from normal practice, such as liaison with the mainstream teacher, defined curriculum-related targets and timetabling which avoids the ESL group missing important mainstream events.

The third conclusion is that to integrate ESL pupils into mainstream provision without support – especially in the later grades – will often be unacceptable. Indeed, in the USA, it is illegal (Collier, 1995). We all know of students who are sitting in mainstream classes, learning little, feeling miserable, not fulfilling their potential and perhaps beginning to withdraw, play up or even truant. The fact is that many mainstream classrooms do not represent a facilitative environment for second language acquisition. To make them more facilitative requires the school to install a framework of language support which will ensure that the necessary changes take place. In order to do this, the school may choose from a range of forms of provision. Figure 1 presents an overview of the main categories; note that terms differ from country to country and those used here may not have exactly the meaning they have in any one of our four contexts.

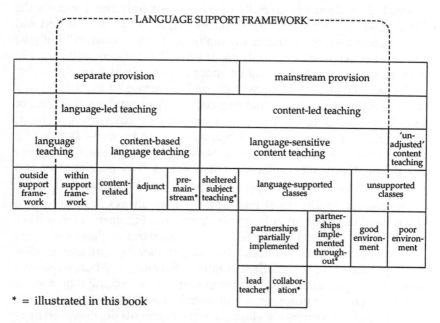

* = illustrated in this book

Figure 1 Forms of language support provision

The first thing to notice is that there are many dividing lines, but that few are hard-and-fast. On the face of it, there would seem to be a rigid distinction between teaching which goes on in mainstream classrooms and teaching which goes on outside them. This, however, is not quite the case. There are forms of separate provision, for instance, which are similar to mainstream work. *Sheltered subject teaching*, for instance, is 'content-led': it preserves the integrity of a subject while taking account of the needs of ESL learners. A subject is taught to an ESL-only group, by a subject specialist, incorporating the linguistic and pedagogical adjustments which ESL learners need and offering credit on a par with a mainstream course. In this volume, Ross McKean illustrates the sheltered teaching of secondary history.

Perhaps, therefore, the more useful division is between teaching which is primarily about content – whether inside or outside mainstream classrooms – and teaching which is primarily about language. In *content-led teaching*, the main pedagogical decisions are determined by the subject, its syllabus, concepts and ways of learning. These decisions may be heavily influenced by second-order influences which arise from the language needs of the students; but the teacher is qualified in the subject and the course provides a subject-matter credit. *Language-led teaching*, on the other hand, is determined by a language syllabus and pedagogy and taught by a language specialist; it may, however, orientate itself to the investigation of a subject, as in *content-based language teaching*. An example of this is the *pre-mainstream* content course which is taught by an ESL teacher with subject-matter expertise, designed in collaboration with a subject specialist, and offered as part of an ESL programme, preparing students for mainstream work. In this volume, Ruth Evans and Anne Filson present pre-mainstream content courses in geography and environmental studies respectively. 'Content shelters' and content-based pre-mainstream work feature in this book as important forms of self-standing bridging provision in which the subject content has integrity. It will be noticed that the differences between the two categories are small enough to blur the distinction between content-led and language-led teaching.

Within the content-based language teaching category two further subdivisions are shown in Figure 1. *Adjunct* classes are not self-standing, but derive from a mainstream class. Students are prepared for the mainstream class or debriefed after it. A language teacher liaises with a subject-teacher, establishes the main language demands (see Section 7(e)) of the upcoming subject-matter and matches these with the language needs of the ESL students. The adjunct class prepares the students for the main language and conceptual demands which the mainstream lesson will make on them. Some ESL teachers also use adjunct classes to teach ESL learners the learning strategies which they need in mainstream lessons, and indeed the assertiveness which they in particular will need to develop in order to hold their own there.

In *content-related* ESL classes, the ESL teacher works to a language syllabus, but imports topics from the mainstream curriculum as hooks to hang the language development on. Teaching is not related specifically to any mainstream lesson and may not involve much liaison with mainstream staff. The topics may only be superficially investigated; they may be derived from a variety of disciplines and do not constitute coherent subject study. They do, however, lend some intellectual purpose and cognitive complexity to language teaching.

'Language-led' teaching clearly also encompasses *language teaching* proper, that is, teaching which focuses on language *per se*, with little reference to its cross-curricular uses. Here, we should differentiate between 'pure' language teaching which occurs outside any language support framework, and language teaching which derives its rationale from an overarching support policy. The former is what most traditional with-drawal ESL looked like and is described in Section 1 above. A language-only syllabus, unrelated to the mainstream curriculum, forms the entire programme for an ESL group for the duration of their withdrawal period. Provision of this kind is no doubt still in existence, but it is on its way out in all our four countries. *Language teaching within a support framework*, however, is a withdrawal facility of a wholly different kind and represents the option to provide a language-focussed course within a mainstream-orientated policy framework, as previously outlined.

Content-led teaching is either *language-sensitive* or it is not. In the latter category, teachers tend not to adjust their practice to accommodate the language needs of learners. This category – shown in Figure 1 as *'unadjusted'* – accounts for very large numbers of ESL children who are submerged in mainstream English and do not flourish; it is thus much larger than it appears in this diagram. Language-sensitive teaching may be formally *'supported'* or *'unsupported'*. Classrooms in which there is no formal language support may be good or bad places for second language learners; as we have seen, there are those which inherently provide a facilitating environment; they need hardly any adjustments for ESL learners. They tend to cluster in the early school years, but also include all those which, for any number of reasons, such as subject or teaching style, happen to offer what ESL learners need.

Most language-sensitive teaching, however, comes about through the operation of a whole-school plan for *language support* which integrates ESL work and provides for formal team-teaching *partnerships* between mainstream and ESL teachers. In some cases, partnerships operate throughout the school; in others they are implemented partially in classes where they are seen to be most necessary. Partnerships may also arise when two teachers work together, not within an all-encompassing institutional policy, but on the basis of an agreement between them.

When we look at how partnerships function in the classroom, they tend to fall into two categories. On the one hand they may tend towards a *collaborative* mode, in which both parties agree to share, as equally as they can, classroom functions such as planning, teaching and assessing as well as responsibility for all the children and thus ultimately, classroom status. Such teachers need to have the openness and diplomacy to tackle a lot of territorial and personality issues. On the other hand, in-class support may be provided by an ESL specialist who may plan with her mainstream colleague but who leaves to her the function of *'lead teacher'* and works particularly to the language needs of ESL learners. In this volume, Cressida Jupp presents this latter variety, while L. Westbrook and Sharon Bergquist-Moody, Elina Raso, Hugh Hooper and Manny Vazquez illustrate the collaborative mode. Julie Reid and Nancy Kitegawa narrate the process of wholesale change which a school undergoes when integrating ESL throughout.

It is clear from this overview that schools do not have a stark choice between the two poles of fully separate and fully integrated provision. On the contrary, there are many types of ESL facility; they range themselves right across the separate-integrated dimension and the boundaries between them are unclear. The separate-integrated boundary emerges as particularly flexible: firstly because forms of content-based language teaching link withdrawal work to the mainstream curriculum; and secondly because thoughtful timetabling and strict school policy can ensure that withdrawal work is a time-limited, focused and effective extension of mainstream language support. It should be noted that boundaries are more blurred in primary than secondary schools. In the former, the language-orientated and contextualised approach to learning makes moving into the mainstream easier; whereas in the latter, the distinction between withdrawal ESL and mainstream subject learning may be sharper. In this volume, Ruth Evans, Anne Filson and Ross McKean show how in the secondary school this boundary may be made more permeable.

Flexibility is necessary in language support. As we have seen, there are many different kinds of ESL learner and many different types of mainstream environment. To match the one with the other a school needs to be able to offer different rates and routes to the same goal of access to the mainstream classroom and curriculum. The authors of this book illustrate several of these. In the next section, we will list some of the common features of their differing approaches to mainstreaming policy and practice.

7.   A Framework for Mainstream Language Support

This section outlines the main characteristics of the approach which the authors take to mainstreaming. The collective picture which emerges gives a good idea of the kind of framework for language support which schools need to set up when they integrate ESL learners into mainstream classrooms.

(a)   Equal opportunities policy

Language minority pupils tend to encounter discrimination of an institutional and personal kind; for this reason, a school policy which regulates their language education is not really understandable unless it is built on the more fundamental principles of a school policy on equal opportunities. Establishing such a policy requires a degree of courage and persistence on the part of the school community which many schools will not be able to summon up. It is not within the scope of this book to show how such a policy might work. Suffice it to say that it will lay down how the school deals with any underlying structural questions to do with the distribution and accessibility of opportunities along the lines of race and gender. It will also encompass the 'softer' issues of multicultural policy, ensuring that school activity reflects language and cultural diversity in such matters as teacher and pupil language awareness, bookstock, visuals, and assessment. It will also determine how the school deals with its relations with minority communities and with specific provisions for communication with parents.

(b)   School Language policy

ESL policy is only part of school language policy and is indeed more effective when coupled with wider language issues, such as whole-language policy. Questions of ESL are certainly inseparable from those of bilingualism and mother-tongue support. This, however, is another matter which is too large to figure centrally in this book; most of the authors work within the context of a school-led or board-led policy on bilingualism, but the authors angle their contributions specifically to ESL practice.

All the contributors highlight the importance of whole-school policy in institutional change; it may be partly developed bottom-up through the dedicated work of individual teachers, and should certainly be arrived at through the sometimes slow-moving processes of consultation and consensus; but it is not reliable unless consistently pursued and funded by principals and education authorities. There are often special benefits to be had from developing policy on a district-wide basis through the stimulus of a district education authority. It is also especially important to monitor mainstreaming initiatives and make changes as a consequence of evaluation (Bourne, 1989).

(c) Forms of provision

A school needs to choose from the range of forms of provision according to its requirements and resources. Provision should be flexible enough to meet the variety of needs which will be present among its ESL learners. The forms represented by the contributions to this book illustrate a good cross-section of the range shown in Figure 1, and are described in detail in Section 6. Six of the contributors present examples of ESL provision which is integrated into the mainstream classroom; three show work which is outside the mainstream classroom, but integrated with the mainstream curriculum.

(d) Partnerships

As we have seen, the contributors illustrate a range of different ways of relating ESL work to the mainstream curriculum. All involve partnerships between ESL and mainstream teachers. In the UK, 'partnership' has a specific meaning which is defined by government guidelines (Bourne & McPake, 1991). Within this formal partnership, specific roles are assigned to the school and to pairs of teachers, and a strict cycle of planning, teaching and evaluation is followed. By and large, the mainstream partnerships described in this book are more informal, but all involve two teachers coming to an agreement about how to share out between them the roles of planning, teaching and assessing. Partners have to be open to change and not too territorial: innovations of this kind have to do not only with logistics but also with teachers' feelings. In particular, it is vital to plan and to have recognised planning time – something which is rarely sufficiently acknowledged.

In any partnership, jobs have to be shared. In this situation it is important to know which duties require specialist language training. In general the rule of thumb is: duties which are more to do with making adjustments at the macro-level of mainstream pedagogy, to make it more accessible, can be done – or soon learned – by mainstream teachers. Those which are more to do with language have to be done by language specialists. Mainstream primary teachers, for instance, are skilled at establishing a rich whole-language environment. Similarly, some language support practices can be learned by a mainstream teacher, such as, for instance, the use of visuals for representing knowledge structures; and a good collaborative relationship with an ESL specialist should result in the transfer of a lot of these skills. Other jobs require specialised training and experience. Among these are many of the task types in the ESL teacher's repertoire, especially those giving practice in specific aspects of grammatical, morphological and lexical and discourse development. Similarly, analysing the language demands of mainstream work, and assessing the language abilities of students are things which mainstream teachers may find difficult to do – at least initially.

(e) Analysing language needs and demands

A lot of good ESL is to do with seeing school work in language terms. Mainstream teachers tend to be rather language-blind; they prefer to see the work in subject-matter terms. A lot of teaching – especially at secondary level – makes complex language demands on pupils, but assumes (Marland, 1977) that they possess the relevant language skills. This is difficult enough for English-fluent pupils, and especially so for ESL learners. A key specialist skill of the ESL teacher is that she can take a language cross-section of any piece of mainstream teaching – a language photograph which reveals the language and learning skills which the teacher expects pupils to be able to perform and sets them out in the relevant terms: vocabulary, discourse, grammatical, functional demands, etc (Levine, 1990). The other side of this coin is to analyse the needs of ESL learners in the same way and then match needs to demands to provide appropriate language support. Good ESL work, especially in the mainstream, requires this kind of simple, routine analysis and it is one of the things which mainstream teachers find most difficult to do.

(f) Adjusting classroom language demands: macro-processes

Classroom processes need adjusting so that the language demands they make on ESL learners are appropriate. Adjustments can be made at the 'macro' level of the overall learning environment, or at the 'micro' level of specific interactions between teacher, student and task. To make macro-level adjustments, a teacher will, for instance, ensure that a lot of visual material is used; that students perform active, manipulative activities; that there is a variety of forms of classroom organisation (whole-class, groups, pairs, individual work); that procedures are clear and orderly and that the general ethos is warm and encouraging.

Planning

Macro-level planning includes setting clear objectives; ESL teachers differ according to whether these higher-order decisions are driven more by topic objectives or by language objectives. A teacher with a more content-led approach might allow content considerations to dominate macro-level planning and deal with language issues at a micro-level as and when they arise. A more language-orientated teacher might plan by reference to language at both macro and micro levels.

Classroom organisation

ESL learners need groupwork opportunities; teachers use lesson structures with a mix of facilitative whole-class work and groupwork. They also take care over the composition of groups, providing peer translation opportunities where necessary and making use of English-fluent peers as well as thinking about group leadership. ESL learners also benefit a great deal from the challenge of making whole-class presentations.

(g) Adjusting classroom language demands: micro-processes

Adjustments at the level of micro-processes are often more exclusively related to language. They may be either relatively spontaneous, involving the quality of teachers' interventions with the class or with groups and individuals; or they may be planned, involving the detail of task design.

Teacher-interventions

Whole-class teacher-talk needs to be interactive, to make naturalistic use of explanations and examples and questions, to mark clearly the sequence of ideas and to be sensitive to students' cultural backgrounds and prior knowledge. In one-to-one talk with students, teachers can pinpoint specific aspects of the language of individuals. They can also organise more fluent peers to provide language models and support. Teacher-interventions, in small-group or one-to-one work should come at 'teachable' moments (Hooper, this volume); this is especially true of language-related interventions, such as corrections or language models: they are useful or not, depending on the point in a child's sequence of thought when they are introduced.

Talking about language can be especially valuable (Gibbons, 1991). It can happen through teacher-pupil talk: the recursive processes of talking about writing are especially helpful, for example, in process-orientated approaches to writing development. Learners, however, do it on their own: students are often very good at working towards an understanding of specialist concepts by talking to each other.

Tasks

At the level of the task, adjustments usually require advance planning: teachers predict the points at which a task sequence will make heavy language demands and prepare language support tasks – often quite finely constructed – to help students meet these demands. Task design is central to language support. A rich whole-language context without careful task design is felt by some (Davison, 1995) to be too loose a pedagogical environment for the ESL learner. Tasks need to enable the learner to engage with cognitively challenging concepts while avoiding over-heavy language demands. Task purpose and structure have to be especially clear. Visuals of all kinds are vital; similarly, manipulative and exploratory activities, outdoor activities and project work provide rich contextual support for meaning. Particularly useful to language and cognitive development are visual representations of conceptual and discourse structures. In particular, Mohan (1986), Early *et al.* (1989), together with Hooper (this volume) and colleagues from the Vancouver School Board have researched and practised this technique and developed it into an overarching 'approach' to ESL pedagogy. ESL learners often need ways of bypassing language to get at concepts. Both ESL specialists and mainstream teachers have developed techniques which strip away text and render concepts accessible by visualising them, often diagrammatically. In addition to giving learners access to concepts, visualising knowledge structures also helps them learn language: a child who is comfortable with a concept has free processing capacity to attend to the language she needs to express it. This kind of task, which helps learners to perform cognitively challenging activities by reducing the second-language barrier, is one of the most powerful tools in the repertoire of ESL teachers, especially at secondary level, and appeals very much to mainstream subject teachers because of its capacity to illuminate subject learning processes.

(h) Credit and Assessment

A language support framework needs procedures to fulfil various assessment functions. It needs rating scales and assessment procedures to assess ESL ability. It needs means of establishing what an ESL learner can do academically and cognitively; this can be a notoriously difficult task, often vitiated by ignorance and prejudice (Cummins, 1984). Language support also requires ways of measuring an ESL learner's progress against national norms. And finally, it requires ways of providing credit for ESL learners within the school. Schools will often very properly wish to establish credits for ESL-only courses as on a par with mainstream credits, but may often encounter tacit reluctance to accept this on the part of both teachers and pupils in the mainstream school.

(i) Staff development

Establishing a language support framework means that teachers need to change their practice, and this means staff development. This happens in various ways. Firstly, staff development tends to occur organically within a well-functioning partnership: the parties learn a lot from each other. Secondly, ESL specialists with a mainstream function find themselves working with staff as much as with pupils and this may well develop from an informal advisory role in planning meetings to a formal INSET function within the school. Observing good practice in neighbouring schools can show the way forward. A local adviser/consultant may help development take place, and a district ESL team may have a similar function. In all our four countries, INSET courses are available, though regional and national standard qualifications do not always exist and much progress has to be made before language support becomes a standard part of pre-service teacher-education.

8. ESL and Education for Social Justice

The teachers who have contributed to this book are attempting to show some of the practical detail of how they go about bringing the education of language minority children into the mainstream school. Clearly, this development is about equality as well as education. As such it can only make sense if it is seen against a wider political background. Australia, Canada, the United States and the United Kingdom are all countries in which ethnic minorities often occupy subordinate sociopolitical status (Cummins, 1988, 1994). They can be routinely discriminated against in education, housing, employment, access to law, and in many other ways. Governments, pressure groups and individuals recognise this to a greater or lesser extent and take measures to counteract such discrimination. As we have seen, in education this often takes the form of multicultural and anti-racist school policies. These constitute the backbone of resistance to racism as it operates through institutional and personal practices within the school.

There are references to such policies in the chapters of this book, but they are not its main concern. In this sense the book may court the common criticism that ESL teachers are not political enough: they think that methodology will improve the lives of their students, whereas in reality nothing short of political change will make any difference. Teachers of ESL often invite such accusations: we are by-and-large members of the ethnic majority and, like other professional groups, probably fairly mixed in our readiness to see our work with second-language learners as part of a broader political movement. In addition, there is the problem of good intentions: institutional racism is not the result of malice. Most of what we do with our ESL students is well-intentioned. What we often fail to see is how the institutional practices of the school as well as our personal practices in the classroom can be powerfully and subtly subverted by the robust structure of political inequality in the wider society.

The authors of these chapters would, however, defend themselves against the charge of political tunnel vision: they see further than the methodological detail. But they would also claim that it is partly upon the detail of good language-sensitive educational practice that the wider principles of social justice in education are built. These teachers' narratives are important as pieces of good practice in the classroom; but they also show how ESL and its day-to-day achievements are inevitably part of the larger picture of social equality and what we do to bring it about.

References

Barnes, D. (1975) *From Communication to Curriculum*. London: Penguin.
Barnes, D. and Todd, F. (1977) *Communication and Learning in Small Groups*. London: Routledge & Kegan Paul.
Bourne, J. (1989) *Moving into the Mainstream*. Windsor: NFER-Nelson.
Bourne, J. and McPake, J. (1991) *Partnership Teaching*. London: NFER/HMSO.
Canale, M. and Swain, M. (1980) Theoretical bases of communicative approaches to second language teaching and testing. *Applied Linguistics* 1, 1–47.
Chamot, A.U. and O'Malley, J.M. (1989) The cognitive academic language learning approach. In *When They Don't All Speak English*. Urbana, IL: NCTE.
Collier, V. (1994) Plenary Address, TESOL Conference. Reported by R.E.W-B. Olsen & B. Leone. *TESOL Matters* 4, 3.
— (1995) Oral presentation at a conference of the National Association for Language Development in the Curriculum, London, UK.

Corson, D. (1990) *Language Policy Across the Curriculum*. Clevedon: Multilingual Matters.

CRE (1986) *Teaching English as a Second Language: Report of a Formal Enquiry in Calderdale LEA*. London: Commission for Racial Equality.

Cummins, J. (1984) *Bilingualism and Special Education: Issues in Assessment and Pedagogy*. Clevedon: Multilingual Matters.

— (1988) From multicultural to anti-racist education: Analaysis of programmes and policies in Ontario. In T. Skuttnab-Kangas and J. Cummins (eds) *Minority Education: From Shame to Struggle*. Clevedon: Multilingual Matters.

— (1994) Knowledge, power and identity in teaching English as a second language. In F. Genesee (ed.) *Educating Second Language Children*. Cambridge: Cambridge University Press.

Cummins, J. and Swain, M. (1986) *Bilingualism in Education*. London: Longman.

Curriculum Corporation (1994) *ESL Scales*. Victoria, Australia: Curriculum Corporation.

Davison, C. (1993) Integrating ESL into the mainstream classroom: Australian perspectives. *Multicultural Teaching*, 11 (3).

— (1995) Oral presentation at a conference of the National Association for Language Development in the Curriculum, London, UK.

DES (Department of Education and Science) (1985) *Education for All: Report of the Committee of Enquiry into the Education of Children from Ethnic Minority Groups* (The Swann Report). London: HMSO.

Early, M., Mohan, B., and Hooper, H. (1989) The Vancouver school board language and content project. In J.H. Esling (ed.) *Multicultural Education and Policy: ESL in the 1990s*. Toronto: OISE Press.

Ellis, R. (1985) *Understanding Second Language Acquisition*. Oxford: Oxford University Press.

— (1992) *Second Language Acquisition and Language Pedagogy*. Clevedon: Multilingual Matters.

Enright, D.S. and McCloskey, M.L. (1988) *Integrating English: Developing English Language and Literacy in the Multilingual Classroom*. Reading, MA: Addison-Wesley.

Erickson, F. (1984) Rhetoric, anecdote and rhapsody: Coherence strategies in a conversation among black American adolescents. In D. Tannen (ed.) *Coherence in Spoken and Written Discourse*. Norwood, NJ: Ablex.

Galton, M. and Simon, B. (1980) *Progress and Performance in the Primary School*. London: Routledge & Kegan Paul.

Gass, S. and Varonis, E. (1986) Sex differences in nonnative speaker-nonnative speaker interactions. In R. Day (ed.) *Talking to Learn: Conversation in Second Language Acquisition*. Cambridge MA: Newbury House.

Gibbons, P. (1991) *Learning to Learn in a Second Language*. Primary English Teaching Association (Australia).

Gipps, C. (1994) What we know about effective primary teaching. In J. Bourne (ed.) *Thinking Through Primary Practice*. London: Routledge.

Harklau, L. (1994) ESL versus mainstream classes: Contrasting L2 learning environments. *TESOL Quarterly* 28, 241–72.

Krashen, S. (1981) *Second Language Acquisition and Second Language Learning*. Oxford: Oxford University Press.

Leung, C. (1995) Linguistic diversity in the 1990s: Some language education issues for minority ethnic pupils. Unpublished paper. Thames Valley University, London.

Levine, J. (ed.) (1990) *Bilingual Learners in the Mainstream Curriculum*. London: Falmer Press.

Long, M. (1983) Native-speaker/non-native-speaker interaction and the negotiation of comprehensible input. *Applied Linguistics* 4 (2).

Long, M. and Porter, P. (1985) Group work, interlanguage talk and second language acquisition. *TESOL Quarterly* 19 (2).

Marland, M. (1977) *Language Across the Curriculum*. London: Heinemann

McKay, S.L. and Freedman, S.W. (1990) Language minority education in Great Britain: A challenge to current US Policy. *TESOL Quarterly* 24, 385–405.

Mercer, N. (1995) *The Guided Construction of Knowledge: Talk Amongst Teachers and Learners*. Clevedon: Multilingual Matters.

Met, M. (1994) Teaching content through a second language. In F. Genesee (ed.) *Educating Second Language Children*. Cambridge: Cambridge University Press.

Mohan, B. (1986) *Language and Content*. Reading, MA: Addison-Wesley.

Mouneimne, S. (1988) Are we enabling level 1 and level 2 ESL learners to function effectively in senior secondary classrooms? Unpublished essay. Ealing College of Higher Education. London.

Pease-Alvarez, C. and Vasquez, O. (1994) Language socialization in ethnic minority communities. In F. Genesee (ed.) *Educating Second Language Children*. Cambridge: Cambridge University Press.

Rubin, J. (1987) Learner strategies: Theoretical assumptions, research history and typology. In J. Rubin and A. Wenden (eds) *Learner Strategies and Language Learning*. New Jersey: Prentice-Hall.

Saville-Troike, M. (1988) From context to communication: Paths to second language acquisition In D. Tannen (ed.) *Linguistics in Context: Connecting, Observing and Understanding*. Norwood, NJ: Ablex.

Skehan, P. (1986) *Individual Differences in Second Language Learning*. London: Edward Arnold.

— (1992) Second language acquisition strategies and task-based learning. In *Thames Valley University Working Papers in English Language Teaching* Vol. 1. Thames Valley University, London.

Snow, M.A., Met, M. and Genesee, F. (1989) A conceptual framework for the integration of language and content in second/foreign language programs. *TESOL Quarterly* 23 (2), 201–17.

Swain, M. (1985) Communicative competence: Some roles of comprehensible input and comprehensible output in its development. In S. Gass and C.Madden (eds.) *Input in Second Language Acquisition*. Cambridge, MA: Newbury House.

Tizard, J., Schofield, W.N. and Hewison, J. (1982) Collaboration between teachers and parents in assisting children's reading. *British Journal of Educational Psychology* 52, 1–25.

Trueba, H. (1989) *Raising Silent Voices: Educating Linguistic Minorities for the 21st Century*. Rowley, MA: Newbury House.

Wells, G. and Chang-Wells, G.L. (1992) *Constructing Knowledge Together: Classrooms as Centers of Inquiry and Literacy*. Portsmouth, NH: Heinemann.

Wong Fillmore, L. (1979) Individual differences in second language acquisition. In C. Fillmore *et al.* (eds.) *Individual Differences in Language Ability and Language Behaviour*. New York: Academic Press.
— (1985) When does teacher-talk work as input? In S. Gass and C. Madden (eds.) *Input in Second Language Acquisition*. Cambridge, MA: Newbury House.
Wright, C. (1985) The influence of school processes in the education of children of West Indian origin. In S.J. Eggleston *et al.* (ed.) *The Educational and Vocational Experiences of 15–18 Year Old People of Minority Ethnic Groups*. University of Keele. Department of Education.

Section 1: Primary Schools

In this section four primary teachers – one from each of our four countries – describe their experience in mainstream classrooms in which ESL learners are integrated with English-fluent students. The *forms of provision* they represent depend partly on the characteristics of the local minority community, partly on *school language policy*, and partly on the quality of the *partnership* they have formed with mainstream colleagues.

Cressida Jupp teaches in a British school in which the majority of children are from minority ethnic groups; however, it is a settled and long-standing community in which most parents are bilingual and thus she provides language support to only a small group. Her mainstream colleague plans collaboratively with her but takes the role of 'lead teacher', while Cressida focuses on the needs of her group. Cressida describes in some detail how she sets language objectives with her colleague and discusses the pros and cons of intervening before, during or after mainstream inputs. She also includes a historical overview of how UK schools shifted towards integration, and a balanced and sobering account of the disadvantages as well as the advantages of in-class language support, reminding us that mainstreamed ESL sometimes comes at a cost.

L. Westbrook and **Sharon Bergquist-Moody** work in an American school with 23% ESL learners from a community of more recent immigrants; thus while the school has a majority of English native-speaking children, they share with Cressida the fact that they are dealing with a classroom minority who need language support. L. and Sharon's school is typical of many in that it reacted to a fast rise in the size of the ESL population by taking a *policy decision* to experiment with mainstreaming. Interestingly in this case, the enterprise was piloted and monitored and L. and Sharon report the heartwarming experience of seeing their good practice spreading and initially sceptical colleagues being convinced (though they hint at the – unfortunately – equally typical occurrence of good practice suffering from budget cuts). L. and Sharon illustrate the key human factor in teaching *partnerships*: the relationship has to be good from the start or at least worked at – what they refer to as the 'marriage' theory of team-teaching! They also typify two other conditions of good partnerships: that a certain philosophy of practice in the integrated classroom has to be agreed on, and that planning time – that scarcest of commodities – has to be found.

Elina Raso describes an Australian classroom in which the majority (20 out of 29) are language minority students. Two important characteristics of her account need highlighting. One is that it illustrates a policy-led approach to ESL on a district-wide basis, in which *whole-school responsibility for ESL* is expected and principals are required to develop documented policy through collaborative processes within the school. The other is that it shows teachers distict-wide working to a common philosophy of mainstreamed ESL through the use of a *planned framework* laying down ground rules for the objectives and sequence of classroom work. ESL and mainstream teachers engage in a careful process of joint planning and teaching.

Julie Reid and **Nancy Kitegawa** tell the story of a school turning itself round. Their school had pursued a policy of withdrawing the neediest, but it was clearly not meeting the requirements of a largely minority-language Toronto community with much recent immigration. They narrate how the school took a *policy decision* to opt for mainstreaming, how later a kind of 'in class' withdrawal developed, and how finally a core team of specialist teachers (ESL, learning support, library and computer) took the lead in language support. This account also illustrates some ground rules for good mainstreaming: get the support of the principal, and pay special attention to the *feelings* which teachers will have about team-teaching. Julie was herself Assistant Coordinator of ESL for the School Board and this account, like Elina's, exemplifies the potential benefits of district-led coordination. It is also notable for its careful *monitoring* of the process of change.

In terms of *classroom practice*, Cressida, Elina, and L. and Sharon represent the variety of ways in which teachers may choose to 'do' mainstreamed ESL. At one end of the spectrum is Elina's class where ESL learners form the majority. *Language planning* pervades both the macro and micro levels of classroom work. She and her colleagues use a commonly agreed format of clearly planned steps in lesson-planning, leading from the more language-focused to the spontaneously communicative. This approach relies on a well-defined model of language use which specifies the language demands of each area of topic work in either lexical, grammatical, discourse or functional terms. These *language demands* are worked out in advance and set out as objectives for each task sequence. *Tasks* supply strong language guidance and Elina and her colleagues make a lot of use of activities which display visually both the cognitive and discourse structure of tasks in hand. These planned sequences rely a lot on visual support and on variety in *forms of organisation*, moving carefully from teacher-initiated input through pair-, group-, individual and whole-class work. They are also directed at the *whole class*, both ESL and English native-speaker students, on the assumption that focused support for linguistic and cognitive processes is a general classroom need.

At the other end of the spectrum is L. and Sharon's class, where ESL learners are in the minority. Although both classrooms partake of the same child-centred, active primary tradition, L. and Sharon's *planning* is driven more by topic; language support is provided more at the point of need. This classroom is typical of the 'discovery' and 'whole-language' traditions, but the teachers adapt it to ESL learners by paying special attention to the *'macro'* aspects of classroom practice. Thus they emphasise visual support, manipulative tasks, cooperative groupwork, student initiative and autonomy, classroom community relations and the alertness of teachers to ESL learners' needs as they arise. At the *'micro'* level of meeting these needs, L. and Sharon offer a lot of one-to-one teacher-child contact, 'buddy' support systems, recourse to bilingual staff and a range of *task* types designed to render the work of the class accessible to ESL learners; that is, to make activities comprehensible and to restrict language production to what is manageable.

Cressida's classroom – where she supports a small group of children with marked ESL needs – combines features of both language-led and topic-led *planning*. She plans with her mainstream colleague by analysing the *language demands* of an area of the mainstream curriculum (weather) and matching these with what she knows of the language needs of her group. This allows her to highlight topics (seasons), learning skills (data handling) and language skills (reading and writing) for which her group will get specific support. Cressida then analyses these areas further to reveal those aspects of language for which she will provide language support at a micro (e.g. lexical, grammatical, functional) level, as the children proceed with work on the topic. The *tasks* and materials she generates as a result of this analysis allow her children to pursue the topic – they investigate temperature, or read and write about 'the Sun and the Wind' – and meet the language demands it makes on them as they arise.

1 Supporting Small ESL Groups in a Mainstream Primary School

CRESSIDA JUPP

This chapter describes teaching on the topic of weather carried out over one term with a group of British bilingual 6 and 7 year olds. The context of such teaching is outlined in the first section, and the main body of the chapter shows how English as a Second Language teaching is integrated into the mainstream classroom and curriculum by ESL teachers working alongside class teachers.

Second Language Acquisition in the UK Mainstream Classroom: History and Pedagogy

ESL teaching in British schools in the 1990s is rooted in the principle that second language acquisition should take place for all children in mainstream classrooms. This is as much a political principle as a pedagogical one. Closely linked to this is the principle that all pupils have an entitlement to the whole curriculum

In earlier decades many bilingual children with limited English were often withdrawn out of mainstream classes to either special classes in a school or, in the case of older pupils, into separate language learning centres, until such time as their English was felt to be sufficiently well developed when the pupils would be placed in mainstream schools.[1] At the time when the first groups of migrant workers were entering Britain in the 1960s, their children were being taught English by methods close to those used in teaching English as a Foreign Language, with an emphasis on acquisition of grammatical structures in a planned language syllabus. The reaction to increasing numbers of children from ethnic minority families in schools was that they should be assimilated into British society as rapidly as possible.

This changed in the 1970s and 1980s; underachievement by minority ethnic children was seen to be a reflection of the fact that schools and indeed society were unwilling to recognise the multicultural and multilingual nature of many urban areas, and the educational implications of multi-ethnic Britain. Very great efforts were made to change the perceptions of teachers, and schools began to reflect the cultural backgrounds of their pupils. This took place at three levels:

- the appearance of a school and individual classrooms in terms of cultural artefacts, appropriate display or the music heard;
- secondly, the curriculum and learning materials incorporating the experiences and knowledge of the whole population, not just those of the white children;
- and thirdly, the recognition and use within school of the languages which pupils were using in the community.

The anti-racist movement pointed out that endemic racism within society led to unequal opportunities for its members, and many schools and education authorities drew up anti-racist guidelines for teachers to use. The introduction of the first ever National Curriculum in England and Wales seemed to many teachers a backward step in this area since opportunities for a multicultural and anti-racist permeation of the curriculum became very limited.

While the whole school environment was changing in order to reflect something of the cultural diversity of its population (and readers must recognise that some schools changed little, others greatly) approaches to ESL teaching also shifted. The terminology altered: 'ESL children or pupils' was largely replaced by 'bilingual children or pupils' so that skills and knowledge of home and community languages were recognised. The term 'bilingual children' will be used in this chapter, denoting language abilities in two or more languages but without specifying any levels of development or capability. The place of teaching changed. Arrangements for teaching English to those children in school with limited English language development came under scrutiny. Special centres or school classes were seen as not only divisive, and giving limited access to the curriculum, but also not the best language learning environments since pupils were cut off from those from whom they could learn English in a variety of contexts: their peers. Research from elsewhere in the world was describing how children learn a second language in similar ways to their first language acquisition. Language teaching focused on the real situations of school and the curriculum, where the children had to learn to communicate in order to learn. During the 1980s language teachers moved into classrooms to support their pupils in mainstream learning as well as English.

This move broke the traditional mould of one teacher working alone with one class. While some teachers felt unease at the presence of another teacher in the room, most welcomed the language teachers who, for part of the week at least, shared the responsibility of enabling teaching to be accessible for all.

The specialist language teachers' role has changed from selecting language items and then teaching them within a chosen context, to looking at the mainstream curriculum and developing language activities around the general learning activities. While this can be described as the functional-communicative approach to teaching English as an additional or second language, the reality in many cases is that no systematic language teaching is possible.

In the mid-1990s bilingual pupils with developing capability in English are taught in the classroom where their mainstream curriculum learning is taking place, and language learning is centred on mainstream curriculum tasks and activities. The main responsibility for second language acquisition therefore lies with the class teacher since learners spend nearly all their time under her guidance. However, many schools have a language support teacher giving extra input for two or three sessions a week to those bilingual children who need it, especially those in the early stages of second language acquisition (SLA). Some of this language teaching may occur in a separate group for a limited length of time, but in most cases language support teachers work in the classroom.

This organisational arrangement implies close cooperation between the two teachers, in order to make links between language development and curriculum learning. In some schools joint planning of the curriculum takes place; in others, not only is there joint planning but also joint delivery of lessons, with both teachers taking a leading role. Where this practice is part of school policy it is termed 'partnership teaching'.

The chief objective of partnership teaching is to facilitate equality of access to the curriculum. The focus of the curriculum is provided by the mainstream teacher, selecting from the National Curriculum. The language support teacher contributes a language development perspective, suggesting approaches to presentation and tasks which support the second language learner. This partnership approach is beneficial not only for bilingual children who are at an early stage of acquiring English but also for all those other children in the class who find the curriculum very demanding. However, in many schools full partnership teaching does not take place, but mainstream and language support teachers may plan together while teaching separately (often within the same room). The teaching which is described later in this chapter is based on this type of collaboration, rather than joint delivery of the curriculum to whole classes.

A further objective of partnership or collaborative teaching is to support the incorporation of the cultures of minority ethnic pupil groups into the curriculum. The topic under consideration, the weather, does not lend itself particularly well to a multicultural perspective with young children, but this is not so for many areas of the curriculum.

Many of the bilingual children in school are born in Britain to first-generation parents. As far as we know, no long-term studies of bilingual learners within British classrooms have been undertaken. We have no theories of second language acquisition which are derived from the sorts of situations our pupils are in, nor do we know whether the organisational arrangements outlined above are effective in ensuring rapid language acquisition as well as equality of access to the curriculum. In spite of this, though, most British ESL teachers would subscribe to the following principles of language acquisition:

- Classroom SLA in an English-medium school follows a similar pattern to foreign language acquisition (FLA) – starting with a period of tuning in silently to the language, moving to short formulaic utterances in response to classroom routines, developing gradually through one or two word utterances to longer output.
- Language is learnt most effectively if it is used in real situations to achieve real goals; a learner needs the language of social interaction as well the language of the academic curriculum, though for young learners the two are inextricably linked.
- Language learning is directed towards the content of classroom topics, with an emphasis on lexical development and the widening of semantic fields, rather than solely focusing on syntactical structures.
- The four language skills of speaking and listening, writing and reading, are all developed within the mainstream curriculum.
- Learners are likely to learn most effectively if they are not pressured to speak in the early stages.
- Learning activities which take place in small groups give opportunities for interaction and collaboration with adults and peers, and can support the pupil who is learning ESL.
- Oral correction is kept to a minimum, in order to increase confidence and motivation.

The work on Weather which is described here attempted to follow these principles; the section which follows outlines the factors which may hinder the children's learning, the context in which the teaching took place and the teaching objectives.

General Factors Which Hinder Children's Learning

This is a wide area of discussion, referred to in other chapters of this volume. Some of the factors which touch particularly upon the education of young bilingual children are summarised below:

- Limited proficiency in English, especially the sort of English used in the acquisition of literacy and in the acquisition of curriculum concepts;
- Lack of communication with bilingual parents at a time when home and school need to be working together in supporting the child's education.
- Lack of parental understanding about the expectations of the school, and vice versa.
- Family difficulties connected with migration, such as racism, low socio-economic status and unemployment.
- An ethno-centric centralised curriculum which is tailored to the majority and leaves little scope for a multicultural or multilingual perspective; this is a particular problem in the UK since the recent introduction of the National Curriculum (although the National Curriculum gives an entitlement that all pupils have access to a broad and balanced syllabus).
- An assessment system based on national tests which are based upon the attainment of the monolingual majority, and take little account of the progress made in learning English as a second language by bilingual children, nor of the language and cultural difficulties which testing brings.
- Class teachers' lack of training in strategies which support language development;
- lack of understanding about the relationship between developing second language proficiency and special educational needs.
- Lack of bilingual support to enable children learn in their home languages.

A central role for the language support teacher or ESL teacher is to counteract some or all of these negative factors. Positive relationships within the school and with the school's wider community support the central teaching task of helping all bilingual children have opportunities to learn successfully and raise achievement.

The Context in Which the Teaching Took Place

The school where I teach is an infants school, that is, a school where children come into full-time education during the year in which they are five years old; they remain in the school for three years before moving on to the next stage (junior school). Before they come to the school full-time, most of the children at my school attend the school's nursery class daily for a year, for half the day. As many of the children at the school are bilingual, and many of them come to school with limited proficiency in English, the year's nursery experience is a valuable contribution to the acquisition of fluent English. As for other young children, nursery education gives pupils a range of educational experiences.

The school is in a suburban area to the west of London, near Heathrow Airport. Many of the families own their own homes and businesses. They have a high expectation of education and nearly all parents would be biliterate and bilingual. This is a settled community, largely originating from the Punjab area of North-West India. Ethnic minority groups in Britain come from diverse backgrounds, and what may be true for the families that my school serves is not necessarily true for other groups.

Profile of the school

Excluding the nursery classes, the figures for the school in the spring term 1992 are as follows:

Number of children on roll	302
Number of children speaking another language in addition to English	179
Percentage of children in school who are bilingual	59%
Number of languages represented in the school	13
Number of speakers of Panjabi (the largest single language)	130

Language support in the school is supplied by one full-time bilingual teacher, two part-time bilingual classroom assistants, and by one part-time monolingual teacher. Approximately one-third of the children receive focused language teaching in the mainstream context during the nursery and first year in school, but few of those continue to need support. The youngest children have opportunities for small-group work with one of the language support staff nearly every day; this reduces to once or twice a week by the time they are in Year 2 at the top of the school. This chapter describes work with 12 children, of whom only half had been in the school since the nursery stage.

The children

Table 1.1 outlines the group of children who were the focus of the ESL teaching. For the purposes of language support teaching, the children formed a group of four within each of the three classes. Selection of the group was made in consultation with the class teachers; in the school where the teaching took place, there were relatively few new arrivals to the school, so children received consistent support over two or three terms, though teachers reviewed group composition periodically. (In other schools, group composition often changes in response to newcomers.) For this topic all the children in the focused groups were bilingual, though in other topics in a collaborative learning situation groups might include monolingual pupils. Each group had nearly two hours support a week, in two sessions, at a time when the rest of the class was also engaged in the weather topic. The usual pattern of teaching would be that the class teacher and I would introduce an aspect of the topic, and then I would gather the group onto one table and continue with prepared work which paralleled that of the class teacher.

Table 1.1 The group

12 children in three parallel Year 2 classes, aged 6–7	
Languages spoken in addition to English:	
Panjabi	7
Urdu	3
Bengali	1
Hindi	1
Place of birth:	
in UK	10
outside UK	2
Level of language development:	
oral:	most children orally competent at the social level
literacy:	below class average (numeracy weak in some cases)

Portraits of two children

Umair is an Urdu speaker; he was born in Britain and entered the school when he was five but then spent 18 months in Pakistan (where he went to school). He returned to our school eager to participate in English-medium education but hampered by little literacy and restricted vocabulary in English. Umair was very keen on gaining maximum adult attention, and used all such opportunities to ask questions and interact in English. He required language support for only three terms.

Amardeep is a British-born Panjabi speaker who had been in the school since the nursery; she received language support for several years. She has always found the pace of classroom teaching too fast, and struggles to understand the tasks she is expected to do. Her oral English is fluent but her level of literacy below that of the rest of the class; her reading and writing were characterised by nervousness and worry about getting things wrong. She could not read or write numbers above about 20. Her knowledge about the weather was limited at the beginning of the topic.

The needs of these children were typical of the rest of the group: to gain greater literacy skills and confidence, and to participate fully in the curriculum through a focus on selected areas of the topic. The support received in the language group enabled the children to understand more of what was going on in the class when the language support teacher was not there.

Objectives

The overarching objective of school-based ESL teachers, in Britain as elsewhere, is to give their pupils access to the curriculum. Language teachers who are working in the classroom in collaboration with class teachers have two sets of objectives for their bilingual pupils: curriculum objectives (shared with the class teacher) and language objectives. For the topic of weather, these can be briefly set out below:

Curriculum objectives (for the whole class including the focused bilingual pupils):

- be able to describe a range of weather conditions, and know the characteristics of the weather at different seasons;
- be able to describe and record the weather over a period;
- be able to measure temperature, rainfall and wind speed and direction.

Language objectives (applied particularly to the focused bilingual pupils):

- vocabulary enlargement (oral and reading/writing) – weather lexis, time lexis (days, months, seasons, yesterday/tomorrow, etc.);
- scientific language functions – observing, comparing, predicting, etc.;
- literacy development.

Setting learning objectives with mainstream teachers is an important facet of collaborative teaching. Detailed planning for the topic was carried out jointly by the three class teachers (with parallel classes) and the language support teacher; the main focus was scientific. Work on the topic of weather, while occupying perhaps a day and a half a week for most of the spring term, was in addition to separate sessions working on reading and writing development, mathematics, music, art, physical education and so on; at the same time, aspects of these curriculum areas were included in the topic work, as will be shown below.

Planning for the Topic: Content, Language and Timing

Mainstream and support teacher planning for a term works down through a number of levels:

JOINT CLASS TEACHER AND LANGUAGE SUPPORT TEACHER PLANNING
considers
Children's developmental stage
and
National Curriculum requirements
and

Literacy and numeracy skills	Cross-curricular themes previously covered

This led to the decision to teach the cross-curricular topic
WEATHER

The joint decision to focus on Weather results in an outline plan that will be followed by all three classes for the term. This is then worked out in detail for six-week blocks, and class teachers decide on their weekly and daily plans.

As the language support teacher, I then looked at three areas and made decisions about what to support:

LANGUAGE SUPPORT PLANNING

considers

language development opportunities in the topic

scientific skills, concepts and attitudes which are needed

children's individual language needs

leading to a decision to support selected areas of literacy and numeracy skills and weather topic:

| 1. VOCABULARY | 2. DATA HANDLING |
| 3. STORY WRITING | 4. WORK ON SEASONS |

The children's individual language needs were assessed informally through continuous monitoring and record-keeping.

Language support involves decisions not just about *what* to teach, but *when* to teach various aspects of a topic in relation to the week-by-week plan drawn up by the class teachers involved. There are three options on timing: before, concurrently, or after the main presentation of facets of a topic. Pre-teaching is appropriate if what is going to be taught by the class teacher assumes knowledge or skills which the focused bilingual pupils are known not to possess in sufficient depth. In the topic of weather, vocabulary development in advance of class work ensures that the supported pupils can participate in class discussion on an equal footing. Concurrent teaching is appropriate when the whole class is learning a new skill or concept, and the supported pupils gain from extra experience; learning to use a thermometer and record data is an example of concurrent teaching. Teaching language or concepts after the class teacher has worked on parts of the topic is necessary when the supported group of pupils seem not to have learnt what has been intended, or gaps in understanding have been revealed. This cannot easily be planned in advance, although a support teacher may already know of likely areas of weakness; the work on reinforcing the children's knowledge of the days of the week, months of the year and so on, was planned to take place towards the end of the topic since many children of this age are unsure of the order of the seasons, etc. If the children have been shown, by on-going assessment, to be competent in this area, then the support teacher can either work on another area of the topic or do something more general such as literacy development.

The following section describes the teaching materials in the order in which they were presented to the children, and their relationship with the work which was happening in the three classes which contained the L2 children I was supporting. It should be noted again that there was little true partnership teaching and sharing of lead lessons, but materials were brought into the classrooms to be used initially with the focused children but also then with other class members. This helps raise the class teacher's awareness of the language aspects of a topic.

Teaching Resources 1: Focus on Building Vocabulary

The first area of language support was in teaching the range of *vocabulary* that the children would need as they worked on the Weather topic. Drawing upon the weather at the time (January), together with photographs of different kinds of weather, in varying geographical locations, the pupils practised the vocabulary necessary for the weather topic. They also completed a simple picture-to-word matching worksheet. Some of this work took place before the rest of the class started work on the weather topic. The main resource was the 'Rainbows and Lightning' game: this home-made game is a variation of Snakes and Ladders and consists of a playing board with numbers up to 50 (which practised reading numbers) with opportunities to go up rainbows and down flashes of lightning. The children then had to read word cards in order to move on in the game; initially these cards were weather words, as shown in Figure 1.1.

Figure 1.1 Weather word cards

The game was popular, and effective in establishing a basic vocabulary of words such as *storm, cloud, windy, freezing, snow*. It was lent to the three classes in turn, with the bilingual children who were being focused on acting as instructors and helping read the cards. It has to be remembered that most of the class were bilingual and also benefited from hearing and seeing the weather words they were working with. A second set of cards was made which included slightly more unusual words such as *hurricane* and *blizzard*.

The game appealed so much (probably because of the competitive element) that I capitalised on the children's keenness and made a large set of core vocabulary words (such as *them, they, because, after, all* and so on) which were used in the reading scheme, and mounted on different coloured card according to difficulty so that within the same game different children could practise words appropriate to their needs in reading.

After the initial use of the game before the Weather topic became fully established in class, it was played at intervals throughout the term, needing little adult supervision.

Vocabulary development was also promoted through providing each child with a home-made booklet in which they could enter the words connected with weather they needed in their class work; this, while seeming a good idea, in fact didn't succeed because the class teachers found it difficult to remember to encourage the children either to add to the word lists or to draw upon the personal weather dictionary.

More successful was a multilingual word chart which was created with the help of bilingual colleagues, which was used as a classroom poster and also, as enlarged strips, as labels for pictures. Language support teachers in the UK seek to incorporate home languages into topic work wherever possible, believing that pupils benefit from the recognition of their mother-tongues in English-medium schools. The school, in common with many others, has a language policy stating support for the bilingual skills brought to school by its pupils, and an equal opportunities policy which values the cultures represented in the school.

Teaching Resources 2: Focus on Data Handling

A great deal of work was then carried out by the three groups of children collecting, recording and interpreting data. The teaching emphasis was on using practical activities to generate spoken English.

The pupils needed to be able to use a thermometer, and to understand that temperature recorded by an instrument has a correlation with the heat of objects which they handle and with the air which they feel. The scientific

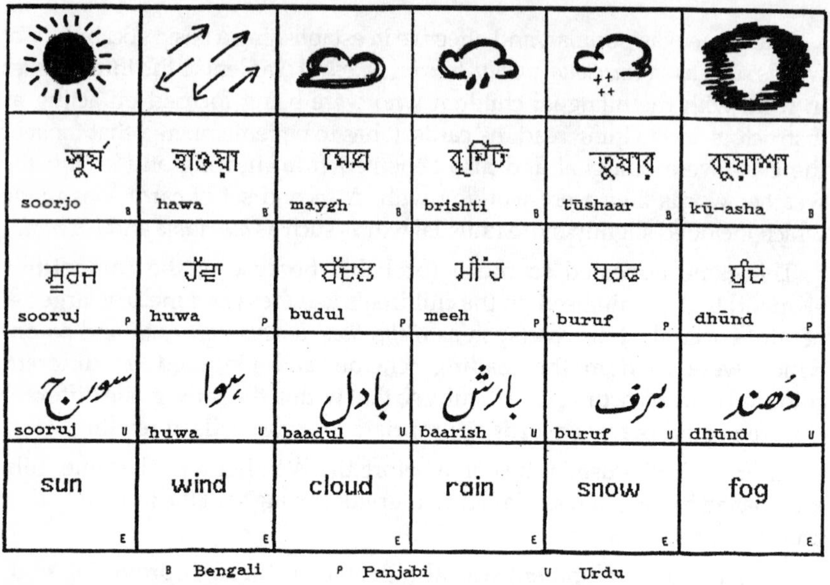

☀	↗↙↗	☁	🌧	🌨	⬤
সূর্য / soorjo ᴮ	হাওয়া / hawa ᴮ	মেঘ / maygh ᴮ	বৃষ্টি / brishti ᴮ	তুষার / tūshaar ᴮ	কুয়াশা / kū-asha ᴮ
ਸੂਰਜ / sooruj ᴾ	ਹੱਵਾ / huwa ᴾ	ਬੱਦਲ / budul ᴾ	ਮੀਂਹ / meeh ᴾ	ਬਰਫ਼ / buruf ᴾ	ਧੁੰਦ / dhūnd ᴾ
سورج / sooruj ᵁ	ہوا / huwa ᵁ	بادل / baadul ᵁ	بارش / baarish ᵁ	برف / buruf ᵁ	دَھند / dhūnd ᵁ
sun ᴱ	wind ᴱ	cloud ᴱ	rain ᴱ	snow ᴱ	fog ᴱ

ᴮ Bengali   ᴾ Panjabi   ᵁ Urdu

Figure 1.2 Multilingual word chart

and geographical skills and the language used are shown in Table 1.2 in the order in which they were taught.

Table 1.2

Data handling	Language focus
1. Measuring temperature using hands to establish relationship to body heat	Comparing temperature/comparatives
2. Using real and model thermometers	Recording temperatures (high and negative numbers); oral descriptions of work to class
3. Recording weather over two weeks	Use of vocabulary and number skills learnt earlier
4. Predicting weather	Predicting (*I think, I hope it will, it's going to.*)
5. Transferring data from class record onto computer data base	Information transfer Adverbials of time (*yesterday, last Monday* etc.)

This work lasted a number of weeks and had to be responsive to the children's needs as revealed by the on-going work. A teacher can establish the language and cognitive learning intentions, but find that something which was assumed to be familiar is not so. This is frequent when working in the mainstream classroom because a number of factors are contributing to the child's growing ability to use language: the class teacher and other adults and children in school, the home and the wider community and so on. A planned and detailed language syllabus is not possible, nor is it possible for a teacher to be completely sure what a child or a group of children knows.

An example of this need for flexibility was Amardeep's difficulties with numbers. Although I knew Amardeep well (described earlier) I hadn't worked with numbers very much with her and wasn't fully aware of the problems she had in reading and using numbers above about 20 (she was six years old at the time); this meant that her work on reading a thermometer had to include many opportunities to look at numbers. Primary language work is concerned with the child's whole education, and language teachers have to be flexible, as well as aware of the curriculum areas being taught by the class teacher. The discussion which takes place during joint planning sessions is a vital source of information for the language support teacher, as is the informal discussion which frequently happens between teachers about individual children and their strengths and weaknesses. Often, with continuity of staffing, a language support teacher can contribute knowledge of a child built up over a number of years.

Looking at the work outlined in Table 1.2, the first section is self-explanatory. We gathered a variety of hot, warm, blood-heat and cold objects, felt them, and placed them in 'heat order'. It will be remembered that the children could use English with reasonable proficiency in the majority of cases but needed enrichment and expansion of their syntax and lexis. Describing degrees of warmth is a good example of this, with the children learning words such as *luke-warm*, *freezing*, and *boiling*, as well as comparatives and superlatives connected with heat.

The next activity involved two types of thermometer and *measuring heat* scientifically. One was a traditional glass laboratory thermometer with a bulb, the other an unbreakable dial thermometer which the children could safely handle (a Thermostik) (see Figure 1.3). The heat-measuring part is contained in a metal spike which can be placed in the ground, suspended in air or put into a liquid or, for example, a cooked potato. Both types of thermometer have only the 10s marked on the scale (0°C, 10°C, 20°C, etc.), and the Thermostik dial in particular is quite small. So I made several model thermometers out of card which the children could easily use; the 'liquid' could be pulled up and down or the hand of the dial could be turned (see Figure 1.4). When we measured water with ice in, the child reading the real thermometer could look at the temperature and then manipulate the model so that everyone could see. Gradually a relationship between a low number on the thermometer and something being felt to be cold was established.

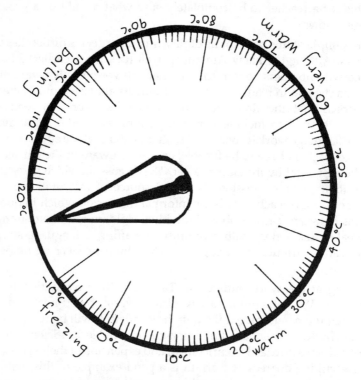

Figure 1.3 Thermostik dial thermometer

Recording the temperature needed lots of practice; it was relatively easy to measure something like water from hot and cold taps, an orange or a baked potato, a beaker of ice or the teacher's cup of coffee, because the children could see the dial or the column of liquid moving before their eyes and at the same time could experience the heat through their hands. It was more demanding to record air temperature since the differences between different parts of the centrally heated school were less dramatic The children found that the hall was colder than their classrooms and that the

Figure 1.4 Thermometer made of card

school offices were the warmest parts of the school, but it was not until we had a day of freezing fog in a fortnight of generally cloudy dull weather that they began to appreciate how something they could not see had a temperature. This led to work on daily recording of the weather.

Giving time for working on an area of skill and knowledge such as this work on temperature is a valuable role for the language support teacher who is working in the mainstream. While one cannot cover every area, small-group work enables all members of the class to succeed in the curriculum. Although all classes in infant and junior schools are mixed-ability, and have been for decades, providing work at varying levels of cognitive challenge is a very demanding task for teachers and one where language support teachers can contribute. Class teachers and language teachers alike need a repertoire of approaches to curriculum areas in order to increase access to skills and concepts. Schools with bilingual pupils at various levels of proficiency in English have to increase their awareness of visual approaches to teaching in order to support language and cognitive learning. The model thermometers described above are examples of this approach, and after the focused bilingual children had demonstrated the models' use to their peers, the models were borrowed and copied by the class teachers for the benefit of all the children in the class.

Standardised national assessment tasks for 7 year olds had recently been introduced at the time of teaching the topic of weather; one requirement was recording air temperature, so the work carried out by the bilingual children in my groups enabled them to fulfil this task satisfactorily.

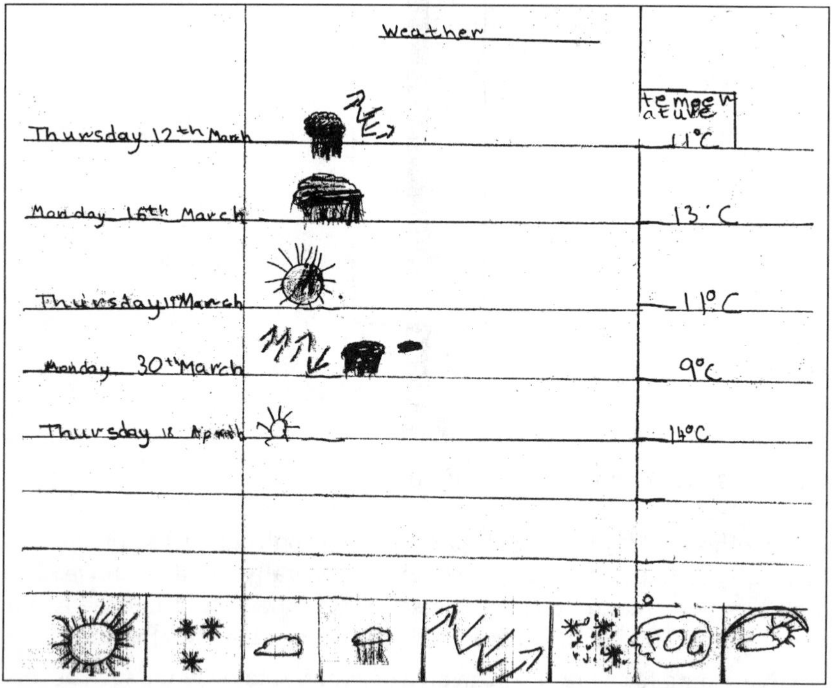

Figure 1.5 Part of Umair's weather chart

An incidental part of recording the weather daily was trying to predict the next day's weather; this gave opportunities for language practice of language items such as *I think it will be cold and foggy, it might be cloudy, probably it will rain* (see Figure 1.5).

The last activity concerned with recording the weather was transferring the information gathered in one class about the sort of weather that had been noted twice a day over a fortnight onto a simple data base which then displayed the information in various graphs. The focused bilingual children did this under my supervision, but while the result looked impressive (see Figure 1.6), it might have been better to draw the relevant numbers of clouds, fog etc and squares of paper and stick them onto a block graph, rather than a rather small computer-produced graph. Language support teachers are often concerned with children whose language level makes abstract concepts difficult to grasp and who benefit from the physical manipulation of objects (or drawings in this case); principles of good primary practice are central to good language support in the mainstream.

WEATHER	Number
RAINY	0
SNOW	0
SUNNY	1
FOG	1
WINDY	1
CLOUD/SUN	5
CLOUDY	11

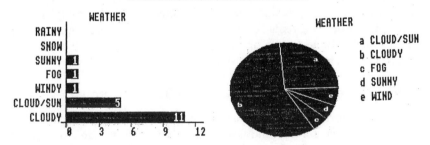

Figure 1.6 Computer print-out

Teaching Resources 3: Focus on Story Writing

Language support teachers have to balance curriculum demands and language skill needs of their children; this is not easy when teachers have at the most two sessions of about an hour a week with each group. The next stage of the term's work on weather sought to bring listening and speaking, writing and reading skills together in a story-writing activity. The story involved was being read to all three classes and was the Aesop fable of *The Wind and the Sun,* where both tried to prove themselves the strongest by getting a man to take off his coat. Small group worked centred on writing is hard in a classroom if the rest of the class is engaged in another activity because of the noise level; for this teaching I took the children to an empty room. Not all language support teachers have or want this facility; I find literacy work with young children who have limited English often more effective in a withdrawal or pull-out situation because they need to concentrate and listen carefully. This can mean working in a corridor, which is a backward-looking arrangement as far as ESL teaching in Britain is concerned since that is where much of the early language teaching took place! However, flexibility of teaching location is one key to success in this field.

The story writing varied somewhat between the three groups, but basically I read them a version of the story and the children either then took it in turns to write a sentence on the computer, aided by group discussion, or dictated their own version to me on a large piece of paper which I typed up. Two activities were devised to help with reading. I cut the stories into sections, mounted them on card and asked the children to sequence the text; when I was sure they could read the text they stuck the photocopied sections into small home-made books which they illustrated and took back into class where the teachers asked them to read their version to the rest of the class. The most valuable part of this activity was the composing – getting the order of events sorted out was difficult, so word-processing with its facility of adding to or changing text was very useful. A copy of the text created for sequencing is shown in Figure 1.7.

Teaching Resources 4: Focus on the Seasons, etc.

The final work on weather was teaching the order of the days of the week, the seasons, months and years. The whole classes were working on seasonal characteristics but it became clear that the focused bilingual children were not sure of the names in relation to the weather. This is not surprising since the children were quite young and therefore had not experienced many springs and summers, and also since the climate in urban London does not have extremes of temperature marking the different seasons! The children do need to be knowledgeable in this area, so I devised some card wheels which indicate the sequences. Two out of the four are shown in Figures 1.8 and 1.9. These wheels have been the most enduring resources which have come out of the weather topic and have

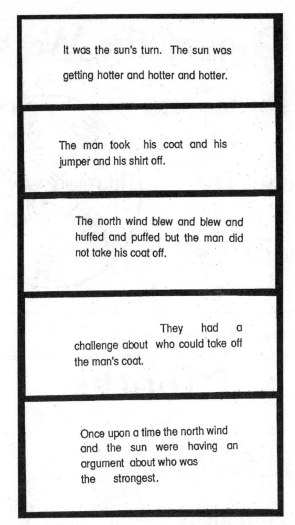

Figure 1.7 Text for sequencing

been frequently borrowed by class teachers over the whole school. As I am working in nine classrooms, I am in a good position to know when I can contribute this kind of visual aid.

The children's knowledge of the days of the week and so on improved as a result of these wheels, but ideally they would be available on display in each class all the time so that pupils could gradually absorb the interrelationship between day, month, season and year.

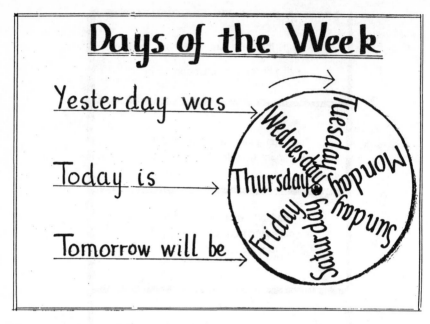

Figure 1.8 Days of the week wheel

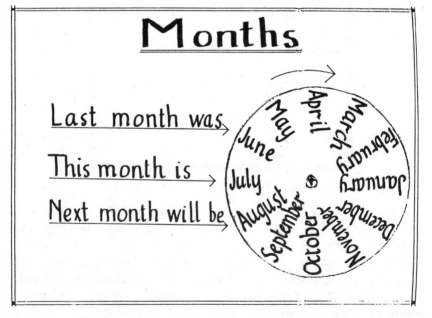

Figure 1.9 Months wheel

The Children's Learning

Limited English can frequently mean limited academic success in the mainstream classroom. The language support teacher's role is to try to counter this, and to devise appropriate learning tasks. Group work which is genuinely collaborative can be an important factor in the children's ability to attain high standards. The joint composing of the Aesop story is an example of successful group work – without the group discussion the sequencing of even such a simple story would have been difficult for the children, and the language of the final versions was much richer than could have been achieved by individuals.

Class and language support teaching together ensured that all the children learnt to use and read a thermometer and to keep a daily record of the weather, and to recognise the words and symbols used on a weather map and chart. They were also able to read and sequence their own versions of *The Wind and the Sun*, to widen their vocabulary in relation to the topic, and to gain increased knowledge of the cyclical pattern of the days of the week, the seasons and so on. Umair enjoyed the work on weather and particularly benefited from the increase in vocabulary which came both from the Rainbows and Lightning game and the practical work on temperature. Amardeep learned to read the basic weather vocabulary of *wind, snow, fog, cloud*, etc. but found the extended weather vocabulary too difficult for her. She used the core sight vocabulary cards introduced later to practise the words which she needed to know for her progress in reading. Her story writing had not been very successful up until this time, and she found the group story composing beneficial. Her ability to write a structured original story developed well in the following term, but one cannot ascribe this directly to the work on weather. The success experienced in the language support group needs to be visible to a class teacher and the pupils' peers if raised self-esteem is carried over into mainstream work. Where a language support group contains children with different levels of English language proficiency it is possible for the status of those children with limited English to be raised.

Conclusion

This topic, with 6 and 7 year olds, is not presented as a model of good practice, but rather as an example to be pondered upon with a view to raising the consciousness of teachers of bilingual children. I have indicated some of the issues raised by language teaching in mainstream classrooms. To those readers who are second language teachers but who are more familiar with working in a withdrawal teaching situation I would say that working alongside mainstream colleagues brings many benefits, not all of which will have been evident from the work described above. These may summarised as follows:

Benefits of in-class support for the pupils

- Children have equal opportunity to participate in the mainstream curriculum as the tasks and activities are made accessible through differentiated materials, and the language teacher knows exactly what is being taught by the class teacher.
- Language teaching is delivered at the point of need, integrated with and tailored to the specific demands of the curriculum; the language support teacher can anticipate needs and pre-teach important elements of the curriculum.
- Home languages are visible in the mainstream classroom (this is particularly important if the language support teacher is bilingual and can use the children's community languages to support concept development).

Advantages of in-class support for the class and language support teachers

- The class teacher knows that some of the children having most difficulties in the class are having intensive support in certain areas.
- Class teachers and language support teachers can stimulate each other's teaching, and share the burden of planning – language teachers can provide language-centred resources and teaching ideas which benefit all children.
- Teachers can share insights into children's learning, not just for the focused children but for the whole class; bringing another adult into the class can lessen the isolation experienced by class teachers.
- The class teacher is able to spend more time with other pupils in her class.
- The language teacher is a fully integrated member of the teaching force, rather than being marginalised as can happen if the children are taken out of the classroom for language lessons and the mainstream staff do not know of the work going on in the group.
- The bilingual language teacher can contribute home languages to the mainstream learning situation, and the monolingual language support teacher can contribute multilingual resources which will aid the whole class.

However, working in a mainstream language teaching situation is not always an optimum situation, especially at a time of cut-backs in the provision of specialist teachers. While the work on the Weather went well, there are other times when there are difficulties which force teachers to reconsider the arrangements for providing effective teaching. Some of the disadvantages are shown below:

Disadvantages of in-class language support for pupils

- Language support teachers may not have sufficient liaison time to plan jointly with the class teachers and may provide inappropriate resources.
- Bilingual pupils in need may get very little focused time because of time-table problems, particularly where language support teachers are peripatetic or where learners are scattered among several classes.
- Individual pupil programmes may not be very easy to plan and carry out because the language support teacher is working with broad areas of the curriculum.
- Basic literacy skills needs are not always easily catered for in a content-centred language teaching situation.

Disadvantages of in-class language support for language teachers and class teachers

- Different teaching styles may mean that having two teachers in one class is difficult; a class teacher may not be willing to open her classroom to another teacher nor accept suggestions about the language demands of the curriculum.
- Dispersal of small numbers of bilingual pupils over numerous classes may mean an inefficient use of language support teachers' time.
- Planning time is essential for successful integrated work, but where this is not possible language support teachers may arrive in class to find that plans have been changed and their prepared materials inappropriate.

In the UK in the mid-1990s we are having to look carefully at the arrangements and pedagogy for teaching English to children for whom it is an additional language. Language support teaching, like all teaching, is not static; schools, classrooms and children change and interact continuously to create challenging situations for all concerned. We have to be flexible in our responses to children's needs and to funding difficulties, but seek always to work towards creating learning situations which help all pupils to succeed.

Note

A full history of the political and pedagogic education of bilingual children can be found in Levine (1990).

Reference

Levine, J. (1990) Responding to linguistic and culture diversity in the teaching of English as a second language. In J. Levine (ed.) *Bilingual Learners and the Mainstream Classroom*. London: Falmer Press.

2 A Whole-language Approach to Mainstreaming

L. WESTBROOK AND SHARON BERGQUIST-MOODY

Introduction

Our story relates some of the efforts made at improving the learning environment for the language minority children and their teachers at one elementary school in a southeast neighborhood of Portland, Oregon. Arleta Primary School serves approximately 500 students ages 5 to 12 years old. Currently our ESL population makes up about 23% of the entire school population. Russian, Vietnamese, and Spanish top the list of 10 different languages spoken by our second-language (L2) students. Between the fall of 1988 and the spring of 1990, the ESL population grew from approximately 7% to approximately 28%. During this time our classrooms had become more whole language, writing process, and hands-on oriented, with a strong focus on developmental strategies. At the same time we were involved in school-wide staff development provided by a three-year grant in which we studied the needs of our low-income population, reflecting on the needs of our ESL students and the multicultural approach of our district. In light of these developments, our traditional pull-out program seemed less satisfactory for the children and staff.

To advance our program we planned two pilots for fall of 1990. The first was a content shelter for the L2 learners ages 8 to 10. Here we used theme studies to simultaneously develop language and social studies/science concepts. The second pilot was a team-teaching model in a second grade classroom: One-half of the students were L2 learners and one-half were monolingual learners. We staffed the class with one classroom teacher, Sharon, and one ESL specialist, Dan (Team 1).

Team 1 implemented the model in a second-grade classroom in the academic year 1990–1, and both teachers felt all their students had benefited greatly: There were very positive interactions between the monolingual and multilingual students; the L2 students were much more involved in the classroom both socially and academically; and the mainstream children became much more aware of how language is used. Outside the classroom we recognized quickly the benefit of two teachers: our discussions around evaluation and assessment led to specific action for individual students. Parents and students responded favorably to the model as well.

The following year, Team 1 decided to 'move up' to third grade with their class. A new classroom was added at second grade and staffed by Team 2 (classroom teacher Donna, and ESL Specialist L.). The third year Team 1 returned to second grade and Team 2 'moved up' to third grade. We, the authors of this chapter, represent both teams, Sharon from Team 1, and L. from Team 2. In order to simplify our story, we have decided to merge the events in the two classrooms, distinguishing activities by grade level only. When we refer to philosophy and teaching strategies, we represent all four teachers.

Beginning Implementation

When a partnership is established, the first step for teammates is to discuss educational philosophy. The model is based on the premise that every learner will participate in every activity, regardless of their level of English proficiency. To do this we maintain high expectations for every child, and use the presence of two teachers to keep students on task. We employ techniques such as teaching from whole to part; using graphic organizers; choosing meaningful, hands-on activities and cooperative learning situations; and modeling thinking processes and problem solving, including how children relate to each other and the adults at school. The class writes about everything we do. Sometimes a teacher will take dictation as in the Language Experience Approach, and other times the children write individually. We use picture dictionaries, illustrated charts, labels on furniture and student supplies more than we used to. Essential to accomplishing this objective of involving every student in every activity is continual checking for understanding: For the L2 learners we use peer interpreters, model extensively, and often ask the kids themselves to explain an activity before beginning it.

Secondly, we ask that all students, L1 and L2 learners alike, take responsibility for their own learning. We recognize the wide range of abilities in any group of youngsters, but particularly within a group including L2 students. We enable students to be responsible by (1) developing class criteria for completing an activity, (2) setting individual, achievable goals, (3) allowing choice within any given activity, and (4) facilitating self-evaluation using the pre-determined criteria and goals.

Thirdly, we believe that depth in study is as high a priority as breadth of topics, i e. while we cover fewer topics in any academic year, the depth of our study will ensure that basic concepts are explored through myriad avenues. Related to this idea is our belief that depth in community relations is beneficial to a group of learners, for which reason we include class meetings in our daily schedule and have stayed with each group of youngsters for two academic years.

We have two thoughts specifically regarding language learning. First, because we know that learning occurs through doing, we believe that peer interaction is essential for language development. Our classrooms buzz with several languages and laughter and learning. Next, we remind ourselves to search out the true cognitive abilities of our L2 learners that may be difficult to uncover due to the challenge these children face in expressing themselves in English. Lastly, if students are able to read and write in their first language, we encourage them to continue. Sometimes we are able to use older students and bilingual aides in the classroom to assist in the L1 literacy process.

In thinking about ourselves, we increasingly appreciate the social nature of learning. Two heads are better than one.

The biggest stumbling block to actually implementing this model has been a lack of time for planning and materials preparation. While we have had occasional release time, most often we have had to grab time before and after school hours, time that competes with the ESL specialist's other responsibilities. Eventually we found a way to work with the music and physical education specialists to schedule back-to-back sessions with our students, giving us two periods of 50 minutes each week for planning.

Our Classrooms

Through the course of an academic year a class schedule evolves. We thought, however, that examples of year-end schedules for one second-grade class and one third-grade class might best illustrate how we have worked within the team teaching model. Following the schedules we describe some specific procedures (see Table 2.1).

Table 2.1

Second-grade classroom		Third-grade classroom	
8.40	Writing workshop/ Reading workshop alternate days with P.M.	8.40	Journals
		8.55	(1) Thematic units *or*
	Writing/reading on corresponding days		(2) Read aloud/Mini-lesson
9.20	Read aloud	9.30	Writing workshop
9.40	Snack and recess	10.10	SSR
10.00	Thematic units	10.30	Reading workshop
10.45	Math	11.20	Class meeting

(Afternoons the ESL specialist is not in the classroom. The classroom teacher covers other curriculum areas, such as art, handwriting, and library visits.)

Writing/Reading Workshop

Arleta students come to second grade familiar with writing as a process (pre-writing, writing, conferencing, re-writing, editing, publishing). To help our second graders recall the sequence of the process we began one year by equating each step of the writing process to an animal with 'similar' characteristics. Pre-writing, when an author's ideas are jumping out in any order, was likened to a kangaroo hopping about; the first draft, when the author pushes ahead to get the ideas into sentences, was thought of as a charging bull, etc. We found these analogies (and the visuals that went up around the room to reinforce them) helped the L2 students in particular to understand and remember the process.

For workshop time in second grade we have used a management tool we call 'The Goal Sheet' (see Figure 2.1). Students write the title of the book they are reading and the topic of their writing in the coinciding section of a given day. The L2 children are often able to copy the book title themselves, once they know what 'title' is. Otherwise they are assisted by teachers or peers. Teachers circulate and give students blue sticky dots by their entries, signaling the students to begin reading. Later, when the kids are writing, we encourage some ESL students to draw first, adding words from the dictionary later. The L2 children may also use picture dictionaries in finding topics they can write about. Some even choose to create their own picture dictionaries as a way to begin.

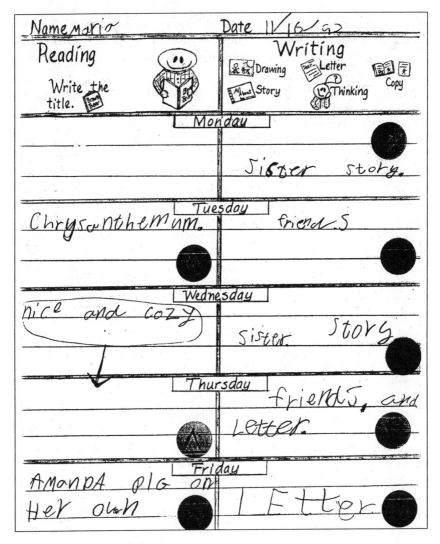

Figure 2.1 The Goal Sheet

In third grade our workshop time was actually divided into two parts, a writing workshop and a reading workshop. To begin writing workshop, students check in each day. Teachers record the title of the work in progress as well as the student's progress through the writing process. The kids' writing may or may not result in publication. If a book is published, it will be presented to the whole class by the author. This sharing of published books gives the L2 kids in particular a chance to be experts on some topic, and is strong motivation for all of the children to write and publish more books. To assess learning, we conference individually with students, and we've been fortunate to have regular help from bilingual assistants during this workshop time.

During reading workshop the two teachers take on different roles. T1 meets with literature discussion groups and guided reading groups while T2 monitors independent work. The independent work time is an opportunity for students to complete book group assignments or to spend time reading and responding to literature of their choice, so the monitoring is essential to clarify tasks and ensure that all students understand the concepts they are working with. In one second grade we taught a variety of activities that the children can use to respond to books. We found *Literacy Through Literature* (Johnson & Louis, 1987) and *Bringing It All Together* (Johnson, 1990) to be great resources for activities that combine graphics and writing, a key combination for the ESL kids. These responses were taught as whole-class activities following a read-aloud story. By third grade the learners were able to choose for themselves from their repertoire of responses (see Figure 2.2). Fridays are reserved for learners to present their book responses to the whole class. These presentations are particularly valuable to the L2 learners: this is a time when the kids have work to share that requires reading aloud and responding to questions and comments from peers. Because the kids themselves have chosen what literature to read and respond to, they really know what they are talking about and are therefore able to succeed in the presentation.

We feel strongly that the ESL children need to be included in the literature discussion groups. Often the books, chapters or novels being studied are beyond the reading abilities of the L2 learners. We have taped books and let the kids follow the text with headphones at a listening center; we have used Silent Sustained Reading time to read aloud while the children followed along, and we have gotten help from educational assistants during independent work time to ensure that the ESL students have 'read' the assigned portions of a book and will be able to participate in a discussion with their peers. At one point we asked more developed readers to buddy up with those who needed help, either doing the reading themselves while their partner followed, or taking turns reading a page or a paragraph. This didn't work, and we have looked at the task of reading aloud to explain it. We hypothesize that reading aloud at first read-through was either too challenging for a less able reader, or too slow for a very interested one. Asking the students to read aloud at a second read-through means asking them to give up significant portions of their independent work time. So we were back to adult assistance. We realize that being read

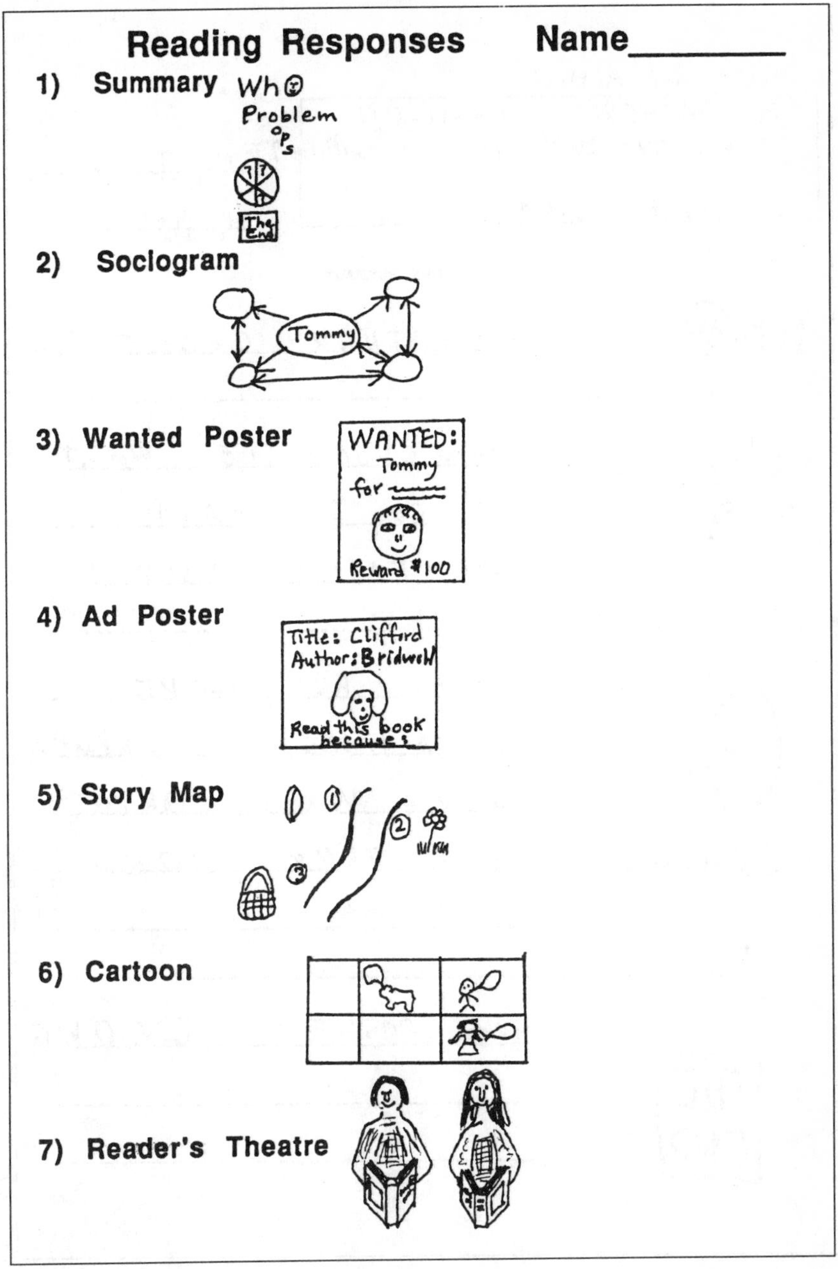

Figure 2.2 Responses to the story 'My Father's Dragon'

Title and Author

MY fATHER'S DRAGON
STORY BY RUTH STILES GANNeTT   NaTalya
                                    NAME

Chapter Nine   4-28-193
                                    DATE

STORY SUMMARY

WH😊

WHO? fATHER   CroCodile

PR O BLEM
    o
    Ps!

PROBLEM? Crocodile waht
IO et The fATHER
BaT FATHER maht to
ktas The raher

(circle with ? marks)

Solutions

SOLUTIONS?   he GaVE
crocodiles   LiLePaPs
ahD   Wan   akras
Tha ther Baks

THE END? faTHER   GoaWa

THE
END

Figure 2.2 continued

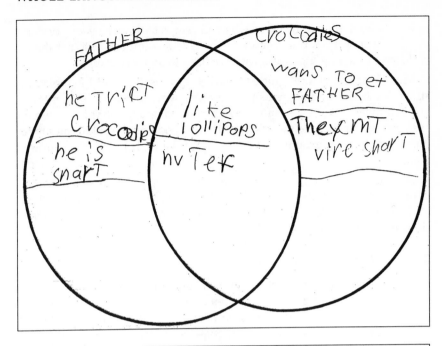

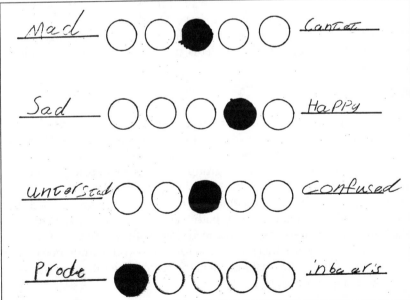

Figure 2.2 *continued*

to is not equal to reading alone, when one stops to think back or ponder a personal connection. But because we believe it is important to get the L2 children discussing literature, we have used this procedure.

The objective of our guided reading groups is to address reading strategies. In these heterogeneous groups we work to help the students use and be aware of the semantic, syntactic and graphophonemic cueing systems. By third grade many students have good reading skills and meet only in discussion groups, but for many of the L2 learners these groups continue.

Assessment records of both reading and writing progress are anecdotal. In one system we made notes on 'Post-Its' about writing conferences which we later transferred to a notebook. At another time we kept track of reading skills in an index card file.

Silent sustained reading

This reading period has changed over time. In second grade nearly all students were sharing books and 'reading' together. ESL students like listening to other students who volunteer to read to them, maybe story books or the lyrics to songs learned in class. One year, by the middle of third grade, the entire class was ready to benefit from a silent reading period. More often, however, we continue to have 'Quiet Sustained Reading'. We use this time for individual reading conferences and special instruction with individuals or pairs of ESL students, much like the time in our guided reading groups.

Read aloud

Students practice predicting, inferring, etc. In second grade we randomly divide the class into two groups to facilitate discussion and to allow us to note listening and comprehension skills of the ESL students who tend to be more reluctant in the larger group. The classroom teacher and ESL specialist alternate between the two heterogeneously mixed groups. Teachers usually choose books that relate to our current theme studies. Eventually all students read with both teachers. In third grade students take turns choosing the book which is read aloud to the whole class. Allowing the children this choice means that the selections will include books that the ESL children can understand, enabling them to be full participants in the large group discussion.

Snack and recess

Students are in charge of selling and purchasing their snacks, crackers that students had donated. We have found many ESL students have not handled US money before and need practice just naming the coins. Every day two students act as vendors, and we often pair an ESL student with a monolingual student who knows about the US monetary system. Buyers keep their allotments of play money in envelopes alphabetized by student names. Snack prices and money allotments increase as the students' mathematical concepts develop (i.e. dimes to dollars).

Thematic units

(a) Nutrition: The Food Pyramid: second grade

Our goal for this unit was to learn how to use the US Department of Agriculture food pyramid (see Figure 2.3) in order to make good food choices. For the L2 learners, we had the additional objective of teaching the names of food.

Figure 2.3 The food pyramid.

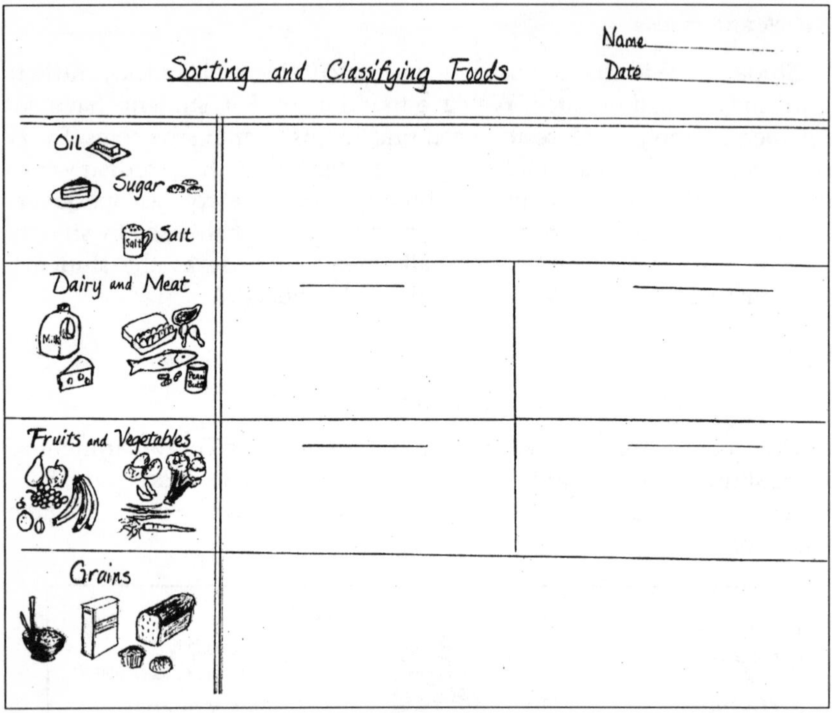

Sorting and Classifying Foods	Name _____ Date _____	
Oil ⬛ 🍰 Sugar 🍬 🧂 Salt		
Dairy and Meat 🥛 🧈 🐟	————	————
Fruits and Vegetables 🍇🍌 🫑 🥕	————	————
Grains 🍜 📦 🍞 🧁		

Figure 2.4 Sorting and classifying foods.

For the initial activity, pairs collected small pictures of food. We paired the students monolingual with multilingual to name and categorize the pictures, which we combined to create a large visual chart. Eventually students made individual charts (see Figure 2.4) and wrote reports using our class experience and picture dictionaries as resources, generalising about the various food groups. One teacher assisted a group of L2 students who needed extra help as they were making their charts.

Next, small groups of students explored the basic structure of pyramids by building them with wooden blocks. The kids discovered the necessity of a large base, and we connected this physical feature to the image of the food pyramid, grain being the foundation of good nutrition. We shared what the children knew about grains, flour and bread, learning about the absence of bread in Asian rice-eating countries, and the existence of a black bread in Russia that is unavailable in Portland. The whole class then taped pictures of food to a large pyramid, and we discussed the results of removing various blocks. Students wrote up their observations and a conclusion (see Figure 2.5).

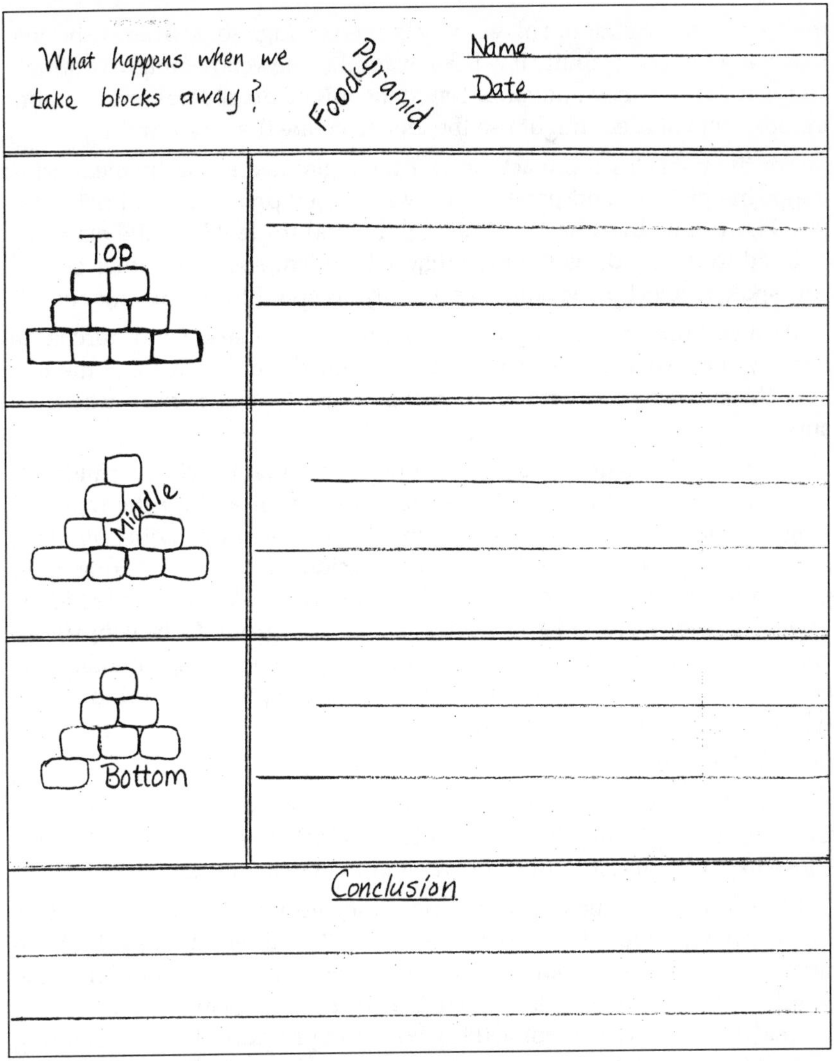

What happens when we take blocks away? Food Pyramid

Name _____

Date _____

Top

Middle

Bottom

Conclusion

Figure 2.5 Writing about the food pyramid.

Another day students wrote about recommended daily servings, optionally using a pattern sentence. For example, the teacher wrote on a large chart 'You should eat _____ servings of _____ every day', and the students used the food pyramid and the chart in Figure 2.4 to complete the information. The pattern could be repeated several times using different food choices in order both to practice the sentence structure and to research the content information. This activity is open enough for learners to be able to work at their own ability level. For example, a newcomer might complete one sentence, a more advanced student might do several, and a more independent student might use the idea to create their own writing.

For the final classroom activity, partners planned a healthy meal using magazine pictures and paper plates which they presented and defended (see Figure 2.6). In some cases the multilingual student held the plate and pointed to the foods as the monolingual student spoke. In other cases a soft-spoken, short paragraph was happily accepted from ESL students.

As a culminating activity we walked to a supermarket and purchased healthy snacks which we enjoyed back at our room, For some of the ESL kids the supermarket with all its merchandise to choose from was truly super.

We merged this unit into a story format based on the classic children's tale, *The Little Red Hen*. The L2 learners quickly picked up the repeated language of the story, ensuring their involvement in the activities, First the children sequenced a teacher-written version of the tale, taking their individual copies home to share with their parents. We also made lifesize paper characters, created a play and videotaped it, ground wheat into flour, and baked bread. The students wrote about everything: making the characters, the personalities ot the characters, the process of grinding the wheat, and directions for making the bread.

(b)   The Big Cats: second grade

Our objective was to have learners research and present a topic. Curriculum requirements at this grade level include animal habitat, so we chose to study cats since they are familiar to many children.

Pairs of students chose to study one of the five big cats in our Metro Zoo. Initially the L2 students were confused about the different types of cats, so we enlisted the help of our bilingual assistant. Students did not know the word 'cougar', but we discovered the Russian speakers had the word 'puma'. Our first classroom activity was using resource books, including pictures, to complete one of our 'cat charts' (see Figure 2.7). Researching is difficult for L2 learners, so some needed teacher help in finding more than one fact about their cats. Other L2 learners got assistance from stronger students.

Students then used their charts to write a report which was edited, typed, and glued onto 5"× 7" index cards by the teacher (see Figure 2.8). Next the kids made papier mâché models of their cats and created appropriate habitats in cardboard boxes. ESL students did this part easily

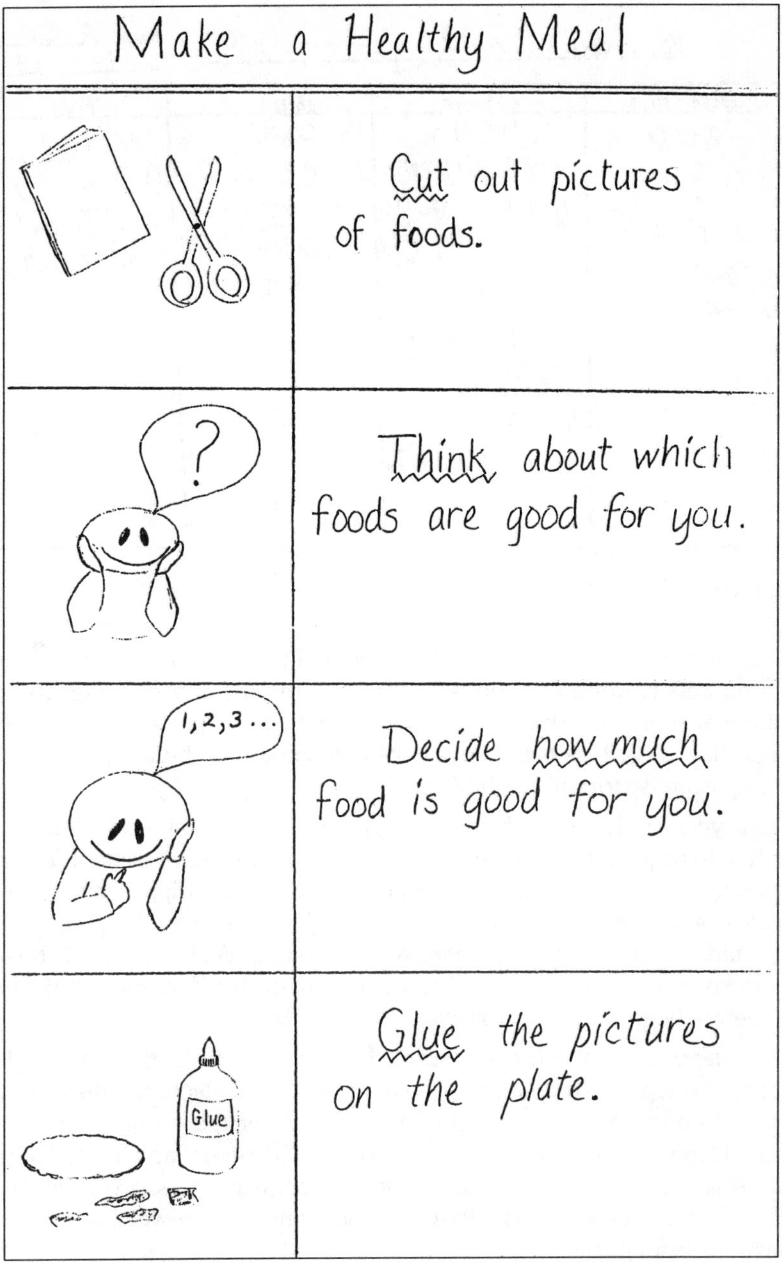
Make a Healthy Meal
Cut out pictures of foods.
?
Think about which foods are good for you.
1, 2, 3 . . .
Decide how much food is good for you.
Glue
Glue the pictures on the plate.

Figure 2.6 Food chart.

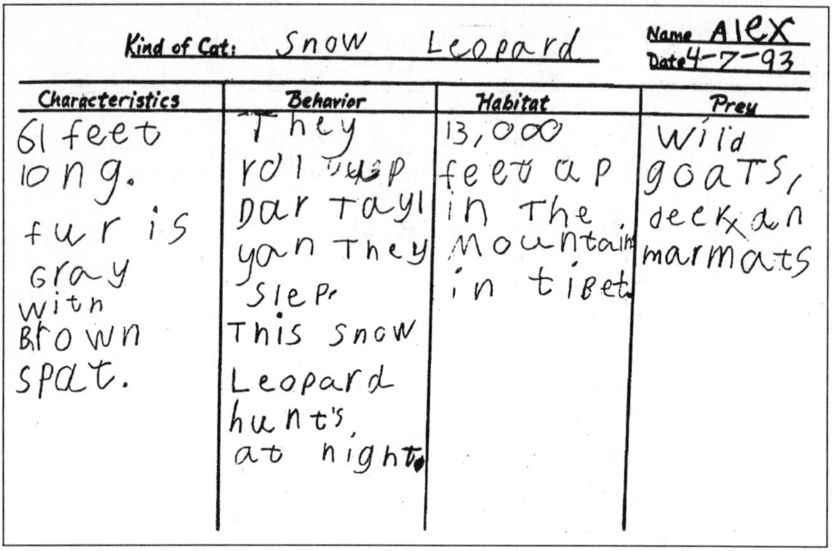

Kind of Cat: Snow Leopard			Name Alex Date 4-7-93
Characteristics	Behavior	Habitat	Prey
61 feet long. fur is Gray with Brown spat.	They rol up Dar tayl yan They sleP. This snow Leopard hunt's at night.	13,000 feet up in The Mountain in tibet.	Wild goaTs, deekxan marmats

Figure 2.7 A cat chart.

with good photographs and library books. Integral to the process were
writing and reading directions for making the cat and creating lists of
needed supplies for the habitats (newspaper, flour paste, string, rocks,
twigs, clay, etc.). This turned out to be a lesson in vocabulary as well as a
writing exercise for the L2 children.

One year a field trip to the zoo was planned for the first week of the unit
but had to be postponed because of rain. When we finally rescheduled our
trip, students had a form to complete regarding the origin, habitat, and
behaviors of their cat (see Figure 2.9). ESL students were helped by the
other kids to get the information from the Zoo signs. We believe the habitats
created by the kids would have been more true-to-life if we had visited the
zoo before beginning the projects.

The learners individually presented their reports to the class while
sitting next to their three-dimensional models. We videotaped the presentations as part of a class record of activities. After the presentations, the
students transformed the classroom into a 'Cat Museum' and invited other
classes and staff to visit. The L2 students were eager to share what they
knew although in some cases they gave only one- or two-word answers to
questions from guests.

The Lion

by Sergey Misiuk

The lion is orange.

The girl lions fight.

The lion lives in Africa.

He eats deer, zebra, rabbit and giraffe.

He eats porcupine.

The Lion

by Pavel Yashenko

The lion is orange. The hair is long hair.

The girl lions fight.

The lion lives in Africa.

He eats zebra.

Jaguar

by Olga Vorobets

The jaguar is black and orange. It is big. It is powerful.

It is an expert swimmer.

It lives in the rain forest.

It eats fish, deer and tapir.

Figure 2.8 Children's reports about cats.

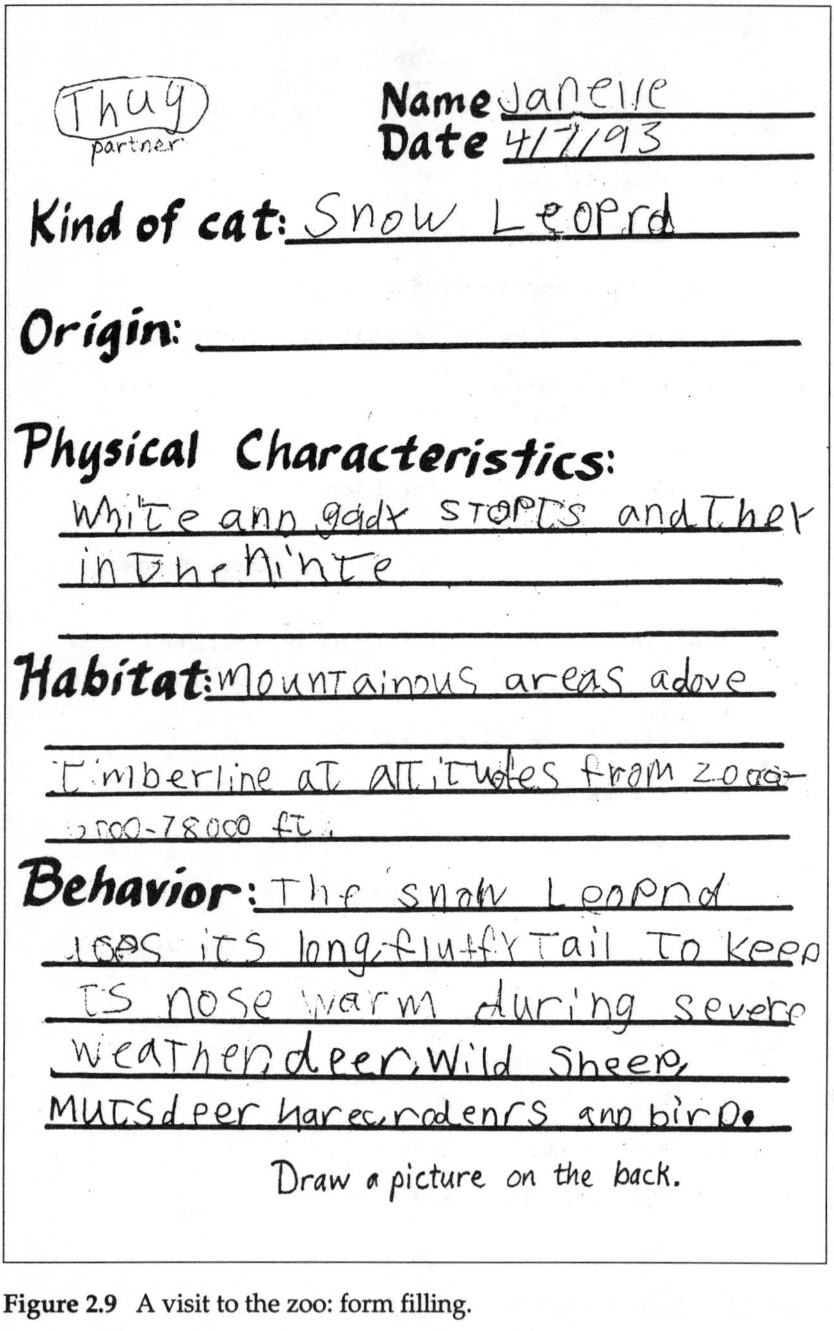

(Thuy)
partner

Name Janelle

Date 4/7/93

Kind of cat: Snow Leoprd

Origin: _____

Physical Characteristics:
White ann gady stopts andTher
inThenin te

Habitat: mounTainous areas adove
Timberline aT alTiTudes from 2000-
2000-78000 ft.

Behavior: The snow Leopnd
ises its long-fluffyTail To keep
Ts nose warm during severe
weaTherndeer,Wild Sheep,
MutsdeerharesrodenrS ano birD.

Draw a picture on the back.

Figure 2.9 A visit to the zoo: form filling.

(c) Little House in the Big Woods (Wilder, 1953): third grade

Third grade curriculum in Portland includes a year-long study of our city. The objective of this mini-unit was to familiarize the students with the way of life of the immigrant settlers. We used the Wilder book two different ways in two different years.

One year we read the entire book with the whole class. On one day the teacher would read aloud a section of the book while the students individually drew pictures about the events in the text. Some kids chose to make one large picture, adding details as the story progressed that day; other kids chose to make a sequence of drawings depicting the action. These pictures demonstrated what the kids had understood without using language, a plus for the ESL kids.

The following day, before continuing on in the book, the class would gather on the rug to recall the details of the previous day's reading. First we made a list of events, and then from the list we created a short summary. We used the discussions to focus on contrasting detail and main idea and to make sure everyone, especially the ESL children, were following the story. Later in the day two students would cooperate in painting a picture to illustrate the class summary.

At the conclusion of the book, we began discussing in detail the natural setting. We used this discussion to move into a mini-unit on trees and the Portland area before the arrival of the immigrant settlers. We researched trees. To begin we walked through our neighborhood and the students measured the circumference of a tree, estimated its height, and took a rubbing of the bark. For some of our L2 learners, this was the beginning and the end of their individual research. The class as a whole cut trees from paper and transformed one of our bulletin boards into a forest. We explored the concept of depth in art and added some animals native to our area. We considered the various ways the pioneer immigrants had used trees and compared them to Indian uses of trees. In this way our mini-unit on trees and early Portland merged into a study of Indians, including some role plays that helped us reflect on our attitudes about the arrival of Christopher Columbus.

Using the Wilder book another year, we used a story-type format, choosing to read only certain selections from the book. To enable L2 learners to follow and read portions of the difficult text, we copied difficult passages onto chart paper and added small illustrations. We used these charts for reading practice, and the students referred to them during independent reading time. This helped clarify the descriptions of life during this time for the ESL students.

To set the scene, we read aloud descriptions of the house. We spent time looking at pictures in books in order for the L2 students to get a visual idea of this time period. A couple of Russian-speaking students related the picture of a plough to their experience on a farm in Russia. Groups of three or four children used cardboard boxes and paper to build models of the rooms of the house, smokehouse and garden, including furnishings. In order to get construction materials, students wrote lists of the materials they wanted. After construction, the children wrote descriptions of the model which they presented to the class.

Next, small groups created the characters from the book. After reading descriptions of the people, teachers wrote out a set of directions on a large chart that included illustrations to help the ESL students understand. By following these instructions the students created stuffed cloth characters. In their small groups later, the children wrote descriptions of their creations. For this writing assignment some ESL students chose to follow a given form (see Figure 2.10) while others wrote narratives.

We then explored the food the immigrant settlers would have eaten, including dried fruit and vegetables. Our media specialist came to explain how her husband smokes salmon, and everyone had a taste of this regional delicacy.

Ws also made apple-head dolls, a traditional craft of this era. To speed along the drying process, we decided to use the clay kiln. Too hot! After the smoke cleared, the teachers wrote an explanation to the students about the now deceased dolls. The letter was on a large chart that the students helped each other understand, in some cases using the students' primary languages. There was disappointment and giggling.

We used a passage from the book that employed patterned language to describe a forest. This was our springboard to creating a mural which could evolve from a simple collection of trees to a modern city. We discussed the fact that there were no Indians on this particular piece of land, making it an appropriate place for the immigrant settlers to build. Next we removed the trees from the mural and added a log house that several students had cut from paper. For our purposes we located the house near the Willamette River in Portland, Oregon instead of by Lake Pepin in Minnesota. Many of our ESL students had not been downtown or seen the Willamette River, so we made a trip downtown.

One night, while the children were at home, there was a fire which destroyed the homestead. This deviation from the Wilder story allowed us to rebuild and thereby create a more accurate replica of early Portland. The kids were surprised at this turn of events, but accepted the fact that a true

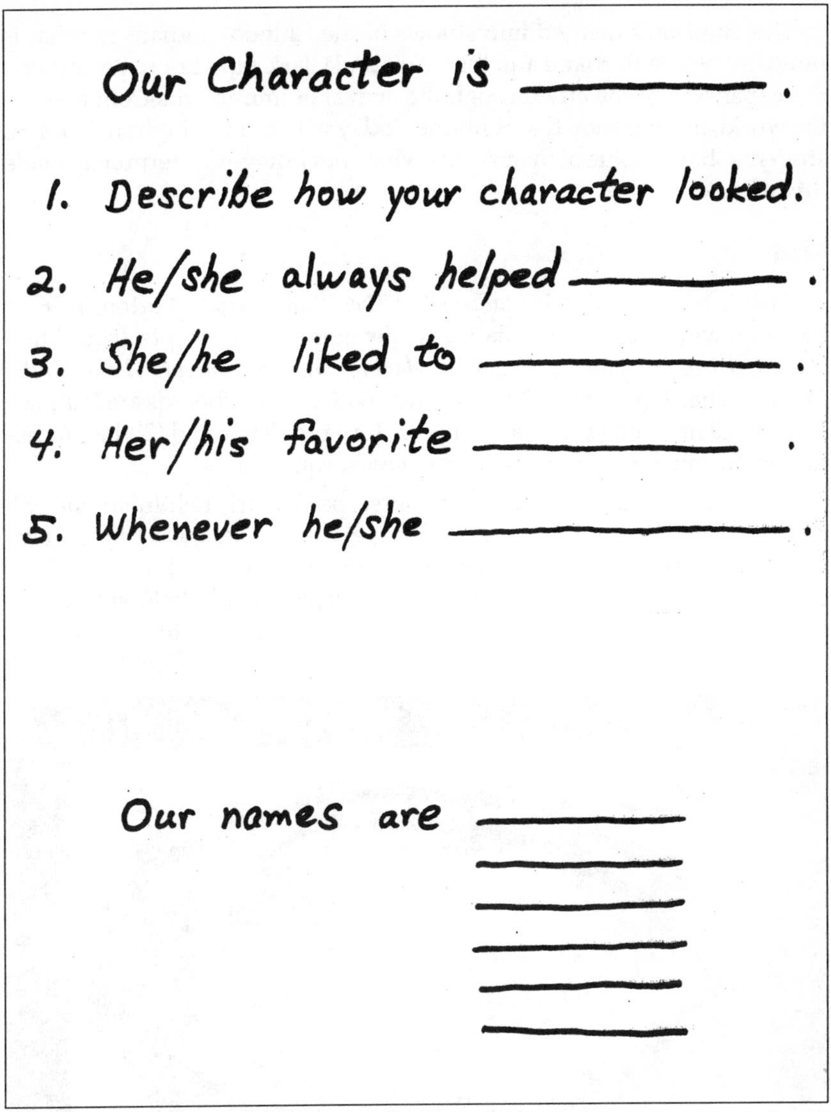

Our Character is _____ .

1. Describe how your character looked.

2. He/she always helped _____ .

3. She/he liked to _____ .

4. Her/his favorite _____ .

5. Whenever he/she _____ .

Our names are _____
_____
_____
_____
_____

Figure 2.10 Guided writing.

city was necessary to meet the needs of the growing population of the immigrant settlers. The changing mural provided visual support for the children to communicate their ideas in writing, and generated contributions to a word bank that the L2 learners could use in their writing.

This mini-unit merged into studies of the Chinook Indians in what is now downtown Portland and the Lewis and Clark expedition. We studied the expansion of the city through the arrival of immigrants from all over the world, immigration that continues today with our L2 children. Our ESL students shared some of their stories which our bilingual interpreters made into a book.

Math

Our district adoption is *Mathematics Their Way* (Baratta-Lorton, 1976), a program which uses manipulatives to develop math concepts. In addition we often use storyboards from *Developing Number Concepts Using Unifix Cubes* (Richardson, 1984). Our objectives with the storyboards are familiarizing students with (1) the language of story problems, and (2) the process of transforming a story into a mathematical equation.

The focus on manipulatives is, of course, particularly helpful for the ESL students. In one activity each table gets an envelope with various storyboards (see Figure 2.11). The assignment is to create a story with cubes representing animals, people, etc. For example, on the field storyboard there might be 10 horses eating, but two run away. To the commercial storyboards we have added key vocabulary (for example, 'Field' in Figure

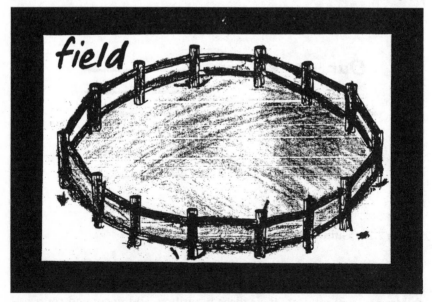

Figure 2.11 A mathematics storyboard.

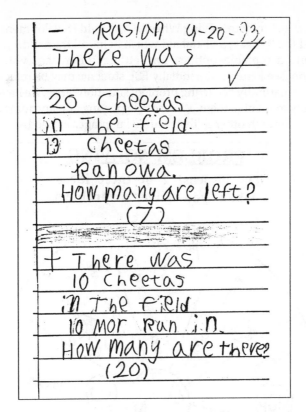

Figure 2.12 Writing in mathematics.

2.11) for the L2 students to use when they write the stories they have created with the cubes (see Figure 2.12). Our groups of six students have various ratios of monolingual to L2 children, but the monolingual students inevitably assist the L2 students at their tables. Additional help is available for the ESL kids In the form of a large chart displaying the basic math questions, 'How many are there?' and 'How many are left?'.

Class meeting

Our goals for this period of time are (1) to develop the feeling of belonging to a group, and (2) to empower students to solve problems.

We sit in a circle on the carpet. We always discuss student-initiated issues, sometimes teacher concerns. The issues might include sharing a story from home, discussing a problem between friends or during games at recess time, or exchanging compliments. Kids school-wide are trained to use the 'Arleta Problem Solving Wheel'. Our Child Development Specialist developed the 'Wheel', a visual aid which helps all the children to see at a glance nine acceptable options for settling differences without adult intervention (see Figure 2.13); initially ESL students may be reluctant to join in, but when naturally occurring problem situations arise, we have a perfect opportunity to involve them. We use role playing and encourage students to translate for each other in their native languages as needed.

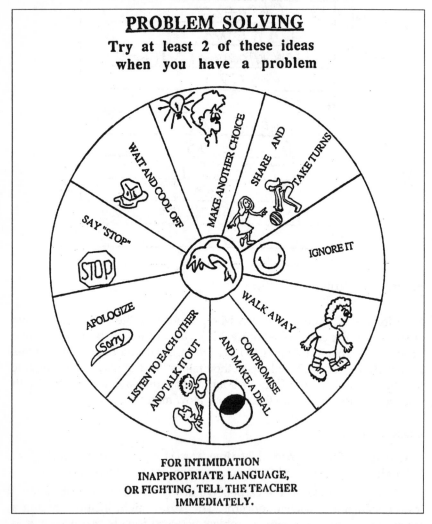

Figure 2.13 The Arleta problem-solving wheel.

One recurring issue at class meetings has been stereotyping. For example, one student raised her hand in class to tell us that she had heard someone on the playground say that all Russian children are stupid. A boy answered, 'Thats not right,' and the teacher responded with 'Why not?' Many students then responded with good reasons about how this statement can make someone feel bad or angry. Monolingual students volunteered to listen for this problem on the playground and to talk to those students or get teacher help as needed.

In third grade we have included self-evaluation as part of our class meeting. Originally we asked all students to participate through oral sharing. This gave the L2 learners a chance to hear how the other kids expressed their thoughts. Later we changed to a procedure in which all students wrote down and turned in their thoughts. At this point we gave the class some sentence starters for optional use. We found many ESL students utilized this tool initially, but moved into a more individualized format as they became comfortable with the procedure. Still later in the year we combined the oral and written approaches, having a pair of students dictate their self-evaluations to a teacher while the others listened and watched. Again this was a valuable opportunity for the L2 learners to hear and learn from their monolingual peers. It was also an opportunity for the ESL students to observe the conventions of print 'in action' as the spoken language was written down by the teacher. We believe this self-evaluation exercise has helped all the kids become more aware of both what and how they are learning (see Figure 2.14, page 90).

Journals

We accept a wide range of writing abilities among the learners: Some students write lengthy entries while others may make a drawing and wait for teacher assistance to add a caption.

At the beginning of one second grade year the teachers suggested a format for the journals that included the date and weather. We gave the kids sentence starters such as 'Last night at home …' and 'This morning before school ...' to encourage sharing of personal experiences. We found that the ESL students relied on this device for longer than other children. During this early period all students read back to the teachers what they had written and received immediate written responses. This was crucial for the L2 learners who were not able to read a written response on their own.

The youngsters could also choose to sign up to share their journals with their classmates. This practice let the ESL kids observe what their

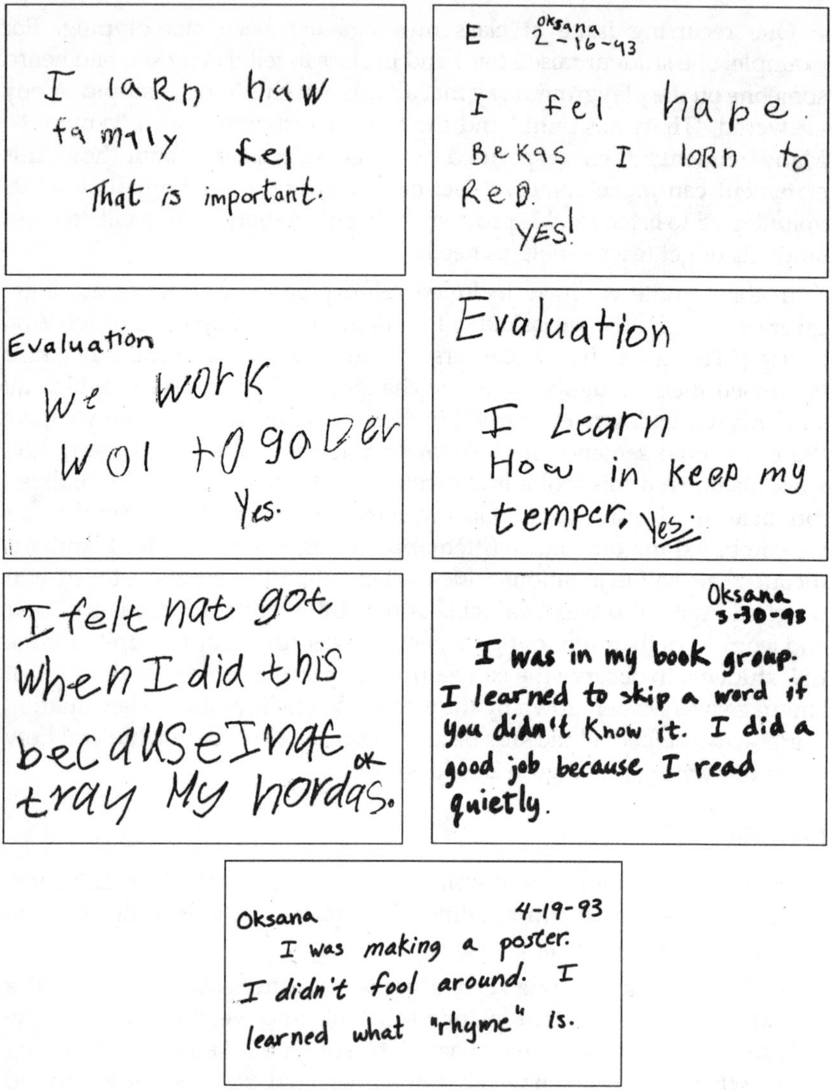

I laRn haw
family fel
That is important.

E   Oksana
    2-16-93
I fel hape.
Bekas I loRn to
ReD.
    YES!

Evaluation
We work
Wol to goDer
    Yes.

Evaluation
I Learn
How in keep my
temper. Yes.

I felt nat got
when I did this
because I nat
tray My nordas. ok

Oksana
3-30-93
I was in my book group.
I learned to skip a word if
you didn't know it. I did a
good job because I read
quietly.

Oksana   4-19-93
I was making a poster.
I didn't fool around. I
learned what "rhyme" is.

Figure 2.14 Self-evaluation.

monolingual peers were writing. The ESL children loved this sharing
because they were successful at reading their own writing.

We eventually took away the sentence starters and stopped the practice
of giving an oral response to the journals except in the case of a few L2

learners. By the beginning of third grade the journals were going home daily with a teacher for a written response which the children helped each other to read the following morning.

Mini-lesson

Mini-lessons may address reading or writing skills, and generally draw on ideas from our current theme study. To include the ESL children we use a pocket chart and sentence strips whenever possible so that the language is actually being manipulated by the students. An example is teaching the use of quotation marks. A familiar text that includes dialogue is copied onto strips with the quotation marks left out. We ask the students to determine which parts of the text require quotation marks and to attach clothes pins to the pocket chart to demonstrate where those marks belong. Another example is using student writing copied onto strips for the chart. The sentences are then easily moved around and the text 'revised'. We also found the overhead projector works well for shared reading if there are visuals to help the L2 learners understand the text.

Conclusion

Four years ago our faculty worked up a school philosophy statement:

'The staff at Arleta provides a safe, nurturing environment where children and adults can learn. We believe that all children are capable of academic success. We are striving to create an environment where all children can develop a sense of competency, belonging, usefulness, and personal power. Children and adults learn together and from each other. Learning responsibility for one's behavior as well as one's academic growth is essential to future success. Our students come from a wide range of interest, experiences, and abilities. We value that diversity. We seek to create a learning atmosphere where all can feel important and successful as they learn.'

We feel our project has helped us come closer to realizing these ambitions. At the classroom level we have many memories of our experiences working in this model, but thinking back to the early days we particularly remember how difficult it was to integrate into our classrooms those ESL children who came to us with absolutely no school experience. Although we were doing our best to ensure they felt safe in our rooms and understood the content of our lessons, we too often found these newcomers daydreaming or making many trips to the restroom. We have since learned how to plan open-ended activities that can be individually modified, and to appreciate the value of peer interactions among the children and between teachers. As we've learned, we've seen children become involved in their classroom communities, feeling capable of their ability to learn and participate, no longer sitting and waiting for their special pullout classes.

We would like to emphasize that this model came into being as part of a school-wide movement to better meet the needs of our particular population. Initially the idea for the model came from the Arleta ESL team. With the support of the school principal and the district ESL department administration, a classroom teacher was recruited to put the experiment into practice. At the beginning of implementation there were some who doubted the value of the model. A few staff members believed we would end up watering down the curriculum, causing the district test scores of the monolingual students to drop. A few others felt, after seeing the high level of involvement of the children in the classroom, that the students chosen for the pilot were not representative of the general school population, but were generally 'better behaved'. To answer these charges, Team 1 invited their colleagues into the classroom to observe. What the observers saw was the curriculum being taught for understanding, emphasizing depth of understanding over breadth of coverage, an approach that lead to more on-task behavior.

It is also important to emphasize that we couldn't have managed any of these goals without the work of bilingual colleagues who have solidified the home/school connection and have created a first-language literacy program to support the children in all their learning. Their program evidences the value we place in multiculturalism, and helps to bridge the gaps between cultural groups.

Lastly, in the fall of 1993 the staff voted for building-wide participation in Project TEACHER, a government-funded inservice program that will help us better understand language acquisition theory, multicultural sensitivity, and techniques for more effectively teaching our L2 learners. This inservice program is not only teaching us new concepts, but it is helping us to see how much we already know.

The Future

The future of this model has taken different turns. Team 1 has worked together for three years now, having gone back to second grade to begin the cycle again with a new group of students. Currently Sharon and Dan are using this model in a mixed-age class, having kept about half of their eight- and nine-year olds and adding half a class of seven- and eight-year-olds. After two years Team 2 has decided to dissolve. L. is working with a different teammate in a mixed-age class with eight-, nine- and ten-year-olds, and Donna is teaching in her own classroom.

Team teaching probably isn't for everyone. Beyond the real difficulty of finding sufficient time for planning, we recognize teaching and management styles as important considerations in putting together a team. We can't imaging a team being created by an administrator assigning teachers. Instead, the two teachers need to reflect and consider their values before agreeing to be a team. Team teaching has been compared to marriage, and we know why! With the right partnership, however, creativity and a willingness to try innovative approaches seem to be increased. We feel that the shared expertise of the classroom teacher and the ESL specialist create a collegiality that improve the learning possibilities for everyone in the classroom.

This model began here. Many people have come to visit and observe, and the teaming model is now being implemented more and more in our whole district. Three years after starting in the first classroom, there are three teams working with different age levels in our building, and other teams are being created in other schools. In addition to ESL teams, the special education teachers have begun going into classrooms instead of pulling their students out. We are sad to report that, because of funding questions, the continuation of our model is in doubt.

Our Thanks

Over time the Arleta staff have contributed much to our efforts to integrate the L2 children into our school community. In addition to the development of the 'Problem Solving Wheel', other staff have developed visuals to help kids remember the cafeteria rules and procedures.

Still others labeled a resource room with an orange triangle, the library with a blue circle, etc., so L2 children could easily locate these places on their own. We truly believe that the success of this experimental model is a result of support and assistance from the district ESL/Bilingual Education Department, our administrators, and the entire on-site staff.

References

Baratta-Lorton, M. (1976) *Mathematics Their Way*. California: Addison-Wesley.

Johnson, T. (1990) *Bringing it all Together*. Portsmouth: Heinemann.

Johnson, T. and Louis, D. (1987) *Literacy Through Literature*. Portsmouth: Heinemann.

Richardson, K. (1984) *Developing Number Concepts Using Unifix Cubes*. California: Addison-Wesley.

Wilder, L.I. (1953) *Little House in the Big Woods*. New York: Harper & Row.

3 A Mainstream Primary Classroom with a Majority of ESL Students: Planning for English Language Learning

ELINA RASO

This article focuses on an approach to planning for English as a second language learning in the mainstream primary classroom. The rationale underlying this approach is described and a practical example of how an ESL and classroom teacher in an inner city Melbourne Catholic Primary School have used this approach in their planning and teaching is provided. A description of ESL provision in Catholic primary schools in Melbourne is outlined to contextualise the discussion.

ESL Provision in Catholic Primary Schools in Melbourne

ESL provision in Catholic primary schools is based on a number of beliefs. Included in these are beliefs that ESL provision is a whole-school responsibility; that ESL teachers need specialist qualifications to be effective in the role and that the needs of ESL students are best met when ESL teachers work collaboratively with classroom teachers.

Whole-school responsibility

All Catholic schools receiving ESL allocations prepare school-based documentation related to a cycle of evaluation and planning which situates ESL language provision within a whole-school planning process. Documents are designed to be developed collaboratively by principals, ESL teachers and classroom teachers. The content of these documents forms a basis for school policy development that is inclusive of ESL students.

Specialist qualifications

A significant number of ESL teachers in Catholic primary schools have postgraduate qualifications in TESL. With specialist knowledge ESL teachers are better able to meet the needs of ESL learners and to provide ongoing professional development to staff.

Working collaboratively

ESL teachers work collaboratively with classroom teachers in assessing students' language development and needs, planning units of work across curriculum areas, and implementing classroom-based work.

ESL provision in Catholic schools includes *direct ESL teaching* of targeted groups of students by the ESL teacher, *joint planning and teaching* by ESL and classroom teachers and *ESL-informed approaches* by mainstream teachers to meet the needs of all ESL students. This provision stems from a belief that ESL students can be taught alongside their native English speaking peers when their specific needs are addressed in the mainstream curriculum. The starting point for meeting these needs is effective planning. Joint planning time with ESL and classroom teacher is generally supported by school principals and built into the schools' timetable of activities.

Planning for Language Learning

A model for planning aimed at improving the language learning outcomes of students learning English as a second language, set out below, guides teachers to develop a sequence of activities with a clear language focus, as part of a topic or theme being undertaken in the classroom.

The approach aims to build success for ESL students through engagement with a range of linguistically connected activities. It also addresses the crucial role teachers play in planning and modelling the linguistic input for students in a range of learning activities in different social contexts, across which the students build experience of the input.

The key ideas in this approach are as follows:

Language focus: Teachers identify the language focus for the sequence based on student needs and the curriculum demands. Comprehensible input, input that is meaningful but challenging, is the starting point of any sequence.

Support:	Students are supported in acquiring the planned language but the nature of support changes throughout the sequence.
Group tasks:	Collaborative group activities involving pair and small group tasks are integrated into the sequence.
Clear visuals:	Concrete and visual materials are used to support understanding and production.
Recycling:	The core language of the sequence is recycled, built and extended across a range of activities before expecting students to produce the language independently.
Language modelling:	Language models are provided at the different stages by teachers, peers and the use of appropriate materials.
Teaching:	The teacher's role changes throughout the sequence from one of actively leading and demonstrating to one of facilitating and intervening when necessary

A brief description of the stages in the sequence of activities follows.

Initial shared experience

The initial shared experience activates prior knowledge and exposes students to comprehensible language input related to the classroom currriculum.

Level one recycling activities

The initial shared experience and level one activities mainly involve groups of students in tasks which broaden their present experience of the language. These activities promote understanding of the content. They also make the core language of the sequence explicit through exposure and modelling. The focus is on interactions with the teacher, materials and content, and on guided interaction with peers. These activities should prepare students to participate successfully in the more challenging cooperative tasks at level two.

Level two recycling activities

Activities at level two provide students with the opportunity to use the core language explored in the initial activities in purposeful ways in a range of diferent tasks. Students are involved in pair and group activities where the role of the teacher is one of intervening where necessary rather than actively leading. Students are more likely to experience success in using English as they have built a considerable degree of familiarity with the language of the tasks.

Level three recycling activities

Once students have had a range of experience at this level they are in a better position to use the language in personal and creative ways in different contexts. The individual and cognitively demanding tasks at level three require students to call on their total linguistic repertoire in order to complete a range of tasks successfully.

The activities do not revolve solely around a topic; they are focused around language and content.

Application of the Approach

The following unit of work, *Australian Animals*, is an adaptation of a unit developed by a group of ESL and classroom teachers in Catholic primary schools in Melbourne as part of a professional development activity.

It was adapted for use and then implemented with a class of seven-year-olds situated in an inner city suburb of Melbourne.

School context

The school population comprises predominantly Australian-born students from families where a language other than English is the main language spoken at home. Although students have varying experience of English outside the school community, for these students the development and control of the language necessary for success in learning needs to take place at school. The class of seven-year-olds is made up of 29 students representing a range of language groups including English, Arabic, Vietnamese, Macedonian, Greek and French. English is the main language spoken at home for nine of these students. Most of the remaining students speak and understand the home LOTE (language other than English). Amongst this group are two students recently arrived in Australia.

The students' proficiency in English ranges from students who are beginning to extend their language use beyond social and classroom language to students who can readily comprehend and produce language in a range of social and learning contexts.

In response to the range of needs in the classroom, the implementation of the unit of work took place in the following ways: it involved the ESL teacher and classroom teacher working together with groups of students on specific tasks; the ESL teacher working with a group of targeted ESL students demonstrating particular needs, and the classroom teacher continuing with some of the activities independently of the ESL teacher.

Developing the Unit of Work: Australian Animals

Observation of students in writing activities and analysis of their writing samples indicated that most students had little experience of producing informational texts. The following piece of writing is representative of the texts produced by students when asked to write telling the readers about koalas (see Figure 3.1).

Figure 3.1 Typical student writing.

As the class had planned to study animals as part of the year's topics, the following sequence of activities focusing on informatinal writing was integrated into the unit. For further information see Greco and Raso (1991).

Most students participating in the unit had had experience with cooperative group work and jigsaw tasks. The class had previously been exposed to informational texts, but had not focused on the linguistic features in detail. They had also been involved in identifying key words in other units of work.

Overview of activities

Activity	Organisation	Language focus
INITIAL EXPERIENCE **1. Brainstorm** Students form into small groups to brainstorm answers to the question *'What do you know about Australian Animals?'* A scribe records the groups' answers.	Small groups.	Activates students' knowledge and experience. Use of language for: *Describing Listing Reporting*
The small group leaders report back the knowledge shared by group members. The key ideas from each group are added to a class list by the teacher. The list may include information about the names and appearance of animals, their eating preferences, how they care for their young and the environments in which they are found.	Class comes together.	

Activity	Organisation	Language focus
2. Grouping the information		
The teacher leads a discussion focusing on how the information can best be grouped. Children suggest categories, e.g. *Food, Habitat, Predators, Body covering, Size, Name of young.*	Class.	Exposes students to the language for: *Categorising information* *Negotiating*
The children are divided into small groups ensuring that the number of children in each group corresponds to the total number of categories having been suggested by the class. For example, if six categories are suggested as above, there will need to be six children in each group. These become home groups.	Cooperative jigsaw task involving *home groups* and *expert groups.*	Recycles language used for: *Categorising* and *Negotiating*
Each member of the home group is designated a particular category from the initial suggestions (e.g. *food, habitat* ...)		Use of language for: *Identifying* *Describing* *Categorising* *Negotiating*
Students then move into new groups, expert groups, according to the particular category they have been designated (e.g. all *Food* children get together).		

Activity	Organisation	Language focus
The task for each of the expert groups is to refer to the class list from the original brainstorm activity in order to identify the animals listed and, for each animal, identify the key ideas corresponding to the category. For example, an expert group considering body coverings will need to identify the words and phrases related to body coverings and match these with the animals listed. Additional items not on the original list may be added if the total group is in agreement. This information will need to be recorded by the group.	Expert groups.	
Students then move from the expert groups to the home groups to report on the task. In this way each home group will have information about each of the categories.	Home groups.	Use of language for: *Reporting* *Questioning for clarification* *Clarifying responses*
Recording information Each expert group organises and presents the information related to its category in written/ diagramatic/pictorial form.		Recycles language from the categorising activity.

Activity	Organisation	Language focus
Each group presents its work to the class. This may be best done by designating the role of reporter and clarifier to students in the group.	Class.	Exposes students to the language of reporting.

3. Sharing a big book

The teacher introduces the big book *Animal Reports* (Latham and Sloan, 1989), and focuses on the text about one of the animals, e.g. the echidna.	Class.	

Predicting task

The students move into small groups to examine the charts of information the class has built. The task is to predict which of the recorded information will be relevant to the animal (e.g. the echidna – *"I think we will find out about the food an echidna eats"*). Students may also predict any other additional information that they expect to find in the text.	Small groups. (Predicting groups with a designated leader.)	Activates existing knowledge to prepare students to maximise the meaning gained from the text.
Student predictions are shared by group leaders.	Class.	

Activity	Organisation	Language focus
Listening task The teacher reads the text twice. This provides students with the opportunity to listen for different detail.	Class.	Exposes students to linguistic features of informational writing.
Students move into small groups (as a predicting task). The teacher re-reads the texts so that students can check the information recalled and the predictions with the information in the body of the text.	Small groups.	Recycles language from previous activity.
Each group comments on its own accuracy.		Introduces language of comparison.
4. Using a grid Teacher models how to transfer the main infor-mation from the text about the echidnas onto a pre-pared grid, as in Figure 3.2.		Recycles the language of classification. Recycles linguistic features of text in point form.

Figure 3.2 Presenting information in grid form (two alternative grids)

	Echidna	Platypus	Wombat
Size (It is ...)			
Habitat (It lives ...)			
Covering (It has ...) (It is covered with ...)			
Food (It eats ...)			

OR

	Echidna	Platypus	Wombat
Size (How big is it?)			
Habitat (Where does it live?)			
Appearance (What does it look like?)			
Food (What does it eat?)			

Activity	Organisation	Language focus
LEVEL 1: RECYCLING ACTIVITIES **1. Identifying key information**		
The students are supplied with the text from the big book *Animal Reports* about another animal, e.g. the common wombat.	Class.	Recycles language of *expository writing* from initial experience.
The teacher reads as the students follow the text. The teacher and students identify key information from text. The teacher records this information as key words and phrases on the blackboard.		Builds concept of noting key words and phrases.
2. Categorising information		
In small groups students transfer the information from the blackboard onto a prepared group grid (see Figure 3.2).	Groups of four (one student designated as scribe).	Recycles linguistic features of text in point form.

Activity	Organisation	Language focus
3. Identifying and classifying information		
In groups, each member is given a new animal text and a personal grid with one area highlighted (i.e. *size/habitat*). Each group member focuses on a different category.	Groups of four *with teacher guidance.*	Recycles language of *classification, negotiation.*
With the teacher as guide, the group reads the text together twice. Each group member identifies key areas for his/her category and records this on his/her own grid.		Recycles skill of identifying key ideas and phrases. Introduces concept of reading for specific information.
The information is transferred onto the group grid, ensuring there is group consensus (members of the group may suggest other ideas that may be added to each section of the grid once the grid is completed).		Recycles and extends language of the initial experience.

Activity	Organisation	Language focus
LEVEL 2: RECYCLING ACTIVITIES		
1. Recording and comparing		
The teacher supplies the text for three new animals (two groups work on the same animal). In small groups the students complete grids of the kind shown in Figure 3.2. In order to do this, the students must read the text, identify the key information, and select what is relevant for the grid.	Small groups.	Recycles and expands language of initial experience. Identifying key information: *Recording* *Reporting* *Negotiating* *Questioning* *Clarifying responses*
The two groups with the same animal come together and compare the information recorded on the grid.		Recycles language of comparing.
The agreed information may be recorded on the class grid by the teacher.		
The teacher discusses the information with the class.	Class.	Revises range of concepts, language and skills introduced to date.
2. Information gap activity		
Two children are given identical grids, each with different information missing (see Figure 3.3).	Pairs	Recycles language of questioning and answering from previous units.

Activity	Organisation	Language focus
Students ask partner questions in order to complete the missing information, e.g. *'What does the black swan eat?'* (Figure 3.4).		Questioning. Introducing reading information from a grid and reproducing linguistic features of text orally.
3. Comparing two texts		
Students are given a copy of one report from the Australian animals text *Animal Reports*.	Class.	Focuses on specific linguistic features and vocabulary used in expository text.
Using an overhead transparency of a similar text, either from the same book or another, the teacher asks students for key ideas common to both texts, e.g.: general information size/weight of animal information about food, habits.		
Students identify similar words and phrases used in both texts. Consider: sentence beginnings verbs (tense) paragraphing The teacher makes a list of these, and discusses whether sequencing paragraphs in a different order maintains meaning of text.		

Activity	Organisation	Language focus
The class examines other texts on animals to see if the same elements are common to these.		
4. Sequencing sentences		
Partners are given a series of sentences related to Australian animals (see Figure 3.5). The sentences are not in the correct order. Partners must work together to sequence the sentences in order to form a paragraph. Students paste or write sentences in order and then compare completed paragraph with that of another pair.	Partner work.	Recycles linguistic features of expository text.
5. Sequencing paragraphs		
Partners are given a series of paragraphs to sequence in order to form a complete text. The teacher places key-headings next to the appropriate paragraphs in order to guide students: *General information* *Size/Weight* *Identification* *Food* *Habitat* *Life-cycle* *Other information*	Pairs.	Recycles structure of expository text. Recycles language of: *classification* *description*

Figure 3.3 Information gap task

	Food (What does it eat?)	Size (How big is it?)	Covering (What is its body covering?)	Habitat (Where does it live?)
White Pointer Shark	The White Pointer eats other sharks and fish.			The White Pointer lives in shallow waters near the shore.
Black Swan		The Black Swan can grow up to 1.3 metres long.	The Black Swan is covered in glossy black feathers.	
Goanna	The Goanna eats insects and small lizards.		The Goanna is covered in scales.	
Penguin	The Penguin eats small fish.	The Penguin grows to about 33 centimeters long.		

	Food (What does it eat?)	Size (How big is it?)	Covering (What is its body covering?)	Habitat (Where does it live?)
White Pointer Shark		The White Pointer can grow up to 7.8 metres long.	The White Pointer has grey skin on top and is white underneath.	
Black Swan	The Black Swan eats grass, water plants and insects.			The Black Swan builds a nest near water.
Goanna		The Goanna grows to 60 centimetres long.		The Goanna lives in burrows between rocks.
Penguin			The Penguin is covered in small stiff feathers.	The Penguin lives in a burrow in the sand.

(for completed chart see Figure 3.4 overleaf)

White Pointer Shark ...	The white pointer eats other sharks and fish.	The white pointer can grow up to 7.8 metres long.	The white pointer has grey skin on top and is white underneath.	The white pointer lives in shallow waters near the shore.
Black Swan	The Black Swan eats grass, water plants and insects.	The Black Swan can grow to 1.3 metres long.	The Black Swan is covering in glossy black feathers	The Black Swan builds a nest near water.
Goanna	The Goanna eats insects and small lizards.	The Goanna grows to 60 centimetres long.	The Goanna is covered in scales	The Goanna lives in burrows between rocks.
Penguin	The penguin eats small fish	The penguin grows to about 33 centimetres	The Penguin is covered in small, stiff feathers.	The Penguin lives in a burrow in the sand.

Figure 3.4 Completed information gap chart

Activity	Organisation	Language focus
LEVEL 3: RECYCLING ACTIVITY		
1. Guided writing activity		
Using the structure of a text and a grid with key information, the teacher transfers information from the grid to the text (see Figure 3.6)	Class. Individuals.	Recycles content and structure of expository text.
2. Building a text		
Students are supplied with the grids completed in previous activities.	Small groups/ pairs. Individuals.	Writing an inform-ational text, using language structures which have been introduced in the range of texts.

Activity	Organisation	Language focus
Using the information and the guide for writing, the group reconstructs the text in order to make a *What is it?* (riddle) book (see Figure 3.7) **3. Individual writing** Students select an Australian animal that they wish to research. They are directed to record the information on a grid as they research (see Figure 3.8). They should look for: 1. *What does your animal look like?* 2. *What does it eat?* 3. *How does it move?* 4. *Where does it live?* Students present their information in a poster format, accompanied by the grid, as follows: Drawing of animal. Did you know that..? .... See Figure 3.9.	Individual.	Evaluation of skills children have gained throughout the unit.

Activity	Organisation	Language focus
4. Oral presentations Students present their work to a group or class.		Use of formal register. Recycling language of the unit.
5. Individual writing/ extension Children invent a new animal by combining information about our Australian animals, e.g. Kangaburra. *What does it look like?* *Describe it, its special features.* *Where does it live?* *What does it eat?* *What is its covering?* *Illustrate.*	Groups. Pairs. Individuals.	Recycles language of unit.
6. Zoo visit If possible students visit the zoo/animal sanctuary. Students work in pairs to build grids about Australian animals at the zoo. They may have a blank space for their own category. They build individual reports based on grids.		

Its home is called a den. (cave)

The dingo is covered in fur, usually a yellowish colour.

It eats rabbits, rats, lizards, birds, wallabies and wombats.

The dingo is the Australian wild dog.

It has pointy ears, watchful eyes and a bushy tail.

It hunts alone or in packs.

Dingoes never bark, they howl.

Figure 3.5 Sequencing sentences

The Platypus

(General information) The platypus is an _____ animal. *(Size/Weight)* It is about _____ cms in length and weighs up to _____ kg. *(Appearance)* The platypus is usually _____ in colour and is covered in _____ . It has four _____ feet. Its eyes are closed under _____ . *(Habitat)* It lives in _____ along the _____ of streams and lakes. *(Food)* The _____ eats yabbies and _____. It lays _____. *(Concluding sentence)* The platypus can be found on the ____ cent coin.

Appearance What does it look like?	grey, fur, bill, four webbed feet
Food What does it eat?	yabbies, fish
Size How big is it?	small
Habitat Where does it live?	Australia, mud and water, edges of streams and lakes

Figure 3.6 Text and grid

Flying Fox – Fruit Bat

Food What does it eat?	fruit, pollen, nectar
Habitat Where does it live?	caves, hollow trees, and any dark place
Covering What is its body covering?	fur, wings are covered by smooth skin
Special features	fingers on the end of its wings, pointed ears and strong eyesight, nocturnal, mammal

From this grid, *What is it?* text may read as follows:

This animal likes to eat fruit, pollen and nectar. It lives in caves, hollow trees, and any dark place. Its body is covered with fur and its wings are covered by smooth skin. It also has pointed ears and strong eyesight.

Figure 3.7   Building a riddle text

Individual chart/ Class chart	**Australian** **Animals**			Name:

Name	It is covered with...	It lives in...	When it moves it...	It eats...
Kookaburra				
Pelican				
Sugar Glider				
Wombat				
Echidna				

Figure 3.8   Grid for guided writing *(continued on next page)*

Name	It is covered with…	It lives in…	When it moves it…	It eats…
Crocodile				
Emu				
Penguin				
Fruit Bat				
Wallaby				
Platypus				
Goanna				

Figure 3.8 *(continued)*

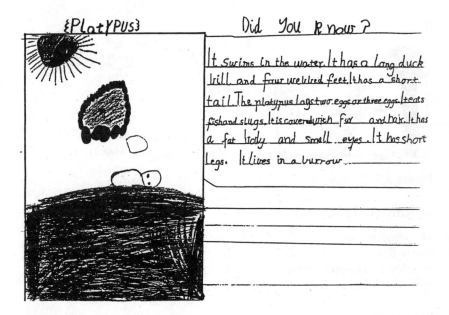

Figure 3.9 Children's posters *(continued overleaf)*

Did you know

Wallabies looks like
kangaroo. Their colour is
grey. They have fur. They
are big. Their feet are
big too. They have a
short neck. They have a
long tail and the tail is
skinny. Wallabies eat grass
Wallabies live under shady
trees. Wallabies move by
jumping. Wallabies do not
lay eggs but they have
live babies

GOANNA

DID YOU KNOW

That a goanna is a
reptile and it makes a
home by burrowing down
in between rocks.
It eats mainly insects also
some small lizards.
The goannas long tail is
covered with spikes.
The female goanna lays
about 5 eggs in the spring
time.

DANIELS and ANGEL

Figure 3.9 *(continued)*

Acknowledgements

The original sequence of activities was developed by Margaret Hanna, Maria Raso, Mandy Doolan and Carmel Sandiford (ESL teachers). It was adapted and implemented by Maria Raso, Geraldine Dalton and Margaret Hill at an inner Melbourne Catholic primary school.

References

Greco, S. and Raso, E. (1991) *About Teaching Languages. Unit Three: Planning for Language Learning.* Melbourne: Catholic Education Office.
Latham, R. and Sloan, P. (1989) *Animal Reports.* Sydney, Harcourt Brace Jovanovich.

4 A Whole-school Approach to Mainstreaming: The Rose Avenue ESL/D Project

JULIE REID AND NANCY KITEGAWA

Background of the Project

Rose Avenue is a junior school situated in the midst of tall apartment buildings in the heart of the city of Toronto just west of the Don Valley Parkway. The student population, which numbers almost 420, is characterized by wide diversity in linguistic and cultural backgrounds. As many as 17% of the children have arrived in Canada within the past two years, and at least 78% have one parent who was not born in Canada. The majority speak their mother-tongue in the schoolyard, at home and in their leisure hours with friends.

The one full-time ESL/D (English as a second language/dialect) teacher who is on staff at Rose Avenue provides a withdrawal program, serving the ESL/D children who are the neediest – those who have very little or no English. In winter 1987 44 children from grades one to six were attending the ESL/D class, but there were as many as 71 others who were identified as needing ESL/D help. Furthermore, the growing population of children in the junior and senior kindergarten classes had little or no English to the extent that they outnumbered the English-speaking children three to one.

Discussions with the Principal shortly after her appointment to Rose Avenue in January 1986 centred around how to best organize human resources to meet the school's ESL/D needs. A plea to the school superintendent for additional staff resulted in the allocation of an additional half-time ESL/D teacher for the remainder of the school year. Although this alleviated the situation somewhat in the short term, it did

MAINSTREAMING ESL

not address concerns about how to best help ESL/D children in a context where 54% of the student population could be loosely classified as ESL/D.

The nagging question about whether withdrawing small groups of children to a separate classroom for short periods of time each day was the best way to tap into the expertise of the full-time ESL/D specialist remained unanswered. The Principal wondered whether this was in fact *a waste of teacher power*. Was there another approach where the ESL/D teacher's work could benefit more of the children and would also encourage greater carry-over between ESL/D and regular classroom activities?

In the recent literature on this question, there is evidence that schools need to be organized to facilitate cross-flow of expertise and understanding between ESL/D and classroom teachers. It suggests that to meet the needs of second language learners there must be close liaison between the two (Johnson, 1988). In fact, it is sometimes argued that a cooperative teaching model where the ESL/D teacher works in collaboration with the classroom teacher, both in the preparation and execution of lessons to all students, not just ESL/D, is more effective than a model where the ESL/D teacher acts as a resource person working only with the ESL/D students.

This claim was substantiated by the Principal's previous experience in a school where the learning centre (Special Education) teacher worked effectively in classrooms with the teachers. All this seemed to point in the direction of trying a new approach to providing ESL/D, one where the ESL/D teacher worked in the classrooms with the ESL/D students, rather than withdrawing them.

It would be hard to pinpoint a single event which actually moved what was at a talking level to reality. However, the ESL/D teacher's agreement to give working in classrooms a try, combined with three willing colleagues certainly helped. Before long the ESL/D Project at Rose Avenue was underway.

Description of the Project

The team members

The ESL/D Project Team consisted of the Principal, the Assistant Coordinator, Language Study Centre – ESL/D, the ESL/D teacher and three classroom teachers. The teachers who were invited to participate were those whom the Principal felt would make a commitment and give the approach a good try and thereby would increase chances for success. All of these teachers also provide an activity-based program which the principal thought would make for easier entry of an additional teacher in the classroom.

Three grade levels were represented – Nancy, Grades 3–4; Dorothy, Grades 2–3; and Maureen, Grades 1–2. All of the classroom teachers were in their third year at Rose Avenue, whereas the ESL/D teacher had been at Rose Avenue for over 20 years, 11 of them as the ESL/D teacher. As it turned out, these teachers had already expressed an interest in working with Kay, the ESL/D teacher, in a collaborative way.

Roles

It was understood that the Assistant Coordinator, ESL/D, would provide support and encouragement and would work closely with Kay. However, role expectations related to the ESL/D and the three classroom teachers were not specified. It was suggested that, for the first visit or two, Kay should observe and become familiar with each teacher's program. What each teacher would actually do in their new partnerships with Kay was left open so that there would be room for their working relationships to evolve.

How the project was structured

It was decided that, to begin, Kay would spend one day each week, on Thursdays, moving from classroom to classroom following this schedule:

9.00–10.20	Dorothy
10.50–11.50	Maureen
1.05–2.30	Nancy
2.45–3.30	Kay's time to reflect, plan, prepare a written record.

What Kay actually did in each classroom varied widely. In two cases she worked mainly as a resource/support person with a primary focus on the ESL/D students. By the end of the school year, she and the classroom teacher were working cooperatively, and planning for the whole class during the time when Kay was in the room.

Kay's Notes

Of the four teachers involved in the project, it was expected that the ESL/D teacher would need a big share of the support that the Assistant Coordinator could provide. It was suggested that Kay keep a personal journal or written record of what was taking place in terms of the children and her working relationship with her colleagues. These notes would in turn provide the content for discussions with the Assistant Coordinator and in the review meetings with the whole team.

Kay kept very detailed notes which tended to focus exclusively on what she did with individual children in each classroom. The following is an excerpt from Kay's notes:

'Thursday May 26, 1988

My Nghi is making excellent progress. She has finished her story and she is elaborating on the first part. Irene copies her story out in good form but elaboration is hopeless as her needle is stuck on the same plot. Omar is trying to add more to his story. He is beginning to lose interest. Nam Ho still cannot get started. Perhaps I'll have him start on a different theme next week. Tuan Die – did not get to today. He was not in the group last week. Melissa is struggling to finish – she won't take risks. Has a fair amount of English, too.'

Throughout the project, Kay expressed her concerns about having a tendency to be judgemental. She worried about reflecting this in her written notes. As a result, in her records, Kay avoided commenting on her working relationship with her colleagues in case these written notes would be misconstrued.

The review meetings

As a formal means of providing support to everyone involved in the project as well as to structure an opportunity to reflect on the project experience, a review process was established. The project team met at regular intervals, once every four weeks, to talk informally about what was taking place from everyone's perspective. The review meetings were characterized by openness and a high level of professionalism. While members were careful to phrase their comments in ways that would not be critical, there was open and honest dialogue. Some of the issues addressed at these meetings included:

• role expectations	'Who does what?'
• territoriality	'Who's the boss?'
• time	'When do we plan?' 'When can we talk?'
• success	'What's working well?'
• problems	'What about the noise level?'
• continuity	'What am I accomplishing?'
• priorities	'Do I work with the ESL/D children only or with the whole class?'

- ownership   'Who has the ultimate responsibilitv in
                               what takes place?'

Other project activities

Opportunities were provided for team members to extend the ptoject experience. Some of these were:

A visit to Daystrom Public School

The project team visited Daystrom Public School in North York to talk with teachers there. At Daystrom, a full-time ESL/D teacher (Verna Duncan) uses a combination of withdrawal and work in classrooms. She assumes the role of ESL/D resource to the whole school. The description in Figure 4.1 (overleaf) illustrates the thinking behind Daystrom's approach to providing ESL/D.

What is unique about the Daystrom model is their use of classroom assistants who speak the languages of the dominant linguistic groups in the school. The ESL/D teacher has the responsibility of training and working with classroom assistants who in turn work with the classroom teachers. For example, while the classroom teacher is presenting the content of a lesson, the classroom assistant, sitting in the midst of the students, translates to facilitate the children's understanding of the lesson. The classroom assistant also works with the students, individually and in small groups.

Cooperative learning seminar

Kay and Maureen attended an interboard ESL/D seminar on coopera-tive learning given by Dr Spencer Kagan. They both commented that the shared experience was a good one and had provided them with new ideas on how they might work together.

Planning for a New School Year

At the final review meeting in June, discussion moved from talk about progress made to date, to concerns and needs that should be addressed if the project were to continue and possibly be expanded in September. It was suggested that the Assistant Coordinator, ESL/D, interview each of the team members individually rather than attempt to discuss all issues raised in a larger group. The interviews would serve a dual purpose. They would facilitate teachers' reflections on their experiences with change, and would identify issues and possible solutions related to the continuation of the project in September.

Withdrawal Program

- emphasis on receptive and expressive oral language skills (small groups) no risk
- assist students with adjustment to new environment
- select and teach topics from what they already know develop oral language skills by providing opportunities to use their expressive language in purposeful, meaningful way (telephones, play centre)
- develop process writing and spelling skills by selecting topics that are of immediate interest and use to them
- give them time to rehearse 'ideas'
- teach the vocabulary of school wide themes by using as many visual aides as possible and to reinforce the content of the classrooms
- assist classroom teachers with program modification to facilitate integration of E.S.L.D. students into the regular classroom program

from Verna Duncan

Integrated Program

- build students self esteem in classroom
- read appropriate books to students and help them choose reading material
- encourage students to work together
- develop activities based on children's interests and expose them to real language at their skill level
- Emphasize process rather than product
- help classroom teacher to design units of study that focus on audio-visual aides, concrete hands-on materials and task cards that span a wide range of levels
- provide language activities that include puppetry, art
- conference with students during various phases of process writing
- individualize spelling program – select words from process writing
- assist with assigned task cards – teach mini lessons
- help with printing and writing skills
- assist classroom teachers in reporting to parents, in identifying special needs of ESLD students and in modifying program to facilitate ESLD students

Balance

Figure 4.1 The Daystrom approach

Planning the interview

All project members were consulted for advice on what questions should be asked. Based on this input, the following were general themes followed in what were semi-structured, informal interviews:

- Reflections on the project initially and over time.
- Surprises as the project progressed.
- Roles of the classroom teacher, the ESL/D teacher, the principal, the assistant coordinator.
- Benefits to teachers and to students.Learrienced.
- Learrienced.
- Hopes for the project in September.

Conducting the interviews

The project team members were interviewed during the final weeks of school in June. The interviews, which were tape-recorded, were about three-quarters of an hour in duration.

Results

Initial reaction to the project

As already stated, the classroom teachers were very receptive to trying the new model, and they welcomed Kay into their classrooms with enthusiasm. Each of them had thought previously about other ways they might tap into Kay's expertise. Because of her previous experience as an ESL/D teacher, Nancy, in particular, had worried about whether withdrawal was the best approach to meeting the ESL/D needs of her students and welcomed the new approach. This is how she put it:

> 'The most attractive part of the project was working with the ESL/D teacher in terms of specific children and possibly how it might spill over to the rest of the class. Even before all this happened, I had thought about how best to tap into Kay as a resource. Because I had a lot of concerns about the kids who were missing so much of the core part of the program by going into the ESL/D classroom.'

But Kay, the ESL/D teacher, has a different perspective. After all, she was the one who would be required to alter her way of doing things the most. She admits that she was apprehensive, but that did not prevent her from trying it out. In her words:

> 'I'm old. And I've been teaching a long time. And I'm set in my ways. And why would I want to bring something new to this? But also, I thought, I've been doing it for such a long time that you can quite easily get into a rut. And I always like to try something new.'

Although Kay's courage in agreeing to a major change in her teaching was highly evident throughout the project, the apprehension she felt resulted in considerable anxiety.

Maureen was concerned about how Kay would react to the reality of her classroom. 'What will Kay think when she sees "John" acting out?' She wondered, 'Will she understand what I'm trying to do?'

The three classroom teachers also commented on the many unknowns they experienced at the beginning of the project. For example, Nancy said she had wondered, 'How will this work? Will I be able to work with this teacher?'

Teachers commented that there was little that was defined about what each person would do. As Nancy put it, 'All the talk was nebulous. And so we had to work it through. The initial days when Kay came into the room we really didn't know what we were doing.'

But everyone agreed that the indefiniteness was important. It left things open so that each of the partnerships with Kay could evolve.

Making the project work

In reflecting on the three months that the project was in place, all of the team members agreed that it had been a success. The following summarizes comments they made:

Conditions that made it work

The project was characterized by a high level of trust and commitment. The principal noted how effectively the teachers went about working together. In her words, 'I was pleased with the openness and honest feelings everyone had ... the support they gave one another.'

And Kay noted how much she valued the constant stroking and support her colleagues gave her:

'They don't feel threatened. They don't look down their noses at me. They don't say, 'Well, here she is, again!' They are just wonderful. They don't make a big fanfare when I come in. They're working. I come in and they don't even see me come in. It just happens. It's as natural as can be.'

Role expectations

At the initial review meetings, talk centred on role expectations. As Kay had asked, 'Who's the boss?' However, at the time of the interviews the classroom teachers appeared to have come to terms with roles. Nancy. who views teaching as an inquiry process argued that the roles should be less defined. 'After all,' she explained, 'we're all teachers. Period!' She believes that rather than isolate teachers through role definitions, teachers should work towards being colleagues.

Similarly, Maureen and Dorothy shared the vision of working with Kay in a collegial way, as a two-person team, rather than with distinct, clearly defined roles. They welcomed the opportunity to put two heads together, to collaborate, to plan, to make joint decisions or just to talk.

Kay continues to grapple with her role and just what is expected of her. She has definite expectations of what she should do as a teacher, expectations which flow from past experience. And so she is still sorting these issues through. Some of the areas she pinpointed include:

- Should she be a disciplinarian, e.g. noise level?
- Is she expected to be the person who brings 'gadgets out of a bag'?
- Should she work with all of the students in the classroom or just the ESL/D students?
- How does what she does with ESL/D students connect with what the other students do?
- What kind of planning time with her new partners is it reasonable to expect, during her free time and during school hours?

Kay also says she is a 'take-over kind of person' and therefore tries hard 'not taking over'. Hence, she tends to hold back at times.

The review meetings

Everyone accorded a high level of importance to review meetings. In Nancy's words, 'The review meetings are vital, absolutely vital. Without them, I think the project would have failed.' They evolved, becoming a formal vehicle for providing the ESL/D project team with a network for encouragement and support.

Dorothy noted that the talk became progressively more open. She suggests this is so because of the principal who 'allows for an open atmosphere so that you don't feel judged for what you say'. There was hope expressed that the review process would continue.

Kay's notes

Although the idea of keeping a journal or some written record was intended to be a vehicle for reflection in Kay's meetings with the Assistant Coordinator, Kay decided to share her notes with all members of the project team each week. Maureen and Dorothy had mixed feelings about Kay's notes. While they found them interesting, they would prefer face-to-face dialogue with Kay.

For Nancy, the significance of Kay's notes changed over time as her work with Kay took on a new shape. In the beginning, when Kay's work was focused on the ESL/D students, the notes were more or less meaningful, 'a record of what was done'. However, she said that as their working relationship began to centre on the whole class the notes became more relevant. As Nancy put it,

> 'I became conscious about how she felt because I had a part in what was happening. It wasn't just my reading about what Kay did. It had to do with what was happening in the room together. So, I had her views of it and I had my own.'

The role of the Principal

The Principal played an important role in the success of the project. Teachers commented on the way Joyce communicated her trust and support and her concern for their adjustment to a new way of doing things and for their professional learning. In Dorothy's words, 'Joyce gave us her blessing ... she recognizes that we're all adults. We're not perfect. We're going to make mistakes. But ... we're learning.'

And Maureen put it this way:

> 'I feel confident that if Joyce thought there was an area of your own professional development that she wanted to help you with, she would lead you gently without putting you down for not knowing already how to do it at this point in your career. To help you improve in that area. She gives you the space to go ahead and do it. Release time or whatever. And that to me, is a very nurturing thing to do. And she encourages working together and teachers sharing their skills.'

For Kay, too, Joyce's role was critical in making the project work for her.

> 'Her role takes the pressure off me. If it doesn't work, it's her fault. She is the overseer of it all. She is putting her trust in me. She's the pilot. And I trust her good sense. She trusts me. And if she trusts me, then I want to make it work! Joyce said, 'Give it a try!' And I said, 'Yes, I'll give it a try. And if I don't like it, I'm not going to do it.' And she wanted me to try it for more than one time. And I thought, 'Well, I'll try it two times!' And, after the second time, I started to look forward to going back the third time.'

Nancy also acknowledged the important role of the Principal in the success of the project. This is how she put it:

> 'Without the Principal initiating (the project) with you, I doubt very much whether it would ever have happened. Obviously the Principal does make the difference in terms of what changes occur in a school ...

through her support – allowing time for visits to other schools, for review meetings, for attending the meetings with us ...'

It was Joyce's hope as Principal 'to be the support, the encouragement, the person who's there if someone needs someone to talk to. That's the role I want to play. If it's not working, let's talk about it. Let's keep open lines of communication.'

The role of the outside consultant

It was the Principal who initiated the Assistant Coordinator's work at Rose Avenue. It is her belief that 'teachers need to know there's someone who has the goods, knows what she's talking about and can be that source. Getting information that I can't get. Acting as a support to principals because principals need that tool. She credits the Assistant Coordinator for having 'planted the seed' about a possible new role for he ESL/D teacher.

Even though it was the Assistant Coordinator who interviewed the team members, teachers also openly expressed their views about the Assistant Coordinator's role. All team members felt that the Assistant Coordinator wanted the project to work, and knew what she wanted to accomplish, which was, as Dorothy suggested, 'a successful project of adults working together.' Nancy thinks the consultant's role is very important in acting as a liaison between teachers and the ESL/D teacher. As she explained:

'I find it enormously beneficial to have that mediator.. So, we do need someone who acts as a middle person. I mean someone who has some background knowledge and seems to know what's going on – and who lets us know that it's okay to flounder. There's somebody there who's steady, to help us through the rough waters – and who knows we're going to get to the other side.'

Other Reflections on the Project

Benefits to students

Team members agreed that it was too early to comment on benefits of the new approach to students. However, Nancy speculates that 'it has made a difference' but she can't label what that is. And Kay has noticed that the children in the three classrooms have begun to view her differently:

'I'm not just the person down the hall who teaches ESL. I've become someone who's part of the school. You see. A lot of those children are new. They've come to the school from another country or another school. And a lot of them don't know me. They know me as the English teacher at the end of the hall. They don't even think I'm a teacher. Now, I get spoken to in the yard more.'

Benefits to teachers

All of the teachers commented on their own learning which was an outcome of the ESL/D Project experience. For Kay, it confirmed that while she sometimes resists change, in fact she welcomes it. Kay admits openly that she considers some of her own personal characteristics as flaws which she worried would make the new partnerships unworkable. First, she says she is very judgemental, and secondly, she says she needs her space, is 'selfish about her own time and as a result is not the easiest person to get next to'. The project experience has given her the opportunity to reflect on whether this is actually true.

Now she says she is learning, because in her words, 'I have to give of myself a little more to other people. Before, I was just giving to the children.' Kay also learned that although she has been 'very fast at judging things previously', she can be flexible. She explains it this way:

'Well, I can adjust. I'm like a tree. I started out in the '50's. And I have firm roots in the '50's. But I'm like a tree. I can bend with change. The winds blow change.'

Maureen had worried initially about being judged. But she found otherwise: 'I've learned that I don't feel very intimidated about the idea of having an extra pair of eyes and hands. I really didn't feel that Kay was judgemental of me – although initially I had some fears about that ...' She said she discovered, however, that 'we are both professionals and can plan together.'

In addition to her own professional learning which was an outcome of working with Kay on a drama theme, Nancy welcomed the opportunity this approach provided her as a teacher, 'for team teaching where that mixture will happen because you've got two adults. The potential is incredible.'

Nancy talked about a time in her career when she had been ESL/D teacher and worked in classrooms. The difference then, she explained, was that she worked with the ESL/D students only, and not with the teacher. 'There was no talking about it with the teacher. And so, nothing actually could come out of it. But this model, where Kay is working with me – it takes the best advantage of learning for kids and for teachers.'

Hopes for the project in September

All of the team members expressed their wish that the project would continue. Although they all have the expectation that it will grow and evolve, they identified a number of areas they hoped could be addressed in September. These include:

- Kay's time   Getting more of Kay's time to talk and plan (Maureen and Dorothy).
- Kay's Notes   Finding a way for Kay's notes to become two-way communications (Nancy, Dorothy).
- A whole-class approach   Finding ways to work together to plan for all students, not just the ESL/D students (Maureen, Dorothy).
- A whole-school approach   Working towards all staff having shared understandings about ESL/D students and what ESL/D is (Joyce). Communicating to parents that this approach is in fact 'ESL help'((Joyce). Reaching a point in time when this approach becomes a natural part of the school (Joyce).

Updates

1992

Rose Avenue School primarily works within an integrated and partial withdrawal model when servicing special needs students. Specialist teachers within ESL, the Learning Centre (Special Education), and the Library now collaborate with classroom teachers to provide support to both students and teachers. Further, many in-service programs, such as drama, are provided within the classrooms. The integration model is part of a whole-school approach and philosophy which was initiated and strongly supported by our principal, Joyce Boucher.

ESL integration is approaching the end of a fourth year. Even within these few short years, there have been many changes. There is greater comfort with classroom teachers. Sometimes the ESL teacher works in collaboration with a classroom teacher and helps in a unit or theme. On occasion, the ESL teacher provides or initiates a program in which the classroom teacher supports the specialist teacher. At other times, individual ESL students or a mixed group of students (some are not ESL) are helped with classroom work. The 'how' and 'what' is flexible and is usually dictated by events within the school and by the calendar, e.g. holidays.

Some things have not changed; the difficulties of timetabling and finding time to plan, time to meet with new teachers who are new to teaching and teachers new to the school and to our approach. Yet, as we struggle and learn together and learn to celebrate the good and moan about the difficulties, we are slowly learning how beneficial it is to all students when an extra teacher is in the classroom.

1995

In 1988 we had 420 students. This year we hover around 600. As an inner city and ESL school, challenges are part of our school life. Within the past three months. approximately 30 new students have arrived. Unlike the pattern over the last three years, where the majority of our new students came from one country, Sri Lanka, most of this year's newcomers come from different parts of the world. They are from as close as Jamaica and from as far away as Serbia, Thailand, Ethiopia and Somalia; and, of course, most of these students speak little or no English, some have interrupted schooling, and one eleven-year-old boy had never been to school.

The integrated model in 1988 was initiated to better service the growing numbers of ESL students. Within five years, integration became less a collegial model to return to that of a withdrawal program. The difference was that of geography – the withdrawal program was located within the teacher's classroom. Also, this trend was happening with at-risk students who worked with the Learning Centre teacher. As the ESL and Learning Centre teachers worked primarily as independent satellites and knew little of what the other was doing, some students were being double-serviced.

Paralleling the growing difficulty of servicing greater numbers of ESL and at-risk students, teacher discussions at division meetings began to pivot around reading and ESL; without exception, all teachers reported concerns as well about the apparent lack of responsibility in our students; i.e. forgetting to bring texts back, not doing homework, forgetting gym shoes and recorders, etc. Many teachers also stated a desire to be able to talk with teachers of other grades.

Our new Principal and Vice-Principal, Linda Reichert and Sue McMurtry, designed a more coherent and efficient system to address these concerns. In consultation with the specialty teachers who had flexible timetables (ESL Learning Centre, Library Resource and Computer), they came up with a plan which they implemented this school year. They harnessed as resources these specialty teachers to form core language support team. All members work with their own group of teachers (save the half-time computer teacher – it was felt she needed to be free to train teachers and students and to test software for this year.

The team's mandate is to work with classroom teachers within their programs, to plan for language development for all students and, where needed, language acquisition. Also the mandate included working with teachers to find practical strategies to help students take greater responsibility for their learning. The language support team meets weekly to ensure commonality of purpose and to discuss issues related to their mandate.

Although the language support team is central to this plan, most important is a system which facilitates teacher discussion of shared concerns. In response to many teachers' desire to have a broader perspective, Linda and Sue placed a strand of teachers (J.K. – grade 6) to work with a language support teacher. Approximately once a month each strand consisting of eight or nine classroom teachers, the language support teacher, and Linda and Sue meet to discuss a previously identified area of concern; e.g. reading. This format is a change. We are accustomed to meet with teachers of similar grades. Even though teachers requested the opportunity to talk with teachers across the grades, as yet they have not taken ownership of these meetings.

It is too early to assess whether the new plan will provide the necessary structure to enable teachers to assess for themselves common areas of concern and to plan effective programs for greater academic achievement for our students. In fairness to all, what needs to be included is the context in which these changes are taking place. In addition to the usual changes which occur in schools: i.e. staff, administration, new students, we had a year-and-a-half of intolerable dust and noise from the major construction of a new wing, a diminished playground area because of the construction coupled with a significant increase in school population, a need to share school space with an expanded daycare centre, the addition of a breakfast program to the daily snack program, and a general cutback in funding, including teachers' salaries. Just as education everywhere is undergoing major 'restructuring' (the new buzzword), we too are reeling from the effects of a magnified examination of education. Accountability has become concrete and etched in print with ever-increasing new initiatives and directives which come from the Ministry of Education and which compete with similar thrusts from our own Toronto Board. These are difficult times. Stress levels have reached new heights. It is not surprising that, with all these demands, changes within the school were not well received.

Despite it all, we survived the first term. Everyone had to be open to shape this new model as we worked within it. Classroom teachers had to work with all their students within their own program in partnership with the language support teacher. The language support teachers had to give up their established individual roles and egos to become members of a team. In retrospect, we can see small and large successful experiences between classroom and language support teachers, e.g. program planning, extension and/or modification program, help with student assessment and general supportive help. We are not out of the woods, but we are definitely more relaxed – this week. Perhaps we need to take another look at our latest effort six years from now. I look forward to it.

References

Johnson, D. (1982) ESL children as teachers: a social view of second language use. *Language Arts* 65, 2.

Section 2: Secondary Schools

Of the five contributors from secondary schools, three represent classrooms which provide solely for ESL students: a sheltered subject course and two pre-mainstream content courses. They thus constitute a waystage to mainstreaming in that they integrate ESL work with the mainstream curriculum, but not the mainstream classroom. The other two illustrate team-teaching between ESL and subject specialists in mainstream subject classrooms.

The three ESL content courses differ considerably in approach according to the degree to which language decisions influence planning at the macro and micro levels of classroom process. **Ross McKean**, teaching a senior *sheltered history* course in a Canadian high school uses a largely *topic-driven* approach. He plans both content and language objectives, but allows the progress of his teaching – lesson shape and task sequence – and his students' work to be influenced in the first instance by the requirements of the subject. The chief means which he uses to adjust his teaching to the language needs of ESL learners are processes at the more micro level, namely the quality of his interaction with the whole class, the organisation of groupwork and the use of student presentations to motivate their attention to accuracy and communicative ability in English. The key features of his *whole-class work* are an interactive talking style, careful staging in the presentation of ideas, the use of visual support to accompany ideas, the use of example and metaphor and appeals to the previous knowledge of the students. In *groupwork* he pays attention to group composition, ensuring a mix of language groups and English language abilities. His own interventions at the drafting stage of written work produced in groups are one of the chief means of focusing on language issues.

Anne Filson works with low-literacy ESL students in a *pre-mainstream environmental studies* course in an American High School. Anne adjusts her teaching to ESL requirements at the macro level by attention to the *overall environment*: she uses a lot of visual material and active, manipulative tasks, ensuring a mix of whole-class, group and individual work, and making full

133

use of colleagues and English-fluent students across the school. She also allows the topic to determine largely the sequence of tasks, but manipulates task design to ensure that content is comprehensible and language production practicable.

Language influences more strongly the level of *micro-processes*, where she is sensitive to students' previous knowledge in whole-class interaction and pays a lot of attention to the detail of their language development in one-to-one teacher-student work. She also uses carefully planned student presentations to foster attention to accuracy, and gets native-speaker 'buddies' to provide help in preparing these. In addition, she uses a range of conventional *tasks* to support students' control of vocabulary, grammar and other basic building blocks of language.

Ruth Evans describes *pre-mainstream geography* in an Australian language centre. Her approach is influenced by language at the level of both *macro-* and *micro-processes*. Her model of language development leads her to work to a well-defined sequence of teaching stages – similar to that of Elina Raso. The geography topic is analysed for the *language demands* it will make on the students; these language demands then influence the sequence of tasks within a given stage – moving from the more guided to the more open. At the micro level, *tasks* are tightly designed to support specific elements of language. She employs a lot of visual support and a variety of forms of classroom organisation and encourages students' capacity for critical comment. Through a sequence of interlocking form- and content-orientated tasks, she directs students' attention ultimately to the subject-matter, but wherever relevant to questions of language.

The last two secondary contributors work in *mainstream* classrooms. Both illustrate the integration of language and science, though in different contexts. **Manny Vazquez** teaches in a school with a 15% intake of pupils who speak a language other than English at home. He and his science colleague collaborate within an agreed *partnership* framework, which we see here working in a classroom with a small group of students with ESL needs. According to the ground rules of this agreement, language development of a cognitive/academic nature is seen as important for the largely English-fluent class in general as well as for the ESL students in particular. Language aims are generated for the whole science curriculum, and the whole of a given lesson is thus informed by language, as well as being made especially accessible for the ESL minority, through the collaborative effort of the partners. Manny belongs to a *district-wide* ESL unit which supplies ESL specialist staff to schools which need it, and thus – like Julie Reid – exemplifies the value of a coordinated district approach. **Hugh Hooper**, as

District Principal for ESL in Vancouver, also illustrates a School Board approach to mainstreaming, which has won a considerable reputation. Hugh describes here a first-time trial of mainstream collaboration between a science and an ESL specialist, in a classroom with an ESL majority. The two teachers share classroom roles equally.

Both Hugh and Manny use an approach to integrating language and content which highlights the cognitive as well as the linguistic demands which the subject matter makes on pupils. Both plan language into lessons at the *macro* level. They do this by looking closely at the conceptual aims of the science subject-matter, analysing what these require students to do in terms of language skills and then matching these language demands with the language needs of the class. Within this procedure, Manny pays special attention to the needs of his ESL minority, which he diagnoses by using district-wide *ESL assessment criteria*.

Hugh uses the *'knowledge framework'* (Mohan, 1986) approach which breaks down any given area of subject-matter into commonly occurring knowledge structures, specifies the key language items associated with them and provides visual as well as linguistic means of conveying the relevant concepts. This language planning strategy at the macro level generates a highly organised sequence of language-informed tasks at the micro level, somewhat reminiscent of Elina's class.

Hugh highlights the importance of small-group work, where the students do a good deal of precise *talking about language* in the process of being exact about defining scientific concepts, and where the teachers need to find the 'teachable moment' at which to intervene. Manny also makes language very visible at the micro-level of *task design*, through the use of a range of tasks which provide support to the development of both language and science concepts, and are differentiated to suit the needs of varying levels of ESL ability.

5 A Sheltered History Course for ESL Students

ROSS MCKEAN

Description of School

Jarvis Collegiate Institute is not a school that can be easily categorized. Officially, we are designated as an Inner City School for funding and program purposes, because we are located in downtown Toronto where there are many subsidized housing complexes. However, we also have students from two other areas which are solidly upper middle class and predominantly white Anglo-Saxon. The majority of English as a Second Language (ESL) students, however, live in subsidized housing or large apartment complexes in the downtown core.

The school's ethnic and racial mix is equally diverse, especially amongst the ESL students. Many of these students are from a wide variety of east Asian countries, but there is a growing number from eastern Europe, the Caribbean, and Africa as well. First languages of the majority of the students are Cantonese, Mandarin, Tamil, and Vietnamese. It should be noted that there are no formal heritage language programs offered at the school. However, there are extensive extra-curricular programs for ESL students where there is ample opportunity for them to speak their first language.

The make-up of the school is even more complex, as there are two separate schools within one building. There are both a French and an English school, each of which functions under separate school boards and with separate staffs. However, the French students are free to take ESL English courses, so they do have an impact on our program.

Inter-ethnic divisions are not very pronounced. Where racial conflicts occur, we deal with them in the first instance by using peers as mediators. We attempt to respond to the needs of parents from the minority community; for example, an interpreter system was introduced in order to

136

attract them to parents' evenings. The Toronto School Board operates both an anti-racist policy and an affirmative action policy for hiring teachers.

Now amid all this diversity, there is one common denominator: over 90% of our students are university or college bound, whether they are in the French or English school, or ESL or non-ESL students.

For the ESL student who enters Jarvis with little or no English but with the desire to go to university or college, it has been our practice to provide sheltered subject teaching for ESL students, particularly in their first two years at the school.

Because of the large number of ESL students at Jarvis, just over 20% of the school's population, we are able to offer a variety of courses (ESL 1, 2, 3 and 4), corresponding to the students' first, second, third or fourth year in Canada. After that, students take Grade 12 and then 13 English, although usually in sheltered classes taught by ESL teachers. Our ultimate goal, though, is to integrate the ESL students into mainstream English classes at the senior level, but this is rarely happens. The curriculum of these sheltered courses is similar to mainstream English courses, but geared to the special needs of ESL students.

Sheltered subject teaching also takes place at the Grade 9 and 10 levels in history, geography, science and in one senior level social science course entitled 'People in Society'. Sheltered classes in these subjects are offered for most incoming ESL students because they do not have the English language skills to function in a mainstream class. Subjects where sheltered teaching is not offered are mathematics, keyboarding, art, music and physical education. While tutorial support is offered in these subjects, including the 'health' component of physical education, the language skills needed for ESL students in these courses are minimal when compared to subjects such as history and geography, where the students are expected to write essays and give oral presentations.

The same rationale is used for the senior social science credit, 'People in Society'. Because of the emphasis in this course on written and oral English language skills, ESL students have opted in the past almost exclusively for the economics course to meet their senior social science credit. Recently, however, the 'People in Society' course has been offered in sheltered classes, in the hope that more ESL students would enrol and thereby learn more about Canadian society while improving their English language skills. At present there are three sheltered classes in this subject. This indicates both a need and desire on the part of ESL students to take a course of this nature.

We have a constant intake of ESL students from September through to May, and they may be anywhere from 14 to 19 years of age, and in some cases adults, at the time of their arrival. Again, the sheltered subject class is the model we use to help these students bridge the gap, but we are well aware of the isolation that often comes with this type of system. For that reason, it is a constant juggling act to find the balance between meeting the language needs of the incoming students and trying to integrate them into the mainstream student body as quickly as possible.

As the focus of this chapter is the Grade 10 History course, I shall outline the average timetable of an incoming Grade 10 ESL student:

ESL classes: ESL 2 (two classes): history; geography; science.

Mainstream classes: mathematics; keyboarding; one of art, music, French or physical education.

I stress the word 'average' because there are many variations on this timetable, depending on the students' language and academic skills, and at what point in the year they entered the school.

Rationale for Sheltered Subject Classes and Other Support Systems

At this point, I will outline a few of the teaching methods used in the sheltered subject classes, which in a number of cases differ from the mainstream classes, and the support that is available for ESL students outside the classroom:

(1) One of the most important things to remember is that we cannot make assumptions about ESL students' knowledge of Western culture, and particularly Canadian culture. This is especially true of courses such as history and English which are so culture-bound. We assume no prior knowledge of the issues, and therefore must remember to explain things which might be taken for granted in mainstream classes.

(2) Wherever possible, we try to draw on students' own cultural experience, because it is something that is familiar to them. This is particularly important in this Grade 10 History course, and especially in the assignment described in the next section. The assignment requires students to question both Canadian values and those of their own culture, in order to create a constitution that might embody the best of both worlds.

(3) We have the students keep vocabulary books, in which they not only find the definition of a word, but write a sentence using the word as well. Sometimes we give the students vocabulary sheets with defini-

tions if we feel that the word is important for understanding a passage, but not essential for everyday use. This, of course, is a judgement call on our part, but it does discourage the students from relying too heavily on the dictionary, which is time-consuming and may take the joy out of reading. This points to the importance of choosing reading material that is appropriate to the language level of the students.

(4) There are several teaching techniques which are also used in mainstream classes, but are especially important for ESL students. These include: (a) a careful step-by-step structuring and explanation of the assignment, so students know exactly what is expected of them. This more structured approach often enables ESL students to be more creative; (b) guided questions which elicit concepts which are important for understanding the assignment. These questions not only draw on students' experience, but also follow a progression, so there is a building-block approach to creating a definition of the concept. At this point, new vocabulary can be introduced, although I try to keep the definition of the concept simple and clear. (c) constant review of vocabulary and concepts, using techniques such as jigsaws, crosswords, and board reviews.

(5) For support outside the classroom, Jarvis has a peer tutoring program which is supervised by teachers who teach English, history, and science. Incoming ESL students may get additional help with assignments during their lunch hour and after school, from both Canadian-born and ESL students. For incoming ESL students, help may be given by peer tutors in the new students' first language, because many of the tutors are senior ESL students. This is particularly important for ESL students who arrive part way through the year, and need to catch up quickly on course material. With other ESL students who have more advanced English language skills, we encourage them to get help in English. This approach not only helps the ESL students, but ESL tutors as well, in improving their English language skills.

One interesting off-shoot of this program is that often the tutors are senior-level ESL users who are Canadian-born and who are having academic difficulties. This serves the dual purpose of helping the ESL students improve their English language skills, as well as giving them contact with Canadian-born students.

Course Exercise

For this article, I have chosen to deal with the Canadian History course, and more specifically the government section which deals with the writing of a constitution. Below is the section of the course curriculum, which describes the rationale, aims, skills objectives, and brief outline of the course content, so that the reader can place the exercise of writing a constitution within the context of the overall course.

Grade 10 Canadian History
for Students who speak English as a Second Language
(sheltered subject course)

I. **Basis of Course**: Ontario Ministry of Education Guidelines for History Intermediate Division 1987.

II. **Level of Difficulty:** Advanced (Academic).

III. **Credit Value:** One credit.

IV. **Rationale:** This is the Canadian history credit necessary for the Ontario Secondary School Graduation Diploma, but has been designed for students speaking English as a second language at the intermediate level who have been in Canada less than three years. This contemporary course attempts to give these students a basic understanding of the issues confronting Canadians today. The course emphasizes the importance of an awareness of contemporary issues and develops communication skills and tools for understanding history. As the course progresses, the students realize their rights and responsibilities with regard to the government (i.e. the role of the citizen). They also gain a perspective on their place in Canada, and Canada's place in North America and the world.

V. **Aims:** This course will provide opportunities for students to:
    - develop an understanding of the Canadian political and legal systems;
    - develop an appreciation of their rights and responsibilities as Canadian citizens;
    - develop the ability to analyze, in historical perspective and in terms of future implications, contemporary issues of concern to Canadians as citizens of Canada and members of the world community;
    - develop an understanding of Canada's historical development in the twentieth century;
    - develop an awareness of the contributions of women and men of all ages and groups to the development of Canada;
    - develop the cognitive skills to process information and to communicate ideas in writing and speaking;
    - begin to develop the skills of the historian;

- encourage personal responsibility, self-discipline, initiative, good work, and study habits;
- develop reading, writing, speaking and listening skills.

VI. Skills Objectives: The course will assist students to:

- distinguish between fact and opinion, primary and secondary sources;
- understand cause/effect relationships;
- draw conclusions based on observations;
- develop generalizations from conclusions;
- develop note-taking skills;
- use various sources of information: people, textbooks, other books, maps;
- use charts, graphs, maps, and pictures in assignments and notes;
- write clear, coherent and correct paragraphs and essays;
- speak in a variety of situations: small groups, oral presentations, role-playing;
- formulate opinions, using supportive evidence;
- conduct an interview;
- identify the main idea and supporting evidence in an editorial.

VII. List of Units and Suggested Time Allotment (in weeks):

(2) 1. Geo-political Orientation of Canada.

(8) 2. Citizenship: Government and Law.

(2) 3. Beginning of a New Century (1890–1910).

(4) 4. Canada and World War I (1914–1918).

(2) 5. Canada in the Roaring Twenties.

(3) 6. The Depression.

(4) 7. World War II (1939–1945).

(10) 8. Contemporary Canada.

Note: Teachers should take time to help students examine and discuss contemporary issues facing Canada as they arise in the media. Newspaper editorials and reports may motivate discussion and written responses. Topics might include:

- political party leadership conventions;
- poverty in Canada;
- environmental issues;
- Canada's relations with China;
- French-English relations;
- Canada's Native Peoples.

Process

The writing of the constitution comes at the beginning of Unit 2 – Citizenship: Government and Law. There are a number of steps to this process:

Step 1. This exercise is prefaced by a *class discussion on why we have government*. At this stage of the assignment, I use the Socratic method of teaching to guide the discussion. I try to relate the discussion to the classroom, by asking questions which enable the students to identify the system of government we have in the class, and why we have it. I begin this way because the classroom structure is something students can relate to. For instance, I ask them if they had any choice in having me as their teacher, and what my function is in the classroom. The students have no problem at all giving the answers to the questions. The difficulty might be that they lack the vocabulary for concepts such as democracy and dictatorship. In this case, it is my role to provide them with the vocabulary, as they already have the concepts, given their experience in the classroom.

However, I am often amazed at the sophistication of the students, because some of them can readily identify the system of government in the classroom as a dictatorship, and use exactly that word. It is at that point that I introduce the term 'benevolent dictatorship', that is – where you do not get to choose your leader, but the leader is kind. We usually have fun in this discussion, debating whether or not this classroom is actually a benevolent dictatorship. The animated nature of the discussion shows me that students understand the concept.

When I ask about my role in the classroom, the answers lead to the themes of maintenance of order. I ask the students what would happen if I left the classroom for a week and let them organize the classes. Again, this often leads to a humorous discussion about all the things that might happen if I were to leave. As they are quick to identify fighting among students as one of the possibilities of my absence, this leads to a discussion of the protection of individual rights and freedoms. This concept is not too difficult for the students to understand, although they would not express it in those exact words. My role in this discussion is to help them articulate those concepts more precisely.

Step 2. At this point it is useful to *introduce students to the idea of different types of government* by further exploring the types of government they had in their home countries, and the type of government we have in Canada. Having just identified the classroom as a type of dictatorship and my role in the protection of rights and freedoms, I then ask the students to identify the similarities and/or differences between classroom government and the governments of their home countries. While the students often lack the necessary vocabulary to actually label the governments of their home countries and that of Canada, they usually have very strong opinions about them.

Many of our students are refugees and have left their home countries because of repressive governments or war. It is at this point that we clearly define a democracy versus a dictatorship, after they have described some of the elements of both systems as they have experienced them.

Step 3. Having identified why we have governments and several different models of government, I then give them the exercise of *creating their own constitution*. Below are two scenarios that I have used for this exercise.

Scenario I*

Spaceship Aurora

Imagine that your class has been selected to join a spaceship, the *Aurora*, on an exploratory trip to a distant comer of the galaxy.

You and your classmates are assigned a central cabin with individual survival chambers. Travelling swiftly through space, you are soon many light-years from earth.

Suddenly the pilot speaks from the control room. The ship has passed through a mysterious cosmic storm that has damaged it and robbed it of most of its power. There is just enough fuel left to land on a nearby planet. A scan of the surface shows that the atmosphere is breathable and there is enough water and vegetation to support human life. However, the pilot does not know the state of the reverse thrust landing gear. She asks all passengers to return to their cabins and prepare for an emergency landing.

Touchdown is violent. In your padded chamber you are safe, but others may not have been so lucky. Cautiously, you emerge to take stock.

All adults, whose cabins were near the outer walls of the ship, have been killed. Only your classmates, in their individual chambers, have survived. No older people are around to give orders or impose rules. You are 'free' to do whatever you want.

But what *should* you do?

At the moment, you have no supplies of food or water. You have no place to sleep and no way to keep warm. It is obvious that you will be on this planet for several weeks, months, or even years.

At first no one seems to know what to do. People make various suggestions. There is much shouting and arguing, but no useful plan of action emerges. Gradually you realise that you can only solve your problems by working together as a group.

You gather in small groups to discuss and answer the following questions:

1. How will you make your decisions?
2. Who will be your leaders. and how will they be selected?
3. What kinds of people do you want as leaders? What characteristics do you think that they should have?
4. What kind of rules will you make? Who will make these rules?
5. What will you do if some person or group refuses to abide by the rules?

As you examine these questions, you are considering the same problems that are faced by any group of people trying to work together. All societies and nations have faced these problems. Different groups arrive at different solutions, but all must meet the same basic needs. They must establish rules, make decisions. and select people to run the organisation. In other words, they must set up a system of government.

* Reprinted with permission of the publisher Fitzhenry & Whiteside from *Canada – The Twentieth Century* by McFadden, Quinlan and Life.

Scenario II

War has just ended between the USA and the USSR, and Canada has been the battleground. While nuclear weapons were not used, Canada was still decimated by the fighting. Having taken refuge in a shelter, you and your classmates have survived. You now have the task of rebuilding society. The immediate problems that you face include a shortage of food, no shelter, and no communication systems (other than the English language of course). In order to prevent chaos, you need some sort of organized system to maintain law and order, and that means A CONSTITUTION!

(1) Your task is to write that constitution. To help you accomplish this, organize your constitution according to the 'four elements of a constitution' that we discussed in class:
(a) Structure of Government
(b) Selection of Leader(s)
(c) Basic Laws
(d) Enforcement of Laws

(2) You will work in groups of four, and each group will present their constitution to the class.

Although the second scenario is dated, I have included it for two reasons. Firstly, it can be adapted for classroom use; for example, the Cold War scenario can be substituted by an environmental disaster. Secondly, and more importantly, it outlines the structure that is used for this assignment – the four elements of a constitution.

I go through these four elements by again relating them to the classroom. For instance, what is the structure of government in the classroom? Who sets the agenda, and how is that person selected? What are some basic rules of behaviour in class, and how are they enforced?

To reinforce what these four elements of a constitution mean, I usually go through the same process using the government of the school and the government of Canada as well. For example, the students and I put a diagram on the board for the structure of school government, so it is very clear what is meant by these terms. I do this using the socratic method by asking who the leader of the school is, how that person got to be leader, and what his or her function is in the school. I put all the responses on the board as the students answer. I do the same thing for the vice- principal/s, at which point the students begin to see the hierarchical pattern that is emerging as well as how these leaders are selected and the basic laws that they enforce.

I then ask the students to come up to the board and continue the diagram with the other leaders in the school, e.g. department heads, assistant heads, teachers. The students seem to have very little difficulty with this lesson except, ironically, for defining the role of the principal.

I use the same series of questions to draw a diagram illustrating the government. The diagram we come up with for the government of Canada is very basic at this point in the course, but it is important as it emphasizes what is meant by the terms 'structure of government', 'selection of leaders', 'basic laws' and the 'enforcement of those laws'. At the same time, the diagram introduces the students to some basic terms like 'parliament' and 'prime minister', or acts as a review of these terms. This is important because these are terms that they will have to use later in the course.

Having clearly defined what is meant by these four elements of a constitution, I then encourage the students to be creative in writing a constitution that would best create a society that they would want to live in. This is not an exercise in which they are expected to parrot back the constitution of Canada or the structure of school government. For example, I want them to give some careful thought in their groups to five or ten basic laws they think are essential for their society to function smoothly. For instance, it is at this point that I introduce the question of their rights, because as ESL students the issue of equality, that is, everyone being treated equally regardless of race, ethnicity, religion, etc., is particularly pertinent to them and is also part of the policy of the Toronto Board of Education. Therefore, they have to give special thought to this issue as one of their basic laws, and to the enforcement of that law.

Because this assignment falls fairly early in the year (mid-October), I select the groups so that they have a good representation of different language groups and abilities. This enables the stronger students to help those students who may have weaker skills. This is particularly important because this is a mandatory course and therefore the language abilities within the classes are generally very diverse. I monitor the groups in order to help them organize their thoughts and ideas for the assignment, as well as give the vocabulary (where necessary) to write the constitution. Although I monitor each group individually, when common problems emerge, I address them with the class as a whole.

The focus of the assignment is the organization and development of their constitution, and an obvious off-shoot of that is vocabulary development. My reason for including three different constitutions in this chapter is in part to show both the success and failure that groups have in organizing and developing their ideas. As I say later in my analysis of the sample constitutions, the first constitution is by far the best organized and developed in its ideas. This is not to say that the other examples do not have their strengths, but they do not achieve the success of the first example with respect to the main objectives of the assignment.

I hope that the structure I have given the students in creating a constitution is firmly embedded from the examples we have drawn on the board. They can then start to discuss what kind of constitution they want, using the structures with which they are now familiar. This is where the role of the teacher is most important, for two reasons: one is to help the students organize and develop their ideas within the structure that they have been discussing. This is done by asking questions of the group which will encourage them to think seriously about the kind of society they would like to create. The second reason is to ensure that they do not parrot back the examples we have been discussing in our class discussions, which were for the purpose of providing a clear structure in which to create their constitutions.

Step 4. Once the rough draft of the constitution is written, groups *re-work the rough draft* with my help, to improve on grammar, spelling and sentence structure. This stage is particularly important to monitor, as it is the students' first oral presentation. If they feel confident about their written work, then they will feel more comfortable about making their oral presentation. While I often help the students with more complex sentence structure, I use a symbols sheet that all the students are given at the beginning of the course. For instance, I will circle on their rough draft where there is an error in subject/verb agreement with 'S-V'. They can look up 'S-V' on their symbols sheet so that they know what the error is, and then as a group, they try to correct it. As the year progresses, the students understand the symbols, and rarely need to refer to their symbol sheets. However, grammatical accuracy is definitely less important than the organization and development of ideas and vocabulary development.

Step 5. The assignment is concluded with *oral presentations* of each group's constitution. As the groups are made up of four students, each one presents one of the four elements of a constitution. Each presentation concludes with questions from the class. It should be noted that before the oral presentations are given, I help the students with pronunciation, so they feel more confident in giving their presentations. For students who have real difficulty with pronunciation, I often give them addition help, one-on-one, during peer-tutoring hours.

The evaluation sheet (Figure 5.1) is given to the students at the beginning of the assignment, so that they know what is expected of them. The content mark is a group mark, while the mark for delivery or the oral presentation is an individual mark. The content mark is a group mark in order to

	Presentations				
	A	B	C	D	E
CONTENT					
Well Organized					
Topic Well Developed					
Creative					
DELIVERY					
Strong, Expressive Voice					
Eye Contact					
Clear Pronunciation, Enunciation					
WRITTEN WORK					
Grammar, Punctuation Spelling,etc.					
Overall Presentation					

A-Excellent B-Good C-Fair D-Only Passing E-Not Passing

Figure 5.1 Evaluation sheet

emphasize the importance of group work in the course, and that working together is essential for the success in the course. The mark for content is also a comparative mark in that each group is evaluated in relation to the other groups.

The mark for delivery or oral presentation is an individual mark and not comparative. Each student is evaluated in relation to his or her own ability. I do this because this is the first oral presentation that the students give in class, and for some, this can be a formidable task, particularly so early in the year. For that reason, I want this mark to affirm and encourage each student in developing their oral language skills.

The mark for the written work that the students hand in at the end of the presentation is worth less than the content mark. I do this because, for this exercise, thought development and creativity are more important than correctness in surface structure of language. In addition, to the mark for each section the students also receive written comments on their work.

It should be noted that while students hand in a written copy of their constitution at the end of the assignment, I encourage them to make point form notes of the oral presentation, so they are less likely to read their presentation to the class.

However, one of the pitfalls of the assignment is that because each group has people with a range of abilities, there is often someone who emerges as the leader in the group work. This person is often the one who keeps the group on track, provides a lot of input in terms of ideas and the organization of these ideas, and who is also comfortable giving an oral presentation. For this reason, I insist that everyone present one section of the constitution to the class during the oral presentation. However, anyone in the group may answer the questions afterwards, but no one is forced to. As I said earlier, the main objective of the assignment is the organization and development of the constitution. The oral presentation is secondary.

This, however, does not deal with an innate problem of group work, that some people contribute more than others. For this reason, I try to monitor the groups constantly in order to ensure that everyone makes a contribution. While there is a wide range among the finished products of the groups, I have never failed a group, for two reasons: it is early in the year and their first experience with group work in this class. Therefore, I want it to be a positive experience because it is an essential component of the course as a whole. Secondly, as this is the first group assignment and I have been monitoring the groups closely, I do not feel it is fair to fail any one group.

Examples of Students' Constitutions

On the following pages, I have included three samples of students' constitutions, which were all written as a part of the Spaceship Aurora assignment. The samples have been reproduced at various stages of the editing process, and therefore you will see a variety of errors in the copy.

After the three samples, I have included a brief analysis of each.

Example 1

The Government of Aurora

Our group consists of 5 people. One will be the leader, another a Chief Advisor, followed by a group of Council of Advisors and the rest will be the ordinary members of the society. We named our government after the spaceship and we have a special symbol to represent our party. There are four colours in this particular symbol and they are red, blue, yellow and black The red represents self-confidence and power while the blue represents cool under pressure. The yellow represents a stable and strong government and the black alphabet 'A' stands for Aurora. The three broken rings signify unity.

Red – Self-confidence and power.

Blue – Cool under pressure.

Yellow – stable and strong government.

Black A – Aurora.

Three broken rings – unity.

(1) Structure of Government

Aurora Party has a democratic system of government. We think that the government should get involved with the people because there are people who are unemployed and the government can help them to find jobs, provide financial assistance if they are out of work, protect them from robbery or unfair treatment, teach them useful skills and pay their medical bills. People under this democratic system of government will have their own rights too. Citizens who are 18 years old and above get a chance to vote their own leader and to run for election. In our system of government established by our group, the person occupying the highest position is the leader. He is the one who heads the whole group. Then comes the Chief Advisor. He or she is to help the leader to make decisions. Below the Chief Advisor is the Council of Advisors. They help the Chief Advisor to collect taxes, plan the education system, maintenance of the group and many other responsibilities to the group of people.

Structure of Government

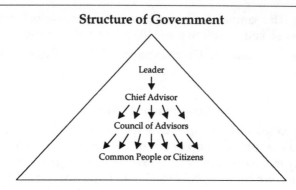

(2) Selection of Leader

Leaders are chosen in elections. Citizens who are 18 years of age and over vote for the leader of their choice. The candidate with the most votes wins. This candidate is a representative of the people who have chosen him or her to make decisions on their behalf. Being a leader requires special qualities and responsibilities. There are a few people who have all the qualities necessary to be a successful leader. A successful leader must be well-educated, self-confident, decisive, determined, flexible, organised, imaginative, careful and financially secure.

(3) Basic Laws

All laws start with ideas about solving problems. When someone demands action from the government, he or she is asking for laws. Laws to prevent or stop this. Laws to provide the money to do that. All groups or societies establish certain basic rules or laws. Laws are very important because if there are no laws or rules, this world will be in chaos. Imagine a boxing game with no rules, or no referee to enforce them. The boxer can use a knife and just stab the opponent and no one will even bother. There is no justice. There are many types of laws established by different groups and societies to protect the citizens. Here are the 7 basic laws that most groups and societies will have:

(1) Equality before the law regardless of race, nationality, colour, religion, sex, age and mental or physical disability.

(2) There shall be no killing amongst each other.

(3) Drug taking is forbidden.

(4) All laws must be obeyed by both men and women equally.

(5) Anyone who disobeys the laws shall be judged and if the person is found guilty he or she shall be punished.

(6) Stealing is prohibited.

(7) No one is allowed to harm people physically.

(4) Enforcement of the Laws

Laws and enforcement must always come together. If there are laws only, people will go against them and nothing will happen but when there are enforcement of laws people will not dare to go against them. Nevertheless there are some who do. The reason why enforcement of laws is important is so that people will learn to obey and respect the laws. For example, if law is not enforced, a person can take along with him a gun and if he feels that he doesn't like someone he just shoots that person. That is why enforcement of laws is very important.

In our group the leader and the police force enforce the laws and if anyone is caught breaking any law, he will be sent to a court and be judged. If the crime is a serious one the punishment will be heavy. For those which are not really serious, they receive lighter sentence.

Group: *U-Jin Hoo   Rolando*
                   Yuan   Natasha

Example 2

Our Government

We are stuck on this planet and we have lost our contact with earth. We do not know how many days, months or years we have to live here. Even with this uncertain future, we have to live. So we should maintain some rules and regulations to form a peaceful and successful community until we return to earth.

The structure of government

Union: contains 5 people

Leaders (2)

Food Administrator | Basic Needs Administrator | Defence Administrator

Organizers (5) | Social Workers | Helpers (10)

Every body will be elected

- Leaders, who will maintain the function of the government, and responsible for the function.
- Food Administrator, who will be responsible for the social health and other basic needs.
- Defence Administrator, who will be responsible for defence and look after that every body obeys the basic rule.
- Organizers – They will help Food Administrator and maintain all activities, which are related to the food section.
- Social Workers – They will help to Basic needs Administrator and serve to people in medical and other needs. So they should have some medical knowledge.
- Helpers – They will protect the community from external forces and internal crisis. So they should be strong enough.
- Union – They will help the government in providing services and maintain the basic laws.

Basic Laws
- No physical assaults or killings
- No stealings
- No misusing the foods
- No smoking and liquor
- Every body should keep the environment clean
- No television or radio at high volume
- Every body should obey the government and union
- Every body (including all government workers) should work in their limited working hours, but exceptions will be allowed by the union
- No misusing anything, which can serve basic needs
- Every body should do their own part to maintain the community
- Any new law should be decided by elections

Enforcement of the Basic Laws

Union will look after that every body obeys the basic laws or not. Helpers will help the union to maintain the rules. If any body does not obey the basic rules, union and helpers will suggest the punishment. But votes of the community will decide it.

- Election is being held once in three months for the government and union.
- Everything should be decided by elections.

Example 3

Introduction

Once a time, the school Jarvis organized a field trip for Mr. McKean's class, period 1. The trip was going to sail in the Atlantic Ocean. Once in the boat that the school borrowed everybody was happy and some felt sick (first time on sea). On board were 30 students and Mr. McKean, he was the one who drove the boat and the one who kept an eye on us. But one night there was a terrible thunder storm. The boat was being shaked by the large waves the sea made. The boat started to sink so Mr. McKean gave the order to leave the boat. After we had swim for about one hour we got to shore and because we were too tired we slept until next morning. After we were already awake we started to count each other and we saw that somebody was missing and it was Mr. McKean; then we figured out that we were on an island big enough to fit 1000 people and live comfortable. At first we had problems in how to organize us, so we planned to make some changes. We set some rules and we chose some leaders and with that we had some obligations and we had to respect them.

(1) STRUCTURE OF GOVERNMENT

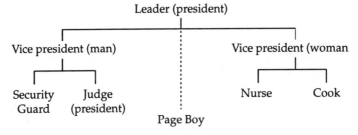

(2) SELECTION OF LEADER

All elected by every body and every one has the same rights to elect.

(3) BASIC LAWS (6)

1. Do not murder
2. Do not steal
3. No use of guns
4. No descrimination
5. No sexual abuse
6. Co-operation

(4) ENFORCEMENT OF LAWS
- You have to obey the leaders
- You have to have discipline
- If murder or bad action is done, the person responsible for it is taken by the security guard (or law keeper) to the judge (leader) and if he or she is guilty, gets a punishment and taken to a room (like a jail).
- Every body has to co-operate.

Analysis of Sample Constitutions

The first constitution, the Government of Aurora, is probably the best piece of writing I have received since I have been teaching the course. It is a final draft which did not have a lot of input from me in terms of ideas, organization or development of those ideas or editing of them. The constitution is well organized and developed and interestingly presented. The students have shown creativity in developing a logo which emphasizes the themes of their constitution. The only area which is a little weak is in their section on structure of government. They tend to use Canadian society as a model; for instance, when they talk of finding jobs and providing financial assistance for the unemployed. This is not appropriate for a society of 25 people who find themselves stranded on a planet.

In contrast, the second constitution (also a final draft) takes into better account the uniqueness of the situation presented in the Spaceship Aurora assignment. The group has clearly defined the basic needs that must be addressed in the situation, and defined the roles of those who have to meet these needs. In that particular area, this assignment is more creatively done than in the first constitution. In other areas, it is not as well developed as the first constitution, nor is it as structurally or grammatically correct.

The last constitution I include is a first draft, so that the changes that the constitutions go through become more obvious, both in thought development as well as structural and grammatical correctness. The editing process both in terms of form and content is very important to the assignment. For instance, the group worked on the development of structure of government in their second draft, so that the roles of the leaders were more clearly defined. What the students did well was their introduction. They were quite keen to create their own scenario. Despite the fact that it resulted in my demise (in the scenario), I thought that it was a clever idea, given that the assignment is not to include any adults who either help create the government or administer it.

Conclusion

The main purpose of this assignment is for students to develop the four language skills, as well as organize and develop their ideas. At the same time, however, this is their first assignment, which is not as content-based as the rest of the course. Therefore, it gives them an opportunity to be creative and have fun, which I think is evident in the introduction of the third constitution.

6 Environmental Studies for ESL Students: School Skills, Literacy and Language

ANNE FILSON

Background

School context

Fairfax County, Virginia, Public Schools system serves 135,000 students in the populous suburbs west of Washington, DC. Currently, 16% of the students in the school system speak English as a second, or third, language. The number of students enrolled in ESL programs has increased by 15% in each of the past five years.

The Environmental Studies unit described here was taught at Herndon High School, one of the 23 high schools in the school system. The student population at Herndon High School, numbering 2,000 in 1993, includes 120 students in English as a Second Language classes plus many others formerly in the program. The school principal addresses the needs of the ESL students, and their growing numbers, with objectives in the school's Annual Operating Plan, through committee assignments, and with inservices on teaching ESL students.

A small farm community only 20 years ago, the town of Herndon has grown rapidly, with single home and townhouse developments, as well as rent-subsidized apartment complexes for low-income families. The high school has expanded along with the town.

Pupils and their needs

The majority of ESL students at Herndon High School are from Central America, with significant numbers also from South America, Southeast Asia, and the Indian subcontinent. The students' families, typically, have low incomes and are struggling to adjust to the fast pace of life and the mix of cultures in this area.

Because of the large number of languages spoken by immigrant students (75 languages in 1993), bilingual education is not a reality in Fairfax County. All students are enrolled immediately in mainstream classes in addition to three periods a day of ESL for Beginning students, two periods for Intermediate, and one period for Advanced.

Increasing numbers of students are arriving in the county with very low literacy skills in their home languages – from no schooling to only three or four years, often interrupted – and limited experience with academic studies. These students are classified, through testing in the school system's Central Registration, as Literacy students. The Literacy students face not only the task of learning English, but also the difficulties of coping with mainstream classes in which at least upper elementary school literacy is assumed.

Special provisions for Literacy students

Recognizing that low literacy skills were a major problem for many high school ESL students, the county school system funded, in 1991, new programs for the Literacy students: Concepts Science, Concepts Social Studies, and FAST Math. The Concepts courses were designed to teach literacy skills in the context of basic knowledge, and English vocabulary, of academic subjects.

Each course has a curriculum developed by a committee of the teachers involved, although a great deal of latitude is given so that teachers can address the gaps in knowledge of their particular students. The staffing demands of each high school offering the courses determines whether the Concepts courses are taught by teachers in the Science, Social Studies, or ESL Departments.

The Concepts courses are each one semester long. The Literacy students, in general, take Concepts I Science and Concepts I Social Studies (beginning level Concepts) the first year; Concepts II Science and Concepts II Social Studies the second year, depending on literacy progress. The students then enter mainstream science and social studies classes with much informal support from ESL teachers, plus a lot of consultation between the mainstream and ESL teachers. In some county schools, an ESL teacher is assigned to co-teach a mainstream class. At Herndon High School our population is growing too fast for staffing to allow this. Even within two years of Concepts classes, the low beginning literacy level of many students continues to be great handicap – a problem we are far from solving!

The Environmental Studies unit was a series of lessons in the beginning level Concepts Science course at Herndon High School in the spring of 1993. There were 16 students in the class, ages 15 to 19, and all but five were Literacy students. Four of the Literacy students were taking the beginning level course a second time because of their slow progress towards literacy. Their two years' experience with oral English, however, allowed them leadership roles. The other Literacy students were struggling with literacy levels of less than second grade in home languages as well as in English. The students not classified as Literacy were assigned the course because of interrupted educations or very recent arrival in the USA. Two students were from Vietnam, two from Afghanistan, one from India, and the rest were from Latin America. As the teacher, I was certified to teach high school Earth Science as well as ESL.

The Environmental Studies Unit

Objectives of the unit

The Environmental Studies (ES) unit grew out of several observed needs beyond the literacy and language needs regularly addressed by Concepts Science. First, few of the students had had any experience producing an attractive, organized, graphic display of learning. In Fairfax County, and elsewhere, students begin early in elementary school making posters, charts, and other displays, and, when students get to high school, teachers expect them to know how to do this. Therefore, one objective of the ES unit was to teach the Literacy students the skills needed to produce a science exhibit: skills that would be useful to the students in their subsequent mainstream classes.

Second, a study unit in the Concepts Social Studies course had introduced the students to the Library Media Center. Another objective was to reinforce and build upon what they had learned about library reference books, computer searches, and using scanning techniques to find information. These skills, it was hoped, would also carry over into mainstream class demands.

Third, at Herndon High School, an active student organization named SAGA (Students Against Global Abuse) has made recycling a major theme of the school. An objective of the ES Unit was to draw the ESL students more into the high school community by focusing on the vocabulary and concepts of this school theme.

Fourth, although their literacy levels are quite low, the Literacy students know a great deal about their home countries and can be frank and objective about the problems the people face. It was hoped that the ES unit, as the last unit in the school year, would lead to discussions about environmental problems of the entire community of nations, thus leaving the students with a broader world view than they had possessed at the beginning of the school year.

The language focus of this unit included (1) broad aims of acquisition of language-in-context; (2) specific science vocabulary development; (3) use of a question-and-answer format to exchange information; and (4) note- taking and rewriting notes into coherent sentences.

Preparation and materials

The ES unit included classroom and library research on specific questions, science laboratory experiments, guest speakers from the community, several video films, and the culminating production and oral presentation of science exhibits. The language/literacy component included group and whole class vocabulary development, reading and writing practice, and oral practice in the group work.

The students were divided into five groups for this unit of study in order to encourage, indeed force, group cooperation and to wean the students from dependence on the teacher as the determiner of when, what, and how much to learn. Group 1 focused on air pollution; Group 2, water pollution; Group 3, land pollution; Group 4, forests and recycling; and Group 5, energy and conservation.

Resources

The textbook *Concepts and Challenges in Earth Science* (Bernstein *et al.*, 1989) provided several two-page 'chapters' useful for vocabulary development, homework practice, cloze exercises, graphics, and an introduction to the five topics. The *Raintree Illustrated Science Encyclopedia* (1984) also was a source for vocabulary and information, and for practice using an encyclopedia.

The students borrowed numerous books from the Library Media Center as much for the pictures, maps, and charts as for the text. They used the library computers to search for materials and to find related topics. In addition to these, the speakers provided a number of unanticipated pamphlets and illustrated materials.

Three of the science lab experiments were suggested by the Concepts curriculum. One was suggested by the electric power company speaker.

One came out of teacher experience. As with much curriculum development, ideas for this unit were globally gathered in from many directions.

There exist a great number of filmstrips and video programs about environmental issues. The county school system's video library had three fifteen-minute videos titled 'Reduce', 'Reuse', and 'Recycle'; a short lumber company film about paper production; and a video about the Alaskan oil spill. A nearby elementary school lent several excellent filmstrips on soil, forests, and conservation produced by National Wildlife Foundation. Various other filmstrips for small group viewing were found in the high school library. Finding specific media titles proved less important than engaging the students in an active viewing process.

Finally, science projects (on tri-fold cardboard forms), made earlier in the year by American students for an earth science class, were used as models for the Concepts Science students' exhibits.

People

The Herndon High ESL teachers have established active, working liaisons with other teachers and staff in order to smooth the transitions needed as the ESL population rapidly grows. For this ES unit, assistance was sought from and given by six other teachers.

The two librarians and the reading teacher gave the students lessons and practice in finding materials, scanning text for relevant information, and using an encyclopedia. Two science teachers supplied materials and advice for the laboratory experiments. A foreign language teacher gave nine of his regular students credit for volunteering in the writing and oral presentation stages of the ES unit.

Lastly, four speakers from the community were invited to talk about careers in, and local applications of, the environmental topics: a speaker from the electric power company brought a large model house with energy saving features; a county soil scientist showed slides of two major local oil spills; a government official showed charts of the metropolitan Air Quality Index; and a commercial arborist demonstrated his craft on a tree on the school grounds.

The relevancy and positive impact of the speakers, and their willingness to come, was such that we regretted not having invited more speakers all year.

Materials

(1) Audiovisual equipment; Apple IIE computers (Appleworks word processing program).

(2) Many large index cards (notetaking and vocabulary), file folders, colored paper, markers, glue, scissors, letter templates.

(3) Lab experiment materials, equipment, and report forms.

(4) Five tri-fold, free-standing, 3 × 4 foot cardboard forms.

(5) Miscellaneous homework forms, crossword and wordfind puzzles, quizzes, and other exercises (produced as the unit progressed).

General Organization of the Five Groups and their Topics

For this unit, during which the students had to make decisions about what to learn, and had to be self-directed to a great extent, each group needed a strong leader and a balance of literacy skills.

The five students who were either true Literacy students were chosen to be group leaders. The five very low-literate students were divided between the groups so that they could get individual help from the leaders. In addition, each group contained one non-Spanish-speaker to promote the group use of English.

Each of the five topics was assigned, in the planning stage, three defined parts: (A) research by each group on its own specific questions (formulated to focus the research and the report writing); (B) an experiment to be done by the entire class; and (C) a guest speaker scheduled for all ESL Literacy and Beginning students. The students also engaged in literacy and language development exercises with their topics of study as the springboard.

Group 1: Air Pollution.

Research questions: What is air pollution? What causes it? Why is it a problem? What can we do about it? Ten vocabulary words (selected by the students) and their definitions.

Experiment: The collection and observation of airborne pollutants on glass slides smeared with petroleum jelly. A 5-day homework lab.

Speaker: A government official to talk about the Air Quality Index.

Group 2: Water Pollution.

Research questions: The same as for Group 1, applied to water pollution. Ten vocabulary words and their definitions.

Experiment: Sand and charcoal filtration of pond water.

Speaker: County Soil Scientist to talk about the local stream valley pollution caused by the oil pipeline break.

Group 3: Soil Pollution.

Research questions: The same as for Group 1, applied to soil pollution. Ten vocabulary words and their definitions.

Experiment: Soil texture laboratory.

Speaker: See Group 2 – speaker to address both topics.

Group 4: Forests and Recycling.

Research questions: What are forests, and where are they in the world? Why do we need trees? What is recycling? How does recycling help forests? Ten vocabulary words and their definitions.

Experiment: Making new paper from recycled newspaper.

Speaker: Commercial arborist to talk about jobs in tree care.

Group 5: Energy and Conservation.

Research questions: What are natural energy resources? What do we use energy for? What are our energy problems? What is energy conservation, and how can we do it? Ten vocabulary words and their definitions.

Experiment: Student survey of energy use by light bulbs in their homes, and its cost in dollars. A 5-day homework lab.

Speaker: Electric power company speaker with model energy-efficient house.

The Environmental Studies Unit Week by Week

The discussion that follows, describing the activities the students engaged in, groups major topics together in order to simplify this presentation. In practice, of course, the group research work, speakers, science labs, and literacy/language activities were intermixed a great deal to maintain interest and because not every activity fits neatly into the 42 minute class period. The groups worked concurrently but separately on the topics for research. For labs, guest speakers and language activities, however, the students sat in their groups but shared the activity with the class as a whole. Careful planning for group work and having language activities at-the-ready allowed us to move forward a little every day.

Week 1: The 'hook'; Accessing students' prior knowledge; Introducing the unit

The 'hook'

It is common practice to find some 'hook' to draw students into a new unit of study. The hook can be an aspect of the unit they are completing, some community occurrence, or news on the world scene.

For this unit we used the week-long school events celebrating Earth Day: posters, contests, morning announcements. The students had to walk through the school corridors in pairs, locate three posters with the words 'Earth Day', and copy the message or sketch the picture. Back in the classroom, the students read the words and added comments if they could. The students also were challenged to listen to and try to understand one Earth Day fact from each morning announcement.

We viewed a filmstrip about recycling. During the viewing, I wrote new words on the blackboard to reinforce the aural learning, and the students copied them into their notebooks. Again, specific titles are not important: many filmstrips or videos can be used as springboards for vocabulary and concept development.

Accessing students' prior knowledge

After the viewing, we talked about *what* recycling is and *why* it is important. Since paper, cardboard, aluminum cans, and styrofoam food trays are the focus for recycling at the school, we asked *where* these materials come from. If we don't recycle, where do the materials get thrown away? Interestingly, not many of the students knew the basic information that paper is made from trees, aluminum cans from certain rocks, and styrofoam (at least in part) from petroleum.

One student said that in his country, Vietnam, unwanted things are reused or sold, not discarded. Other students expressed genuine surprise that there were any problems. The suburban materialism they see all around them, and the vision of American life they see on television, has not encouraged recognition of environmental problems. This filmstrip and discussion introduced the forests and natural energy resources topics and allowed the students to begin using new words to tell what they already know about them.

A video about the Exxon Valdez oil tanker disaster in Alaska hooked the students even more and introduced the topics of air, water, and soil pollution. In addition, a major oil pipeline had broken three weeks previously close to the school and had spilled 400,000 gallons of diesel oil, forcing the evacuation of many homes and requiring rescue operations for many of the animals living in the streambed of the nearby parkland. The local newspapers and *The Washington Post* were full of pictures to cut and post.

Throughout the next four weeks, the students viewed other filmstrips or videos, or, more typically, parts of them. The students were required to talk about what they were viewing, draw pictures, write new terms, form phrases and sentences. They were learning to be engaged actively in their own learning process.

Introducing the unit

The last activity of the week was to show a half dozen sample science exhibits, ones that American students had done for a regular science class, and five blank trifold cardboard forms. Seeing these colorful, uncluttered, graphic displays, and learning that they would be using the blank cardboards to make their own, was extremely motivating to the ESL students. They wanted to start right away.

I announced the group memberships and gave them time to reseat themselves in their groups. Then I gave each group a 5 × 7 card with their group topic and the word *vocabulary* written on it. The assignment: to go through their week's notes from the school posters, filmstrip, video, and newspaper clippings, and to write down terms that they thought pertained to their topic. Two weeks later, after adding more terms to their vocabulary card, each group had to select five to teach the class. Then all students were responsible for exercises and quizzes for the 25 terms.

Week 2: Beginning research; Taking notes; Tackling vocabulary

Beginning research

The week began with the groups reading aloud the four research questions assigned to them. It was important for the students to grasp that these were the central questions to be addressed by their work with books and media and to be answered in their exhibit.

Each group was given a topical sound filmstrip with viewing equipment. The students had to work together to find five relevant vocabulary words and five interesting facts. They were encouraged to write the facts as diagrams or to copy entire filmstrip frames. After each group finished its filmstrip, the members were all responsible for seeing that each member copied the five words and the facts.

The next activity took place in the library. The reading teacher took the three groups studying pollution, and I took the forests and energy groups. We each gave a generalized lecture about 'key words' using library books and flip-chart paper. We pointed out key words in the tables of contents and indexes and wrote them on the paper. The students' task was to write the title of each book, its library call number (Dewey Decimal number), and the key words.

We turned to page numbers associated with key words and scanned bold print headings, picture captions, the pictures themselves, and graphics for recognizable information. The students were encouraged to be active participants in our search. Then they had to duplicate this exercise in their groups with two or three more key words. They used stick-on papers to mark pages containing the key word information.

With the librarian's help, and using call numbers, the students located more books on their topics and repeated the key word and stick-on papers exercise in order to determine which three to five books were useful for their group to borrow for classroom work.

On another day, the reading teacher conducted a simple, standard exercise in recognizing the alphabetically arranged subject organization of a science encyclopedia. She also had the students practice seeing and using the bold print and italic numbers and letters of the index of the encyclopedia.

This rather intense beginning research stage was an important period for development of group cohesion. The students now began to accept and identify with their groups, not always a comfortable task when the groups are teacher-selected.

Taking notes

The students also began to write notes and sentences on the group research question cards (see Figure 6.1, next page). Difficulties in deciding what information to transfer from a book to a notecard is not specific to ESL students. But ESL students, especially ones with low literacy, must struggle first with making meaning from the pages of words. Using the strategy of scanning for key words, the students then must decide how much to copy. Rewriting in their own words is not possible because the words are not 'their own' yet.

Edison copied, '*The largest forests are found in South America, Asia, and Africa.*' Edison had not yet learned the passive voice, but he may have recognized *found* as the past tense of find. In reviewing his notes orally with him, I remarked, 'I see. We find the very big forests on these continents.' Reinforcing that his notes gave the location of forests was important; a grammar lesson was not.

Sandra copied, '*One cause of air pollution is factories that release smoke and chemicals into the air when they burn fuel.*' When we read her note together, she confessed she did not know the words *factories*, *release*, *burn*, or *fuel*. She needed help, and her notes, chosen and written by her, were the perfect vehicle for my assistance.

Edison had not written complete information about location of forests, and Sandra never found all the causes of air pollution. What was important was that they were recognizing the correct key words and were gathering information in an independent research mode. This was a totally new

experience for most of the students, and it gave them great encouragement
that they indeed lacked schooling, not intelligence.

Nineth enjoyed her 'ownership' of her notes so much that she resisted
adding the teacher's words. She answered the question *'Why is soil pollution
harmful?'* with *'Soil pollution can kill people.'* I wanted her to be more specific
about pesticides and chemical pollutants, and more general about the
objects of harm, but she had written about those for the first research
question, and the words, as far as she was concerned, did not need
repetition. Her decision was a grand step forward for a student who had
always depended on The Teacher for what to learn.

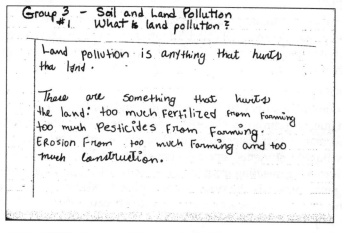

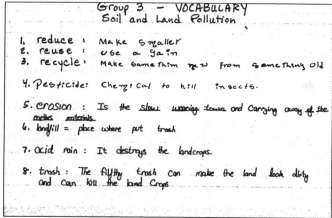

Figure 6.1 Notecards.

Ghulam, educated to grade five in Afghanistan, and with one year of English, tried out his own words with an 'if' dependent clause and a comparison: *'If we recycle we will not use forests so much than before.'* He was ready to learn to put a comma after *recycle* and to change the comparison words to *as much as*. In our discussion, he refined the sentence to be trees-specific by adding after recycle: *'things that made of trees'*. I reread the sentence, adding *are* before *made*; he heard the small word and inserted it in the writing.

Tackling vocabulary

Ibrhim's task in the energy group was to find definitions for words. He came up with these:

geothermal energy = heat from inside earth

photovoltaic = from sunlight

coal = has been used as a form of fuel from early roman times.

The last definition was not useful as 'early roman times' meant nothing to Ibrhim and was far outside the present context. The first two words, however, opened an opportunity for a minilesson in building words.

Similarly, Berta's difficulty in dealing with the words *groundwater* and *oilslick* was a minilesson opportunity.

One of the major advantages of teaching English vocabulary through science is the ease in breaking down many science words into prefixes, roots, word combinations, and cognates. In doing this, the students learn not only new words but also the strategy of making meaning by looking at parts of words. They increase their linguistic awareness.

With Ibrhim's words, we could recognize *geo* from *geology* (earth studies) and *therm* from *thermometer* (heat measurer), both of which he had previously learned. Similarly he knew that he needs *light* for *photography* and that *electricity* is measured in *volts*. So: heat from the earth; electricity from light. Similarly, we connected *hydro* to *water* by way of a *hydro*plane boat for the meaning of *hydroelectric*.

Berta's group drew a picture of motor *oil* running from a road into a stream and a handsome young duck *slick*ing back its feathers. They drew another picture of rain flooding the den of a rabbit for *groundwater*.

The prefix *re* for *recycle* and *reuse* was easily learned by using a drawing of bicycle wheels going around with the words 'wood pulp – white paper – trash' and 'aluminum – soda cans – trash' written around the rims.

The linguistic development of most Literacy students seems to prevent their hearing English cognates of words in their languages. Once the Spanish cognates of energy, chemical, conservation, and contamination were pointed out, the Spanish-speaking students learned and retained the words more quickly. Interestingly, the frequent discovery of Spanish cognates was a challenge to the Farsi and Vietnamese speakers, and they worked hard to find English cognates for their languages.

Week 3: Guest speakers; Literacy/language exercises; Homework

Guest speakers

The speakers were scheduled for the last period of the day when all Literacy and Beginning ESL classes (about 40 students) could gather. This gave a larger audience for these business volunteers to reach, and it ensured that students with more English would be present to attend to and ask questions of the speakers. None of the speakers had had experience communicating with a group of Beginning English learners; all were nervous beforehand, but gratified afterwards about the reception of their messages.

In the Concepts Science class each day before a speaker's visit, we spent the last half of class brainstorming the speaker's topic and formulating possible questions the students could ask, such as 'Do you like your job?' 'What education do you need?' 'Is air pollution in Herndon a big problem?' Then the students practised reading or saying their questions. The students could earn credit by asking a question appropriately and by taking notes on the presentation.

Although the four speakers were unique to this unit in time, their presentations included some aspects of general application.

The soil scientist gave a slide show of the recent local oil spill that had caused the closing of one Potomac River water intake station and consequent water rationing for Herndon, impacting on the students themselves. He also showed slides of a devastating leak at an oil tank farm 10 miles away that had polluted groundwater and soil of a housing development. The students were interested in the costs and in the jobs created for the year-long cleanup task. The young men saw people who looked like themselves and their fathers and uncles working in local jobs that they had not known existed.

The electric power company speaker was a young woman in public relations, friendly and knowledgeable about the kinds of energy-using appliances – televisions, hot water heaters, hair dryers, stoves – that the students use daily. She told the students what their daily activities actually cost in dollars. She had brought a large 'doll house' model home which was something for the students to touch, manipulate, look into, and point at with questions. She also distributed pamphlets, about energy use in homes, for the students to read and share with their parents.

The third speaker, an arborist, wore his work clothes, which linked him immediately to the working-class status of the majority of the students. His short video showed both men and women working in tree care occupations in a town like Herndon. After the video, we moved outdoors, and he demonstrated the use of his equipment. He showed how arborists climb trees without injuring them and then buckled his harnesses onto several students and sent them up into a large tree. This was true learning by doing. Although he had not addressed, strictly speaking, Group 4's topic, this speaker opened new employment options and a new awareness of trees as part of our lives.

Finally, a government official addressed the topic of air quality in the Washington metropolitan area. She used the vocabulary the students were learning: pollution, exhaust gases, pollen, and so on. She also used flip charts with maps of the area and various bar, line and circle graphs that clearly gave information about the parameters of the AQI, the Air Quality Index. The students could see the usefulness and application in the working world of graphic displays.

The value, then, of having speakers was in the students' exposure to ideas, information, points of view, and job fields, and in their seeing connections between school education and their lives. The sessions also allowed the students a 'safe', rehearsed opportunity to practice listening and speaking in meaningful exchanges.

Literacy/language exercises

Throughout the first four weeks of the Environmental Studies unit, the students did literacy skill and language development exercises like those in their ESL language classes, but with science content. Some examples follow.

The textbook provided for Concepts Science, *Concepts and Challenges in Earth Science*, with its grade four reading level, and frequent use of passive voice, was far above the level of most of the students; but the graphics, illustrations, and clearly-organized two-page layout of each topic made it useable for a number of exercises. For sentence structure practice, the students would copy a selected passage and circle the periods and the capital letters. The students experienced the approximate length of English sentences (at least in a textbook) and the formation and use of capital letters.

Second, I would photocopy a passage, blank out about every sixth word, and photocopy it again. The students had to use the textbook to find and write the missing words. They would repeat the exercise with a selection of words, instead of the text, for the blanks. This cloze activity forced the students to be accurate in following a line of words, and it brought vocabulary to their attention. It also provided valuable practice for the nationally normed reading tests the students take every year.

A third exercise with the textbooks was for the students to copy the captions of the graphics. Each student would select one graphic in secret from one of four pages, copy the caption, and hand the caption to a classmate. That student would have to read the caption and find the graphic to which it belonged. Points were given for accurate copying. This activity gave students practice in recognizing the existence, placement and utility of 'captions'.

Using the library books chosen by the students, I would select appropriate passages, different for each group, and challenge the students to find all the forms of the verbs *to be* and *to have* (or all 'action' words). They would copy each verb and the word before it, presumably the subject. Then we could have a minilesson on grammar. Most of the Literacy students had had no experience with grammar.

Science topics are easily adaptable to category exercises, which are a good literacy tool to teach students how to organize information. With strategies to organize written work, Literacy students gain confidence in their learning.

For a vocabulary category exercise, I selected 25 of the terms the groups had collected, put them in alphabetical order on the blackboard, and drew five columns on the blackboard with the group topics as titles. Then we played a common game: Each group, in turn, had to move one term on the blackboard to the correct column. If the term, such as *pollution*, could apply to more than one topic, the students could write it in each appropriate column. They had to be able to justify their decisions. Points were awarded and subtracted for correct or incorrect answers. The resulting chart was copied onto large chart paper and posted. Over time, students added more words.

Homework

Two of the science labs were 5-day homework labs (see below). The students also copied their corrected lab reports for homework. Other assignments focused on literacy and language acquisition. Again, the models were exercises done regularly in ESL classes: writing several times the science terms and definitions; alphabetizing words; cloze exercises; crossword puzzles; and so on. Several students took pride in making up crossword puzzles and wordfinds on graph paper. These I reproduced for all the students to complete for homework.

Three days a week we did brief dictation exercises for listening and spelling practice. One day a student handed me these sentences she had written: *'Most of the water is salt water is unfit for drinking. People drink fresh water. Cities build huge reservoirs (REZ-er-vwahrs) to collect and store fresh water.'* I cleaned up the sentences minimally and used them for the day's dictation. Writing sentences for dictation became a popular, student-invented homework exercise.

Week 4: Science laboratory experiments

An integral part of the Concepts Science course is the inclusion of hands-on laboratory experiments. The objectives are to present science as a discovery process and to prepare the students for the lab experiences of mainstream science courses. Because of the importance of the labs, each was a whole class activity. Two were take-home activities that spanned a week each.

Each lab activity followed a very basic lab report form that included:

(1) Title of lab.

(2) Hypothesis (What am I showing?).

(3) Equipment.

(4) Procedure (What am I doing?).

(5) Observations (What am I seeing?).

(6) Conclusions (What am I learning?).

A generalization true of many of the low literacy teenagers is that they are still concrete, not abstract, thinkers. This means that, whereas they could complete the simple, concrete labs, they had difficulties imagining larger applications of the principles demonstrated. It was hoped that our discussions of the applications helped to move the students along the thinking taxonomy scale.

Take-home labs

(1) Air Pollution The hypothesis: 'The air in Herndon is not 100% clean.' Each student took home a clean glass slide and a small amount of petroleum jelly. They were to put the jelly on the slide and the slide on a windowsill or some outdoor location accessible daily for observation. The assignment was to note down daily what they saw: objects and color changes. Their data sheet was the Observations part of the lab report.

After a week, the students brought the slides to class, and, using small hand lenses, looked closely at the particles in the jelly (pollen, seeds, parts of leaves, dirt), and completed the lab reports. Our discussion ranged over allergies, surprise at the demonstrated level of airborne particles, and air pollution in their home countries.

(2) *Light Bulbs and Energy* The hypothesis: 'Using light bulbs costs money.' The students, in class, examined a wide array of lights bulbs and learned the terms *incandescent, fluorescent, watts,* and *volts.* Their data sheet was a separate 'semantic chart' with columns to write the wattage of two or three light bulbs in their kitchen, to note if bulbs were incandescent or fluorescent, and to record the approximate number of hours per day the light bulbs were on.

After a week, the students, in class, totaled the 'hours on'. We then put the totals on a large chart, multiplied by the wattages, changed the numbers to kilowatts, and multiplied by the cost per kilowatt hour (obtained from the electric power company). The mathematical computations were very intimidating to some, but the clear results in dollars per week was of great interest. One of the students with fluorescent lighting realized quickly the implications of his lower costs over time and requested that we do the further calculations to show annual costs.

We enunciated the connection between *electricity* and *energy,* and the students in the energy and conservation group were happy to formulate the conclusion that turning off light bulbs conserves energy.

In-class labs

(3) *Sand and Charcoal Filtration of Pond Water* Hypothesis: 'We can filter dirty water to make it clean.' Equipment: clean gravel (small), clean sand, powdered charcoal (washed), styrofoam cups, pond water.

Procedure: Punch a half-dozen small holes (with a thumb tack) in the bottom of a styrofoam cup. For sand filtration, pour in about two centimeters of gravel, then six centimeters of sand, then two centimeters of gravel. For charcoal filtration, layer two centimeters of gravel, two of sand, two of charcoal, two of sand, and two of gravel. Gently pour pond water into the cups. Catch the filtered water in another cup as it drains out.

Observations and conclusions: Observe the color, appearance, and odor of the pond water before and after filtering. Discuss the differences, and make whatever guesses or generalizations are appropriate to the class. The water pollution group had found a large poster, useful for this experiment, of the movement of water from river through city filtration plants to home faucets.

(4) *What is Soil?* Hypothesis: 'There are different kinds of soil.' Equipment: sand, silt, clay, loam, test tubes, masking tape (for labeling test tube contents), water, timer.

Name: Nhidys

KITCHEN LIGHT BULBS — ENERGY USE

Hours per day my kitchen lights are turned on.

		Wed. May 19	Thurs. May 20	Fri. May 21	Sat. May 22	Sun. May 23	Mon. May 24	Tues. May 25	Total
Incandescent	#1								
	watts								
	#2								
	watts								
	#3								
	watts								
Fluorescent	#1 40	4	3	3	4	7	3	3	27
	watts								
	#2 40	4	3	3	4	7	3	3	27
	watts								
	#3 15	4	1	2	2	4	3	2	18
	watts								

Name: Bertha Madril
Date: 3/16 93

SCIENCE LAB

1. Title of Lab: water Filtration.

2. Hypothesis (What am I showing?) We can Filter dirty water to make it clean water.

3. Equipment
   gravel   water from a creek
   charcoal
   cups

4. Procedure (What am I doing?) Put ½ in of 1 gravel in the cup. Put ½ in of charcoal in the cup 2 inches in of soil in the cup. pour dirty water from creek into cup. The water filtered into a bottom up. make observations.

5. Observations (What am I seeing?)
   The filted water smelled cleaner.
   the water was a little black.

6. Conclusions (What am I learning?)
   gravel charcoal and gravel are good water Filters make a good cleaner water.

Figure 6.2 Worksheets for labs.

The standard laboratory plan included preliminary observations of soil color, particle size, and texture (feel – both dry and moist) that we skipped because of time constraints and because of language barriers to detailed descriptions. We looked only at the suspension and settling characteristics in water of each soil type.

Procedure: Fill test tubes halfway with water, and label them 'sand', 'silt', 'clay', 'loam'. In turn, drop a pinch of each soil type into the appropriate test tube, shake the test tube, and immediately observe the contents. Record what you see. Set the timer for two minutes. Observe and record what you see.

The discussion and conclusions focused on the susceptibility to erosion problems at construction sites of the different soil types. An excellent follow-up would have been for the students to collect soil from actual construction sites in Herndon to discuss relevant local applications.

(5) Making Recycled Paper Hypothesis: 'We can make new paper from used paper.' Equipment: clean newsprint paper (to avoid messy ink problems), empty coffee cans (with ends cut off), fine mesh screen, deep tray (to catch water), hand lenses, water, blender. Optional: food colors for dyes.

Procedure: Tear newsprint in small pieces, add to water in blender, and blend to a fine pulp. Position coffee can over screen with catch tray underneath, and gently pour the pulp into the can. Remove can, allow mat of paper to drain and dry. Finish drying on flat newsprint or paper towels.

Encourage students to experiment with different amounts of blending (from chop to puree), different water to paper pulp ratios, and different quantities of pulp poured into cans. Students can add food colors to the pulp in blender. They can examine the paper fibers with the hand lenses. They can use their handmade papers for displays – or love notes.

This lab, demonstrating the making of recycled paper, was for fun. We combined it with a short film on industrial paper making from the cutting of trees to the many finished paper products.

Weeks 5 and 6: Completing the research; constructing the exhibits; Presenting the exhibits

Completing the research

With speakers, labs, films, and exercises behind them, the students felt the need for closure for the ES unit. They were eager to begin filling in those blank cardboard exhibit forms. But the groups all needed help, simultaneously, organizing their notes, matching answers to the appropriate questions, filling in gaps in information, constructing reasonable English sentences, and ensuring that each group member was engaged.

At this point, nine American students volunteered for four class periods. Their teacher, the SAGA Club advisor, wanted to support this unit of environmental studies. The student volunteers were invaluable in giving the Literacy students one-on-one help in writing up their findings and practicing for their oral presentations. The volunteers said, "This is how we do it in an American high school", and the ESL students were glad to learn the conventions. The volunteers, for most of whom learning a foreign language is simply an academic exercise, expressed appreciation, and new respect for the efforts of the immigrant students functioning daily in a foreign language.

With the volunteers' help, each group pulled together its notes into sentences and paragraphs, some very rudimentary but on target. The group leaders conferred with me about exhibit parameters: First, each group needed (1) a title, members' names, and date; (2) answers to the four research questions; (3) vocabulary list with definitions; (4) a 'reuse, reduce, recycle' applications card; (5) labelled illustrations. Second, the exhibits had to be artistically arranged. Third, every group member had to contribute to the final product.

It may be noted that the science labs were not included in the final exhibits. The students had already taped and stapled the lab reports to a large bulletin board, and the students unanimously chose not to disturb the display. Nevertheless, the exhibits could have benefited from inclusion of samples of the labs.

The students enjoyed and learned a great deal from the construction of their exhibits. None had engaged in such a project before. Working closely in groups, including allowing the less able members to put their marks permanently on the product, taking pride in the overall effort, even using letter template (a new experience for most) – these were positive outcomes for each student.

Constructing the exhibits

Group 1 – Air Pollution. Two students took turns at the computer typing all the written work. With editing and corrections, this took three periods. Meanwhile, the very low literate member drew and colored pictures projected from a filmstrip onto white paper taped to the wall. She was very pleased to place her pictures front and center on the exhibit. The three students worked cooperatively to color the title and mount all the papers.

Group 2 – Water Pollution. The group leader assigned the tasks firmly, assembly line fashion. One student typed the written work on the computer. Another traced a 'water pollution cycle' diagram and did all the scissors and glue work. The leader wrote the title, added labels and decorative borders to the displays, and supervised. This group pointed out that they had illustrated world pollution (a map) and local pollution (a newspaper clipping), that the 'cycle' drawing added a scientific cast, and that the small pictures of water bodies added color.

Group 3 – Soil Pollution. This group was dominated by one student who quickly wrote all the cards and glued them on the cardboard down the center and at the top of both wings. She also traced, cut out, and glued the title letters. That was the exhibit – her exhibit. It was not until the other exhibits began to take form that the other two members of this group were able to assert themselves and add pictures and a graph. These students may have learned, in the long run, more about group dynamics than about soil pollution.

Group 4 – Forests and Recycling. The student signatures, written boldly across the bottom of this interesting exhibit, attest to the pride taken in the work. The leader, a responsible older boy, made sure that his two 'workers' were each employed fully: one writing, in his best handwriting, two pages of terms and meanings; the other tracing and coloring a map and a diagram. With the guidance of the leader, this group consciously achieved balance in the information presented and in the overall visual effect.

Group 5 – Energy and Conservation. Group 5 also benefited from a strong leader. Instead of being directive, however, she facilitated the self-selection of tasks by the three other members. The resulting written and illustrative information was not as balanced as that in Group 4's exhibit, but each student felt valued and capable of making a good contribution.

Presenting the exhibits

The last activity of the Environmental Studies unit was the oral presentation of the exhibits. With the help of the student volunteers, the Concepts Science students wrote out, on 3×5 index cards, what they would say and in what order the group members would speak. Then they practiced energetically.

The presenters had to participate, understand what they were saying, use the vocabulary of their topic, and be able to answer questions. The audience had to pay attention respectfully and ask appropriate questions. Each group took five to ten minutes for its presentation. We had invited several other teachers, a guidance counselor, and an administrator so that

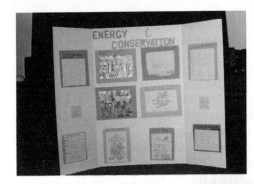

The energy and conservation project.

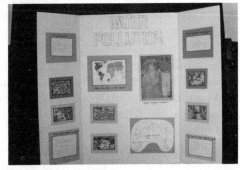

The water pollution project.

The air pollution project.

Pupils at work.

the students had new faces in their audience to address. The second day, when the last group was finished, we had a party.

Brief Comments on the Work as a Whole

This unit was by far the most complex unit of the year. In addition to the stated objectives concerning exhibit production, library research skills, and understanding the recycling school theme, the unit was planned to draw together activities using the map, graph, chart, and diagram skills that the students had been learning all year.

The most difficult part of the unit for the students was the language-intensive research. It was useful to schedule time for the less stressful literacy and language exercises and the short films within the days set aside for research.

Before and after each laboratory exercise and each speaker, it was important to rehearse orally with the students, by questioning and by reading the day's objectives from the blackboard, which group topic was being addressed. This repetition helped give purpose and meaning to the studies.

The Literacy students, it was hoped, would experience learning from their own efforts, rather than from the imposed efforts of a teacher, and would take pride and pleasure in this learning. A number of the students achieved this aim, partly because of the synergistic effect of group work. The students had often worked in groups during the year, but never before had their groups produced such a complex and handsome display of their learning.

Although the unit took a great deal of time and effort to organize initially, once underway there was time to work individually with the groups because everyone knew the steps and the destination.

References

Bernstein, L. *et al.* (1989) *Concepts and Challenges in Earth Science.* Globe Book Company
Raintree Illustrated Science Encyclopedia (1984). Milwaukee, WI: Raintree Publishers.

7 Content-based Language Teaching: Geography for ESL Students

RUTH EVANS

Background

The Topic Approach is a content-based approach to language learning which was developed in the late 1970s in Melbourne, Australia, by B. Cleland and R. Evans. English language centres had been established by the Victorian government to provide intensive English classes to newly arrived immigrant and refugee school children aged between 12 to 18 years. These students came from S.E. Asia, the Middle East, Europe, South America and Africa, and attended the intensive English classes for six months prior to being placed in mainstream classes. Many of the feeder schools which sent their new arrivals to the language centres had very high numbers of immigrant children; in some cases the Anglo-Australians were in the minority. The language centres were often located on a separate site to the main school.

Initially, the ESL classes within such centres tended to focus upon language structures and functions needed for social interaction and 'survival' in their newly adopted country. However, it soon became apparent that the students also needed to develop their Cognitive Academic Language Proficiency (CALP) (Cummins, 1984), if they were going to be able to deal with the language demands of the mainstream school curriculum. The Topic Approach was designed to address this issue. It sought to provide a strategy for integrating language learning and content based units. It did not replace general English classes, but operated concurrently with them. Out of a total of 25 hour per week, 10–12 hours would be spent on 'topic' work. The units were designed in consultation with teachers in the main school but the ESL teachers actually taught the units as part of the language programme.

Within the centres, we took great care to take into account the cultural background of the students. Some topics were written specifically for certain groups: Ancient Assyria, The Muslim World, Rice-growing in Asia, etc. Even within a topic, care was always taken to draw comparisons across cultures, and to utilise the knowledge of the students. We also did our best to accommodate various religious practices and to educate the various groups about the values and customs of each other, not only that of the Anglo-Australian society.

At the time, a content-based approach was very innovative, particularly with 'beginners' in English. Today, the language 'centres' have changed but they still prepare new arrivals for mainstream schooling. The school curriculum has changed too; however the Topic Approach is still a valuable way of integrating language learning with content areas in the mainstream curriculum.

The Topic Framework

Most topics were developed with four stages in mind, as outlined in Figure 7.1. However, the framework was not intended to be rigid and teachers may modify it to suit their particular group.

Stage 1: The visual presentation

This is by far the most important stage in terms of understanding the main concepts associated with the topic, and in terms of using the language to describe and explain the visuals. Through the experiments, models, pictures or maps which demonstrate the concepts, students are actively involved in building spoken and then written sentences about what they have learnt.

Stage 2: Building a reading passage

Here the students are asked to assess true/false statements about the visual stage. These true statements are prepared by the teacher and form the main propositions needed to make a reading passage about the visual presentation. Students may be asked to write the true statements on sentence cards in order to sequence them into coherent discourse. Other activities, such as joining sentences together, substituting pronouns for nouns, and adding logical connectives, may be carried out. The students

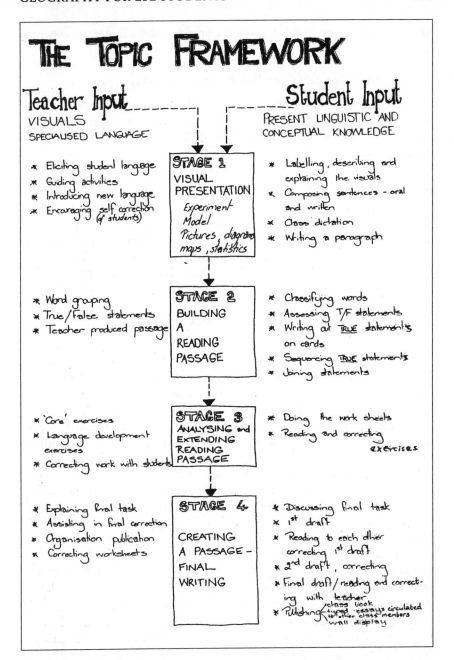

Figure 7.1 The topic framework

are thoroughly prepared for the teacher-produced reading passage which follows.

Stage 3: Analysing and extending the reading passage

In this stage, the focus is on the important language forms and functions in the reading passage. Various exercises consolidate and extend the students' knowledge of English in the context of the topic, preparing them for the final writing task.

Stage 4: Creating a passage – the final writing

In the last stage, the students are given the opportunity to write about a slightly different topic based upon some kind of visual stimulus; however, the material used for this final writing is closely related to the concepts and language built up in the previous three stages. Students are encouraged to write drafts, to revise and to publish their work. For complete sample topics, refer to the topic books in the reference list at the end of the chapter.

Sample Topic: Australia: Physical Geography

Target group

This topic is aimed at recently arrived immigrant and refugee students, who were referred to the Brunswick Language Centre by the surrounding high schools in the Brunswick/Coburg area of Melbourne, Victoria, Australia. These schools had high migrant densities. Most students were between the ages of 13–16 years and were of mixed ethnic and language backgrounds. The predominant groups were: Turkish, Kurdish, Assyrian, Lebanese, Vietnamese, Cambodian and Chinese. Some students had experienced quite serious interruption to their schooling in their home country, and so they had missed out on acquiring basic concepts in some subject areas. Furthermore, a proportion of students were not functionally literate in their first language. It was necessary to develop a series of topics covering some basic geographical concepts, and the associated language to describe and explain these concepts. The students had completed three months of intensive English at the Centre, and were at a lower intermediate level.

As Figure 7.2 shows, this topic involves the teaching of some basic geographical concepts and skills as well as various language structures and functions. Furthermore, it builds upon two previous topics: *Using a Magnetic Compass* and *Australia: Political*; hence students have already learnt about directions and they are familiar with the concept that different types of maps convey different information. The main language structures and functions focused upon in the topic are those which arise naturally out of the context and which communicate information about the geographical concepts.

Objectives

- To enable students to describe the physical geography of a country.
- To familiarise students with the colours and symbols used on a physical map.

Visuals/Materials

- A large chart-sized outline map of the main physical features.
- Pictures, photographs of physical features.
- An outline map of physical features for the students.
- Word cards of the main nouns and verbs.
- Atlases, colour pencils.
- Video film strips as follow-up.

Concepts

- That a physical map shows features such as river systems, lakes and mountains.
- That these features are marked on the map in a particular way.
- That the height of the land and the depth of the seas are shaded in.

Skills

- Using an atlas.
- Drawing and marking in information on a map.

Language functions

- Identifying physical features.
- Asking questions about the map.
- Describing the physical features (oral and written).

Language structures

- Nouns, adjectives, verbs, prepositions.
- Interrogative.
- Simple present tense.
- Definite article.
- Adjectives of comparison.
- Relative clauses.

Figure 7.2 Sample topic: Australia: Physical geography

Preparation of materials

The teacher needs to prepare the following materials:

(i)   A large chart-sized map of Australia showing the main physical features.

(ii) A smaller outline map of the above for the students.

(iii) Coloured pictures or photographs, mounted on cardboard to show deserts, coastal plains, forests, mountain ranges, etc.

(iv) Word cards of the main nouns/verbs needed to label and describe the features.

(v)   Videos, film strips or slides could be used as follow-up material.

In respect of (i) and (ii) above, both the chart-sized map and the students' map are unlabelled. The features are marked, but they have to be named and shaded in. The ESL teacher should discuss the topic with the mainstream social science teacher and should also consult relevant current text books and maps.

Teaching The Topic

Taking into consideration the background of these students, it was found that the intensive work described in the visual stage was necessary if students were to fully understand the concepts and if they were to acquire the appropriate geographical language. Much attention is given to oral work before the written word is introduced in order to allow students to focus on meaning.

The teaching and learning process outlined here is Stage 1 of the topic framework (see visual presentation) and takes three to four hours of class time. This is the most crucial stage, as in it the main concepts are taught, together with the language required to communicate about such concepts.

During the visual stage a variety of tasks and activities are carried out, with the main emphasis being upon meaning rather than form, although this focus changes from time to time, depending upon the activity. The role of the teacher and the students also changes according to the task and activity. Initial activities concentrate upon the spoken word with written forms being introduced at a later stage.

Task 1: Identifying the key physical features

The coloured picture/photographs of the physical features/scenery are pinned up. The teacher points to common features such as mountains, rivers, lakes, deserts and forests and tries to elicit the names from the students.

With a beginner group, the Silent Way technique (Gattegno, 1976a) is particularly effective as it concentrates upon reducing teacher talk and increasing student talk by placing the emphasis upon getting the students to contribute the words they may already know.

More specific terms, such as mountain *range*, river *system*, coral *reef*, coastal *plain*, and *gulf* are introduced.

If the students don't know the terms, then the teacher supplies the names and ensures that they understand the difference between terms like *river – river system; mountain – mountain range*. The teacher goes around the class until the students are able to identify the features.

This is a teacher-fronted activity, involving the whole class as a group. However, the teacher and the students are in close proximity to each other with the teacher taking care to foster a cooperative learning atmosphere by encouraging students to learn from each other.

Once students feel confident in identifying the features and understand what they are, the teacher can then focus more specifically upon pronunciation, if this is appropriate. The activity can be varied by allowing the students to take over the role of the teacher. In other words, a student can point to the various features and elicit the names of her/his classmates.

The written word can then be introduced by distributing the word cards (labels) which the teacher has prepared, to the students. Individual students can then come out and label the appropriate features with the word cards, at the same time ensuring that they can say the name.

Task 2: 'Reading' the physical map of Australia

The students' attention is focused upon the large chart-size outline map of Australia's physical features (see Figure 7.3 on the next page). Individual students are asked to place one of the coloured pictures/photos used in the previous activity onto the outline map, in a location where they think such features would be found.

This activity stimulates a lot of interest and promotes the use of 'incidental' language as the students try to puzzle out where the features would be located. It provides the teacher with an opportunity to discover how much the students already know about Australian geography.

If a student places a picture of a tropical rain forest in a flat desert area, the class can discuss this and work out, with the teacher's help, why such a feature would not be located in that region. In this way, students will be relating their understanding of climatic factors to physical features, even though this is not directly focused upon.

The pictures/photographs are removed from the map in order to concentrate their attention upon the green and brown shading for the land mass and the blue shadings for the seas. The teacher is trying to find out if the students understand that the shading on the land refers to height (in metres) above sea-level and that the blue shading refers to the depth of the seas. The students may use words like *high, mountain, flat* or *plain* to communicate their understanding. It will probably be necessary for the teacher to introduce terminology like: *height above sea-level; the coastal plain is 0–500 metres above sea-level*, and so on.

Students practise giving the heights (and the depths) of various locations on the map. Other features on the map (such as the way in which dotted blue lines show intermittent flow) can also be taught. However, the main point is to relate the different shadings to the height of the land.

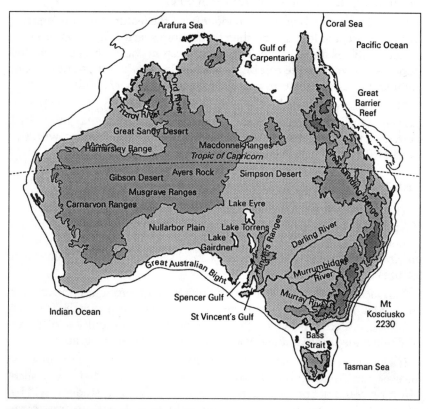

Figure 7.3 The labelled physical map.

The students are then shown how Australia can be divided into four main regions: Deserts; Central Lowlands; Great Dividing Range; Coastal Plains.

Task 3: Labelling and shading the students' maps

This task enables the students to consolidate their understanding of the topic, and it switches the focus from oral work to shading and labelling their own map.

The teacher provides the students with an outline map and a list of significant features such as: Ayers Rock (Ulluru), the Nullarbor Plains and the Great Barrier Reef, which are marked on the map. Working with an atlas, each student labels the features. Their map can be checked as the teacher moves around the class or they can be collected at the end of the session (see Figure 7.4).

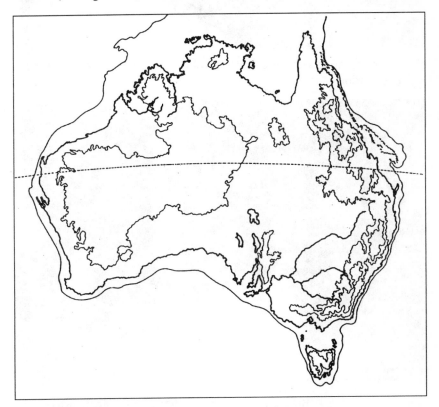

Figure 7.4 Task 3: Labelling and shading the students' map

Here students are composing sentences about the visuals to contribute to a class dictation.

Here students are writing their corrected sentences onto large cards which can be used in a class composition.

Task 4: Asking for information about Australia's physical geography

In this task, students are focused upon communicating with each other about the subject matter. They have to ask for and provide information about the visuals. The kinds of questions students may ask are:

Where is the Great Barrier Reef?

How high is Mount Kosciusko?

Which state is the Simpson Desert in?

Which river system is the longest?

Students learn to use key question words such as *what, where, how, which* in relation to the geographical features. The teacher also introduces key verbs such as *flow, run, stretch, cross, locate, find, mark.* Inevitably, as students try to describe where something is they will have to use prepositions such as *from, to, between* and so on.

The information exchange can be done as a whole class first in order to learn the key verbs and prepositions, but afterwards it could be done in pairs or groups. This task allows the students to exercise their communicative capacity as they are focused upon getting their meaning across, rather than focusing upon form.

Whilst the students are asking each other questions, the teacher can move around the classroom and note any difficulties they may be having. At the end of the activity, the teacher may then decide to focus on any misunderstandings or language errors which have occurred.

Task 5: Describing Australia's physical geography

This involves three main activities:

(a) Composing oral statements about the visuals.

(b) Composing written statements about the visuals as a class dictation.

(c) Composing a class composition.

(a) *Composing oral statements about the visuals.*

Students are encouraged to contribute their own sentences. This is usually done as a teacher-fronted activity because the students will probably need guidance in making up their sentences. However, the students should be given as much freedom as possible. They may compose sentences such as: 'Australia has many deserts in the centre and west' and 'The Great Dividing Range stretches from Victoria to Queensland'.

The aim of the activity is to build up a description of Australia's physical features so that students are moving beyond words and short answers to sentences and eventually the discourse level.

(b) *Composing written statements/class dictation.*

As with the map labelling activity, in composing written sentences about the visuals the students have the opportunity to consolidate their knowledge and to use the written language. Students can write three or four sentences like the ones in the oral phase.

Then, as part of a class dictation, each student selects his/her 'best' sentence and reads it out to the class. The whole class, including the teacher, writes the sentences. The teacher should ensure that there is a spread of sentences which can be used to form the basis of a class composition.

In respect of 'errors', if the *students* notice an error in one of their classmate's sentences as it is read out, the teacher should allow them to correct it at this stage: otherwise, she should write the sentence as it is, without correcting it.

In correcting the class dictation, it is important to create a supportive, cooperative atmosphere so that students don't feel threatened by their mistakes. If students see that mistakes are an integral part of learning, and that the purpose of this activity is to learn from one another, then the class dictation is a particularly rewarding activity.

Students are actively involved in correcting their dictation; one student reads out the sentence while another one writes it on the white-board or the overhead projector. While the student is writing the sentence, it is better to instruct the others not to call out any corrections until the student has finished writing it down, otherwise he/she can become very distracted.

The whole class can then focus upon the finished sentence, trying to spot both semantic and grammatical errors. The teacher should intervene when a mistake has been overlooked or when the meaning needs to be clarified.

(c) *Composing a class composition.*

The sentences composed by the students in the class dictation form the basis of a class composition. This activity takes the students beyond the sentence level to the discourse level. The students are asked to write their corrected sentences onto a sentence card, large enough to be read by the whole class. These sentences are posted up for everyone to see. The teacher then guides the students into creating a composition by asking the students various questions such as:

How could we begin the description?

Which sentence would be the best one to follow on?

How could we join these sentences together? etc.

During this activity, it may be necessary to move some sentences around; to write some new sentences; to join some together or to leave some out. While the students are focused upon meaning, they are at the same time learning some very important features of written discourse. For example: Join the following sentences together by using the connectives which are given:

(a) *The light green colours show the low land*

(while)

The brown to dark colours show the high land.

(b) *The Murray River forms the border between N.S.W. and Victoria*

(which)

The Murray River is important to farmers in this region.

The class composition represents the culmination of the visual stage during which the students have been taken from spoken to written language through a range of tasks and activities which constantly create a spiral of learning.

Depending on the level and needs of the group, the teacher may continue through stages 2, 3, 4 of the topic, where in stage 4 they are asked to draw a map and write a physical description of their own country or a country of their choice (see Figure 7.1).

Two examples of this final writing are shown in Figures 7.5 and 7.6. Both descriptions were based upon the physical maps of those countries, using the geographical language which was taught in stages 1, 2 and 3 of the topic. While students are doing the final writing, they can use dictionaries or refer to other sources, but only to complement the main information contained on the map. They are encouraged to revise their work and to publish it in a poster or essay form. Sometimes their work is put into a book which is made available to all the class members.

In Figure 7.5 overleaf, the description of the United States, the student has incorporated some political details which she/he has gleaned from another source. An interesting point in the final paragraph is the way in which the student has included a personal comment about the democratic system in America. Whilst this comment is not appropriate in the context, it is to be expected that students will take some time to distinguish between genres.

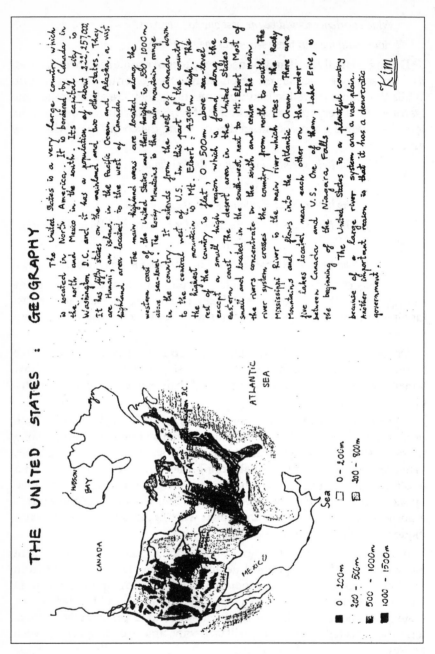

Figure 7.5 Sample of final writing on the topic – done in Stage 4

The description of Vietnam (Figure 7.6, overleaf) also incorporates some additional information (the quantity of water in the river systems), which the student has obtained from another source. The last section, where he describes the river systems, should not have been divided into so many paragraphs; it also lacks a conclusion. Such features of written discourse, though, can be improved upon in subsequent topics.

Sometimes students publish their final writing on a topic in the form of a class book

Evaluation of the Topic Approach

The criticism that has been made of the Topic Approach is that it is 'only as good as the teacher': if the visual stage is not properly understood or taught, then the whole topic fails. Surely this criticism can be made of any 'approach'. If the teacher doesn't have the expertise, then nothing will work. In my view, the Topic Approach has been very successful in the context for which it was designed. It helps to prepare students for the mainstream classroom by demonstrating, in a practical way, how language learning can be content-based even at a very early stage in the language acquisition process.

VIET NAM PHYSICAL

Viet Nam is a country which has an important position in the peninsula of South - East Asia. To the North of Viet Nam is China. The West of Viet Nam adjoins with two countries, Laos and Cambodia. Viet Nam has a very long curved coast line which extends from the North to the South. It forms a figure which looks like the letter 'S'.

The natural geography of Viet Nam can be divided into three parts. The Lowland runs along the coast line from the North to the South. In the South, there is a wide Lowland stretching from the West to East which is very suitable for rice cultivation.

Viet Nam has two main mountain ranges, called the Hoang lien Son and the Truong Son. The Hoang Lien Son Range is situated in the North. However, The Truong Son Range in the centre stretches Southwards. It is the longest range in Viet Nam. On the map, the highlands are shaded with a dark brown colour to indicate that the highland is over 2,500 metres above sea level. For example, The Lam Vien highland in The Truong Son Ranges is 2,658 metres high.

Finally, the river systems in Viet Nam are very closely interlaced. They carry a huge quantity of water about 300000 km3 yearly.

There are two main river systems in the North. The Red River and the Black River. Both of them rise in the Hoang Lien Son Ranges and flow through the Lowland into the East sea.

South Viet Nam has two main river systems. They are The Cuu Long River and The Dong Nai River. When The Me KongRiver flows into Viet Nam, it is divided into nine big branches. Because of this, it is called 'Cuu Long' which means nine Dragons.

The Cuu Long river system runs South -East into the Eastsea. While The Dong Nai river system rises in the Truong Son Ranges and flows through the Lowland of central Viet Nam into the East sea too.

By: THUAN - NGUYEN

Figure 7.6 Sample of final writing on the topic – done in Stage 4 *(this text accompanies the map on the opposite page)*

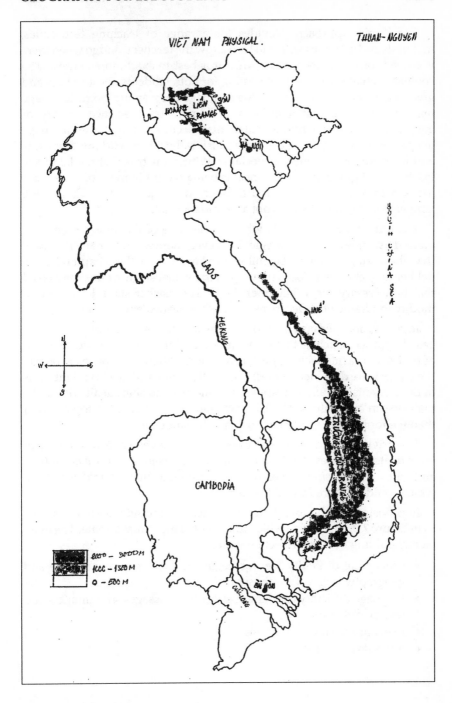

VIET NAM PHYSICAL .

THUAN-NGUYEN

The Topic Approach provides for a range of teaching techniques, materials and activities which in turn allow the teacher to judge when there is a need for more freedom or when it is best to exert more control. The content is challenging and interesting for both students and teachers and gives a real sense of purpose to the language programme. Some language teachers may feel that it is beyond them to teach science, history or geography. Here the fundamental misconception is that the language teacher is replacing the subject specialist, rather than working alongside and in consultation with the specialist. Whilst it is true that the language teacher must grasp the basic concepts being taught in the topic, the main focus is to communicate in and through the subject matter. Combining language and content is thus not a formidable task.

The four-stage framework, which is the basis of the topic structure, is viewed by some as being too rigid. However, there was never any intention that these stages had to be followed slavishly. In this chapter I have deliberately chosen to focus only upon the visual stage, as this may be all that is necessary for a 'beginner' level. The teacher should feel free to modify the framework according to his/her particular class or context.

In conclusion, perhaps the most vexing question surrounding a content-based approach such as this is the question of the sequence and selection of topics. In the intensive English programme where this approach began, the topics were developed in response to the perceived needs and interests of the students, usually in response to concepts and skills dealt with in the mainstream curriculum. The language developed out of the topic, rather than the topic being written to 'display' the language.

The driving force was thus at the conceptual level where a sequence of inter-related topics evolved: for example, 'The Compass', 'Australia Political' and 'Australia Physical'. Over time, a substantial 'topic bank' was built which could be shared by all teachers.

In choosing which topics to teach, the teachers could refer to an outline as in Figure 7.2, and decide which unit was the most appropriate. The main factors guiding the topic selection were:

- conceptual difficulty (i.e. for beginners more concrete science and geography topics were chosen);
- language difficulty (the length of reading passages, grammatical and lexical difficulty);
- relevance to students' future schooling;
- interests of students.

In the Topic book series published by Longman-Cheshire, the topics are graded mainly according to the abstractness of concepts and language difficulty (Cleland and Evans, 1984, 1985, 1988). A fully-fledged content-based syllabus was never formally written for the programme, so this is an area which still needs to be attended to.

References

Cleland, B. and Evans, R. (1984) *Learning English Through General Science*. Melbourne: Longman-Cheshire.
— (1985) *Learning English Through Topics about Australia*. Melbourne: Longman-Cheshire
— (1988) *Learning English Through Topics about Asia*. Melbourne: Longman-Cheshire.
Cummins, J. (1984) Wanted: A theoretical framework for relating language proficiency to academic achievement among bilingual students. In C. Rivera (ed.) *Language Proficiency and Academic Achievement*. Clevedon: Multilingual Matters.
Gattegno, C. (1976a) *Teaching Foreign Language in Schools the Silent Way*. New York: Educational Solutions, Inc.
— (1976b) *The Common Sense of Teaching Foreign Languages*. New York: Educational Solutions, Inc.

8 Integrating a Small Group of ESL Students into Mainstream Science: Partnership Teaching

MANNY VAZQUEZ

This chapter focuses on a piece of classroom work developed in partnership between an ESL specialist and a Science department in a secondary school. It describes the work carried out over a sequence of lessons in which the ESL teacher shared the planning and teaching with a science teacher in the regular mainstream class.

The work took place in Gunnersbury Catholic School for Boys, in West London. It is a school with an intake of approximately 1,000 students, 15% of whom speak a language other than English at home. A further 9% of the school population have an African/Caribbean background. Many of these students were born in the UK, but some arrive new to the country and to the language: over the years, these have included students from Europe (Poland in particular), South America, Vietnam and the Middle East.

In order to help meet the needs of the ESL learners, a teacher from the Local Authority Language Team (Hounslow Language Service) is attached on a permanent basis to the school. The work of this teacher reflects the underlying philosophy of the service, which is to support ESL learners principally by developing successful partnerships between teachers within the mainstream classroom. The development of the oral and literacy skills of ESL learners is seen as taking place primarily within a mainstream context. The role of the language specialist is one of negotiating with the mainstream teacher how the content is to be presented, and then developing differentiated tasks in order to meet the range of abilities.

This approach to language support work has been developing over recent years within the Authority's schools, and it reflects the service's own Equal Opportunities Policy. The opening paragraph of the document is included here (Figure 8.1):

HOUNSLOW LANGUAGE SERVICE
Equal Opportunities Policy

The Service helps schools to provide EQUALITY OF OPPORTUNITY and access to the curriculum for Bilingual Pupils in particular. It encourages and supports schools in their efforts to initiate, develop and evaluate policies and practices within an overall framework that promotes cultural diversity and race equality.

In its working practices and its employment policy, the Service is committed to equality of opportunity in all issues of race, gender and disability.

Equality through Quality

Figure 8.1 Language Service equal opportunities policy.

The Language Service works very much in partnership with the school, with the aim of providing equality of access to the curriculum for ESL learners. This is achieved through joint planning and teaching; development and sharing of resources; contributions to school in-service training; and empowering parents as active partners in the learning process through the forging of strong home/school links.

Traditionally within the service, ESL learners have been prioritised according to their level of need. In order to help make informed decisions as to how resources should be equitably distributed, the service uses the following criteria to differentiate between the different levels of ability in English amongst ESL learners. Pupils are initially assessed and then monitored against a series of stages designed to show progress in their learning of English. The use of such stages as a tool for measuring needs has been common practice within the UK context and has traditionally been a way of arguing for funding from central government for ESL projects. Hounslow Language Service currently uses four stages to assess ability in English: Stages 1 to 3 include those pupils deemed in need of extra language support, and Stage 4 assumes a level at which support is no longer required. The first three stages are described below:

Stage One

Some beginners may arrive non-literate and new to the British educational system. These pupils contrast with literate, educated beginners who may make relatively rapid progress through, for example, level 1 ATs (Attainment Targets) for English.

Listening   *Pupil is beginning to respond to simple commands but more complex instructions are difficult to follow. Pupil may only understand simple peer group talk.*

Speaking   *Pupil is beginning to produce utterances and participate in a basic one-to-one conversation, but takes little part in class discussions or group work.*

Reading   *Pupil displays some recognition at word level and at simple sentence level. Text at this point may have little meaning.*

Writing   *Pupil is beginning to write some vocabulary items and simple sentences which initially are copied. Some pupils may have difficulty forming letters or Roman script.*

By the end of this stage pupils can write simple sentences unaided that relate to their experience, displaying varying degrees of difficulty or ease with English script depending on their educational experience and first language. They will be able to understand basic information in a fairly simple text and will have grasped some basic rules of the English sound system. They will be engaging in conversation although utterances will be incomplete. They will be more competent in identifying elements within the flow of natural speech.

Stage Two

Listening   *Pupil is beginning to identify and remember sequences in the flow of natural speech and is listening with understanding to peer group talk. Pupil may still experience difficulties with some teacher instructions or when the talk involves words or ideas expressed in such a way as to be beyond their linguistic capability.*

Speaking   *Pupil is able to hold a one-to-one conversation but may still be unwilling to talk in front of the class. Pupil may not yet be an initiator in group work but may choose to take a fairly passive role.*

Reading   *Pupil extracts some meaning at text level and has an increased sight vocabulary. When reading aloud, intonation patterns sometimes suggest a lack of meaning in what is being read.*

Writing   *With guidance the pupil is able to write at paragraph level to convey meaning and is able to display an increasing knowledge of grammatical structure. However, writing will still include many inaccuracies, e.g. tenses, articles, spelling, linking words.*

By the end of Stage Two, pupils are engaging in most (if not all) learning activities. Their oral abilities are developing well. However, their literacy development in English is such that they need considerable support to operate successfully in written activities in the classroom as well as coping with the range of different types of text used across the curriculum.

Stage Three

Listening   *Pupil understands instructions and can cope well with most classroom tasks. Pupil may still have difficulty with certain types of more formal discourse, e.g. TV documentary.*

Speaking   *Pupil engages in group discussion, initiates ideas, occasionally answers in class. Speech may well be more competent where context and setting are more informal. Formal speech (i.e. as in a presentation or lengthy exposition) may be more limited.*

Reading   *Pupil reads carefully, may occasionally be unsure, but makes intelligent guesses and has sensible strategies. Pupil reads narrative with some ease, but may find it difficult to read more abstract material: this involves the interpretation of more complex text where links between ideas are more deeply embedded and not explicitly expressed.*

Writing   *Pupil can handle a variety of written tasks reasonably well but with evidence of some errors, e.g. tenses, spelling, occasional structural mistakes. Pupil may handle narrative and personal writing with greater ease although in some cases the style may be more pedestrian and may also lack a proper sense of audience. Pupil may experience problems with writing accounts and with argumentative/persuasive essays.*

At Stage Three, learners are often superficially indistinguishable from their peers in oral and aural skills. The difference is more apparent in written work.

In this section we describe the work carried out jointly by the Science teacher and the ESL specialist over a sequence of six lessons in one particular class. The presence of the ESL teacher had followed a previous request by the Science department at the school to help develop additional teaching materials. Essentially, the language support teacher was there for three reasons: firstly, in order to provide extra in-class support for those pupils speaking English as an additional language; secondly, to produce differentiated teaching materials for the department for use in other Science classrooms; and finally, as part of an agreed curriculum project in which language aims were to be written alongside the content aims for *all* pupils.

Developing Communication Skills in Science

It is clear from the reading of the National Curriculum Science document that it places considerable importance on the development of communication skills. This is also strongly echoed in the original Non-Statutory Guidelines (NSG), where explicit reference is also made to the valuable contribution which a language support teacher can make in Science classrooms:

> The science teacher perhaps in consultation with a language specialist may be able to ... widen (pupils') vocabulary and powers of communication ... through carefully structured group discussion during science lessons linked to planning and reporting activities. (NSG para A7.6).

The importance of developing the communication skills of bilingual learners cannot be over-emphasised, particularly in a subject area where there is often a genuine need to communicate and pupils are often exposed to an input which is rich in directives. These are recurring themes throughout the Guidelines. For example, paragraph A6.5 in the Non-Statutory Guidelines states that:

> Pupils' scientific ideas do not develop only through first hand experiences. Communication with others plays an important part in the learning process. Their learning is supported and extended through discussion with peers and adults. Through talk and informal writing they are able to make their ideas clearer to themselves as well as making them available for reflection, discussion and checking. As they get older, pupils extend what can be learned from first-hand experiences to include ideas from secondary sources such as books, computers and videos.

This is an endorsement of the view of writers such as Driver (1976) who, while acknowledging that 'Science teachers now build courses around a background of practical experience', points out that 'the value of the experiences is little unless they relate to the pupils' thinking.' Yet, while research scientists make no progress without theorising, speculating and discussing their own and others' work, many Science teachers seem to believe that pupils can learn by doing, without reflecting on new experiences and linking them to existing understanding through talk and writing.

This does not, however, mean that the central position of group practical work in the science curriculum is being challenged. Clearly, practical and associated problem-solving skills are basic to Attainment Target 1, which is to be 'interwoven into the science curriculum' and 'not in any sense separable in the teaching programme from the exploration of knowledge and understanding.' Rather, it means that the high proportion of time which may be spent on non-practical work is used, not for passive activities such as listening, note-taking and copying diagrams, but in ways that involve the pupils in active learning. This will not only develop the required communication skills, but also result in a better understanding and more personalised knowledge of the subject matter. It also means that with particular reference to the needs of bilingual learners, every opportunity is taken to use content to teach language. We now describe how some of these ideas were put into practice over the course of the six lessons.

The Class

The composition of the class included a mix of native speakers with developing bilingual learners of English – two pupils from Papua New Guinea and two from the Indian sub-continent. These four pupils were developing well in their use of social English, but were in need of increasing their range of English for more academic tasks. These pupils were designated as being at Stage 2.

Two more pupils, from Poland, joined the class during the teaching of the topic (at the start of Lesson 3). Both were at a very early stage in their learning of English. However, both were literate in mother-tongue and highly educated. In terms of Hounslow's stages, these two pupils were designated as being at Stage 1.

The particular topic being studied was 'Plant and Animal Cells', and the pupils were working towards Level 6 of Attainment Target 2 of the National Curriculum, within the strand 'Life processes and the organisation of living things'.

The content aims the Science teacher was working to are summarised here, along with the particular practical skills being learnt:

Aims

(1) To realise that all living organisms are made up of cells and that cells are similar in their general make-up.

(2) The pupils will be able to draw and label a simple plant cell.

(3) The pupils will be able to draw and label a simple animal cell.

(4) The pupils will know the function of each of the major parts of a cell.

Skills

The pupils will be able to:

(i)   correctly set up a microscope;

(ii) make up a slide for observation;

(iii) relate/interpret their observations to what they draw and label.

Given the nature of the content, and following the discussion between both teachers on *how* the content was to be presented, the ESL teacher then drafted the following language aims to complement the content aims.

Language aims (general)

(1) The pupils will be able to note down the key facts arising from a piece of spoken text.

(2) The pupils will have practice in describing, both orally and in writing, the following two types of discourse:
     (a) The listing of parts of a system (i.e. *'An animal cell consists of ..'*)
     (b) The function of each part (i.e. *'The nucleus controls ..'*)

Language aims (specific)

(1) The pupils will understand, read and be able to spell the following: *cell membrane, nucleus, cytoplasm, cellulose, cell wall, vacuole, chloroplasts.*

(2) The pupils will be able to describe each word in one sentence, incorporating function and/or location (i.e. *'A very thin skin called the cell membrane forms the outer boundary of the cell'*).

(3) The pupils will be able to write an extended piece which describes, in coherent manner:
     (a) The general characteristics of plant/animal cells.
     (b) The differences between plant/animal cells.

The following summary of the lessons described gives an overview of how both the science and language tasks were pursued in parallel.

Table 8.1

	Science input	Language input by ESL teacher
Lessons 1/2	Introductory exposition by Science teacher to introduce topic 'Plant and Animal Cells'	Agreed text written out by the ESL teacher to be read out to class: pupils do structured listening exercise. This leads to the practising of note-taking skills re: general facts. Pupils have to *listen and do*.
	Pupils draw and label and learn the parts of the plant cell and animal cell.	Information transfer exercise encouraging pupils to learn new vocabulary items for themselves.
Lessons 3/4	Pupils set up a micrscope and make up a slide of an onion cell.	(Two beginners from Poland join class). Unsequenced diagrams of method of making slide given to pupils: pupils in pairs discuss/sequence the order of pictures. Sequence checked verbally, then written instructions matched to pictures. Alternative written access worksheets also provided by ESL teacher for the two early stage pupils.
Lessons 5/6	Pupils choose text book to research topic further for an extended written assignment.	Text books at different levels of difficulty available. Pupils given a matrix to help them choose appropriate text book. Guided writing materials provided by ESL teacher on offer to help pupils organise and write an extended piece. Alternative written access worksheets also provided to help consolidate the topic content.

The topic was taught during six lessons over a period of three weeks. What follows is a description of what took place, including a rationale for the language activities used.

Lessons 1/2

Introductory exposition by Science teacher to introduce the topic

The preferred teaching style of the Science teacher was to introduce new topics by giving a general 10 to 15 minute opening talk. In order to ensure that all the pupils, particularly the four Stage 2 pupils would be active listeners, the two teachers agreed on a prepared text which could be read out to the class, thereby allowing for structured listening tasks to be planned in advance. The text for the listening task, the tick sheet and the notes of guidance on the materials are shown in Figure 8.2.

The rationale behind this approach stems from the fact that all pupils have different concentration spans. For some, responding to the instruction 'Listen!' when faced with 10 to 15 minutes of teacher talk may not be enough to ensure their understanding of the matter at hand. Key points may be missed. Thus, listening exercises are so designed to ensure that pupils *Listen and Do*.

The next stage required the pupils to draw and label both a plant and animal cell. One traditional approach is for pupils to copy passively either from the blackboard or from a text book, usually after a brief oral presentation from the teacher.

Our aim, however, was to create a learning situation in which, as far as possible, pupils would be allowed to work out the meanings of (relatively) unknown words for themselves. The pupils were divided into pairs, with each of the four Stage 2 pupils deliberately paired-off with a native speaker. The animal cell work card was attempted first, followed by the plant cell card. On completion of both tasks pupils then drew and labelled both cells in their exercise books. The materials, procedure and rationale are outlined in Figure 8.3.

Lessons 3/4

Practical: Pupils set up a microscope and make up a slide of an onion cell

At this stage in the topic, the Science teacher was now moving on to the practical (the reason for this taking place now had been largely determined by the availability of equipment). The two Stage 1 pupils from Poland had joined the class, a factor which made both teachers re-assess how the

PLANT AND ANIMAL CELLS (TEXT FOR LISTENING EXERCISE)

Cells can be described as the 'building-blocks' of life. Like the bricks which make up a wall, cells are the basic parts out of which most of all living things are made. But bricks are non-living objects, identical in shape, and quite large, whereas cells are alive, vary enormously in shape, and are microscopic in size.

Cells are made up of many smaller parts, and some of these parts are found in plant cells and in the cells of animals. Essentially, all cells have the following parts in common: a jelly-like material called cytoplasm; a very thin skin called a membrane; and a special part which controls all the activities in the cell called the nucleus.

However, there are some very important differences between the cell of a plant and the cell of an animal. Animal cells do not have cell walls, whereas plant cells have a tough layer surrounding the cell made from cellulose. Plant cells also have tiny objects within the cytoplasm which are called chloroplasts.

Animal cells do not have any chloroplasts. The other major difference between plant and animal cells is that in a plant cell, the cytoplasm contains a large space called a vacuole which contains a liquid called cell sap. However, the cell of an animal is mostly made up of cytoplasm and does not contain any vacuoles.

A: LISTENING EXERCISE
LISTEN AND PUT A TICK ✓ NEXT TO THE ANSWER
PLANT AND ANIMAL CELLS

1. Cells (a) are all the same shape and size
    (b) can vary in shape and size
2. A cell (a) is made up of two parts
    (b) is composed of many smaller parts
3. All cells have (a) 2 common parts
    (b) 3 common parts
    (c) 4 common parts
4. Plant cells and animal cells (a) are the same
    (b) are different
5. Plant cells (a) have a thick wall
    (b) do not have a cell wall
6. Chloroplasts are only found (a) in plant cells
    (b) in animal cells
7. Animal cells (a) do not have vacuoles
    (b) have vacuoles

Figure 8.2 Lessons 1/2. Activities and notes for listening tasks *(continued overleaf)*

NOTES ON THE MATERIALS

Listening Exercise – Text and Ticksheet 'Plant + Animal Cells'

(1) Pupils read through the ticksheet in preparation for the passage which will be read out.

At this stage they can make an informed guess at some of the answers.

(2) Tick sheets turned face-down. Pupils listen to the first reading. Note taking is allowed.

(3) Tick sheets turned over. Pupils listen to the second reading and tick off the answers as they listen.

(4) Quick check through answers.

Figure 8.2 *(continued)*

lessons were now to proceed. The ESL teacher was keen that the learning environment now offer the following opportunities in order to assist the development of communicative and grammatical competence for both pupils:

(1) That there should be opportunities for peer group interaction involving the use of transactional English.

(2) That there should be opportunities for some structural practice and focus on form within the context of the lesson content.

(3) That both Stage 1 pupils be actively involved in a highly-focused task.

(4) That both pupils receive highly-focused feedback.

Pupils were now asked to set up a microscope and make up a slide of an onion cell. We decided to arrange the pupils in pairs and allow them to work out the order of steps involved in carrying out the experiment. The two Polish boys were each paired off with a native English speaker. Pairs were then given the eight pictures in Figure 8.4 on page 210, representing unsequenced diagrams of the method, and asked to discuss the order in which they though the experiment ought to be conducted. This was followed by a brief general whole-class feedback.

Once the sequence of diagrams had been established, each pair was given the set of instructions in Figure 8.5 (page 211) and asked to match these to the diagrams. Additionally, for the two literate Polish speakers, key words (e.g. imperatives and nouns) were underlined, inviting both pupils to look these up in their bilingual dictionaries and list them.

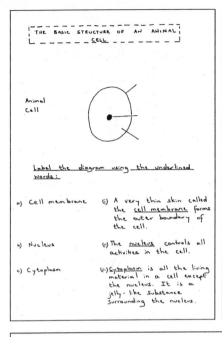

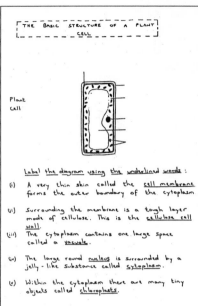

NOTES ON THE MATERIALS

B Workcard: 'The basic Structure of an Animal Cell'

1. (pupils divided in pairs). Each pair writes out three labels on three separate pieces of paper: The labels are: *cell membrane; nucleus; cytoplasm.*

2. Pupils place the labels in the right places using the written information on the card.

3. As pairs finish, the teacher can make a quick spot check of the answers.

Rationale

The diagram forms a communicative base from which judgements can be made. The sentences act as cues which, when allied with the diagram, allow the reader to make tentative judgements about the labels, reflecting one of the processes by which new vocabulary is learned, i.e. through tentative grasps at meaning. By working in pairs, the pupils can corroborate their findings and reach common agreement.

Note: This exercise usually takes about five minutes to complete and pupils have little difficulty in completing it. However, it is a very necessary prelude to Workcard C.

C Workcard: 'The Basic Structure of a Plant Cell'

Use the same procedure as for workcard B, and include three new labels: *cellulose cell wall; vacuole; chloroplasts.*

Note: Pupils are now applying knowledge gained from workcard B to a different situation in workcard C.

Figure 8.3 Lessons 1/2. Drawing plant and animal cells.

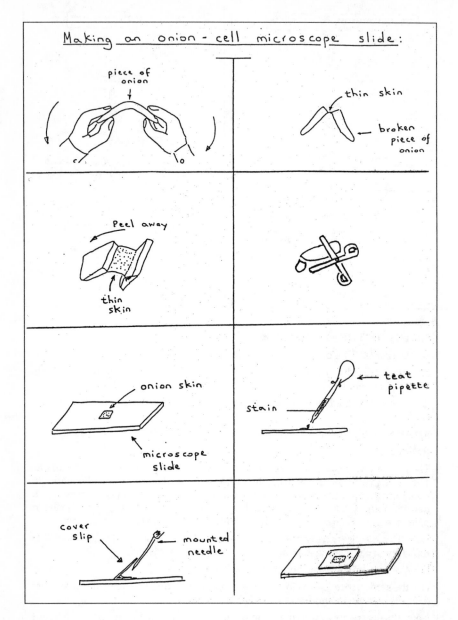

Figure 8.4 Lessons 3/4. Sequencing diagrams

Hold the onion as shown. Gently break the piece in half.

The halves should be joined together by a thin skin. This skin is only one cell thick.

Gently peel one of the halves away from the skin. Be careful not to twist or fold the skin.

Cut off a small piece of skin with the scissors.

Lay the small piece of skin flat on a microscope slide.

Place a drop of stain on the skin.

Place a cover slip at one side of the drop of stain. Hold it up with a mounted needle.

Gently lower the cover slip down so that there are no bubbles of air trapped underneath it.

Figure 8.5 Lessons 3/4. Matching instructions to diagrams

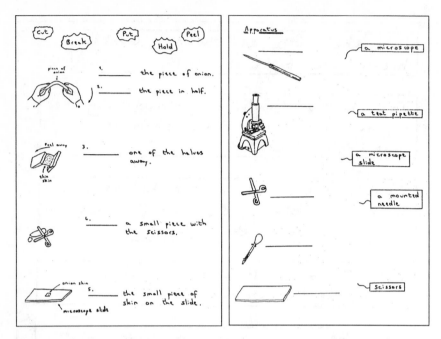

Figure 8.6 Lessons 3/4. Worksheets for instructions and naming objects

For the actual practical, both pupils worked with myself in order to ensure opportunities for focused input and highly focused feedback. This included identifying and naming key objects and listening to, acting upon and rehearsing instructions. The two worksheets in Figure 8.6 were used to follow up the oral work.

Lessons 5/6

Further reading, and extended written assignments

The aim for the final lessons was to spend time in revising and consolidating the content. There were also to be opportunities for further reading. The Science teacher wanted each pupil to end up with an extended written piece, describing the similarities and differences between plant and animal cells.

In order to cater for the mixed ability needs of the class, text books were provided covering three levels of ability. Pupils were then invited to choose the book they felt most appropriate for them, using the table in Figure 8.7.

Here is an exercise to help you practise deciding if a book is going to be suitable. You will be given a pile of books. Quickly *skim* through them, filling in the chart as you go.

Title	Date of publication	Contents page?	Index?	Pictures?	Diagrams?	Clear headings?	Readability?		
							Too easy	Reasonable level	Too hard

Figure 8.7 Lessons 5/6. Choosing books

Pupils were also asked to tabulate information in the following way:

Name of Part	Location	Property	Function
cytoplasm	around the nucleus	jelly -like	?
nucleus	?	?	controls cell
cell-membrane	around the cytoplasm	thin skin	?

Figure 8.8 Lessons 5/6. Reading for information

The rationale behind this lies in the fact that not all pupils may be proficient users of information texts, and this activity helps pupils focus on the relevant information slots. In this particular case, the four information slots are typical of 'structure'-type texts in science (see Davies and Greene).

In additional, some pupils worked in pairs using these cards to place in the relevant information slots. The cards marked with a (?) invited pupils to cross-reference with more difficult texts to find information that was not available in their chosen text book.

The four Stage 2 pupils completed the task by using the cards, and were then given the worksheets in Figure 8.9 in order to establish tense continuity and to help them produce a coherent piece of writing.

The two Stage 1 pupils were given more limited but more structured alternative written tasks, as in Figure 8.10 (page 216).

Conclusion

The following questions are useful in attempting to marry language aims to content aims in the science classroom, for the benefit of *all* pupils in the class.

(1) Listening

How can the Language teacher turn a 'passive' activity where the pupil is required simply 'to listen' into a more active one during a demo, during an introductory exposition, or while the focus is on instructions for experiments?

(2) Speaking

Probably more pupil-pupil talk goes on in Science than in any other subject area. How can we help to focus, as effectively as possible, the nature and direction of that talk?

(3) Reading

The type of reading and the amount of reading which goes on in the lower school is crucial in determining how well our pupils will perform in years 10 and 11. What can we do to ensure that our pupils are practised readers and familiar with different science text types by the time they reach the upper school?

(4) Writing

How much help, and of what kind, do we give to our pupils?
What is the policy in your science department regarding the style of report writing they require in different years, in relation to use of the passive; use of method/results/conclusion; use of past tense for reports; and appropriate writing for description?

Using the information in the tables, write two paragraphs under the heading ' Plant and Animal Cells'

Here is a plan to help you :

Paragraph 1
    The general characteristics of all cells

Paragraph 2
    The differences between plant and animal cells

Here are some ideas on how you might begin the first paragraph. :

* Cells are the units which make up all living things. .....

* Cells can be described as the 'building-blocks' of life. .....

Here are some ideas on how you might begin the second paragraph :

* Although plant and animal cells are similar, there are some differences. ....

Figure 8.9 Lessons 5/6. Support for writing

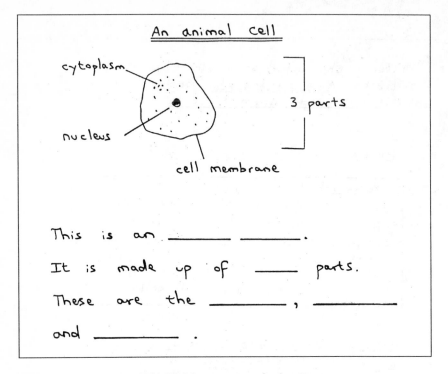

Figure 8.10   Lessons 5/6. Writing support for beginners

Acknowledgements

Thanks are extended to Morgan Higgins, Science Department, Gunnersbury Catholic School for Boys.

References

Davies, F. and Green, T. (1984) *Reading for Learning in the Sciences*. London: Oliver and Boyd.
Driver, R. (1976) Journey in thought. In *Non-Streamed Science: The Training of Teachers* (ASE Study Series No. 8).
Sands, M.K. (1981) Group work in Science: Myth and reality. *Schools Review* 62, 221

9 Mainstream Science with a Majority of ESL Learners: Integrating Language and Content

HUGH HOOPER

Integrating Language and Content in a Science Unit

For years now the Vancouver School Board has had a high number of students for whom English is an additional language: 55% of all the immigrants and refugees who settle in British Columbia settle in Vancouver city. In 1990 significant increases to our immigration numbers were introduced by our federal government; accordingly the number of ESL learners in our school system has increased dramatically. Today, of our 54,000 students (approx.) over 28,000 students speak a primary language at home other than English. Within this group of students over 100 primary languages are represented. Our top 7 countries of origin are: Hong Kong, Taiwan, Vietnam, China, Philippines, Korea, India.

Traditionally settlement of immigrant families has been on the east side of Vancouver. The schools on this side of the city have adapted to the changing demographics over time; however, on the west side of the city we have experienced dramatic demographic changes. For example, in some schools the population has changed from 15% ESL to over 70% in less than four years. In one school, used to having upper middle class English-speaking students, one kindergarten class was made up exclusively of ESL learners. These dramatic changes have put a great deal of pressure on schools.

For the past several years we have been struggling to build programs and services which address the ever-increasing complexity of the social and academic needs of our ESL student population.

Policy Matters

We have had a race relations policy and an ESL policy since 1982. The race relations policy is currently being revised, and while the ESL policy remains the same we are undergoing a review of ESL programs and services, and a number of recommendations have been made.

We have an employment equity policy in place as well; parts of this policy have been implemented already. A consultant was hired to examine how the school board can move towards embracing this policy more effectively.

We have a curriculum project underway in the district which is focused on broad equity and inclusion issues along culture, gender, race and ability lines. The point behind this project is to help teachers reflect these different perspectives in their teaching and choice of resources. For the students, this will provide opportunities to see themselves in the curriculum.

The school board recognises that there is both institutional and interpersonal racism within the school system. Policies are being revised to provide stronger, more current direction. Programs and projects are being created to deal with these issues in very practical ways.

The province of BC Ministry of Education (MOE) has released an updated policy on language; the MOE acknowledges the value of first language/heritage languages, but does not provide the basis of funding. Within our school district we encourage the use of first languages. There are many after-school programs offered in the city. Both the school board and the MOE will admit the value of maintaining L1 but they are reluctant to put this in policy because this would require many resources. In Vancouver alone we have over 100 first languages represented.

The VSB and the BCTF (the teachers' federation) have collaborated to develop a document entitled 'Respecting Linguistic Diversity'. We are hoping this document will help school staffs debate the issue of supporting first language development. In some of our schools this has become a contentious issue.

The Science Unit

Research suggests that it requires ESL students anywhere from 4–8 years to reach grade level norms in core academic courses. Consequently, ESL students face extreme difficulties when it comes to coping with the academic demands of content classes. Since the majority of ESL learners in Vancouver schools are in mainstream classes, it is clear that mainstream teachers need to take responsibility for ESL learners as well. Increasingly classroom and ESL teachers are working collaboratively to meet the language and content learning needs of ESL students.

This unit was designed in accordance with the general objectives of the BC Ministry of Education and the Vancouver School Board for Grade 7 Science. The underlying goal of the curriculum was Biology content: the classification of living things. A Grade 7 Science teacher, Peter, and an ESL specialist, Brenda, taught the unit at Beaconsfield Elementary School. In addition to helping design the unit my role as District Principal ESL was to support the collaborative planning and teaching relationship that Peter and Brenda were developing.

Peter was the home room teacher for the Grade 7 class who took part in this project. Brenda's role was that of an English Language Centre teacher. Prior to being involved in this unit, she had provided support to ESL learners on a withdrawal basis. This was the first time both Peter and Brenda had been involved in such a collaborative venture. The average age of the 28 students was 12.5; 18 out of the 28 (64%) students were acquiring English as a second language. The range in English language ability is from low intermediate to near native like proficiency. There were 14 boys and 14 girls. The first languages spoken by the students included: Cantonese, Portuguese, Greek, Tamil, Hindi, Fillipino, Mandarin, Italian and Vietnamese.

The unit has two major parts. Part I of the unit follows the chapter on 'The Classification of Living Things' in the Ministry of Education prescribed text *Exploring Living Things* (Smith, 1977). Peter and Brenda took responsibility for this section of the unit. The students spent much of their time working out definitions of animals, plants and protists.

Part II of the unit focuses on the *classification of vertebrates*. Brenda, Peter and I developed the unit using Mohan's (1986) knowledge framework approach to simultaneously integrate language and content as a means to orchestrate the integration of biology content and English language development.

The Knowledge Framework:

This systematic approach for relating language and content applies across the curriculum and provides ways for developing academic discourse, thinking skills and content knowledge. Mohan asserts that 'topics' or content can be broken down into the six major types of knowledge which make up the knowledge framework: classification-concepts, description, principles, sequence, evaluation and choice (see Table 9.1). Each of these types of knowledge have unique or distinct semantic/ linguistic features which structurally set them apart from each other (see

Table 9.2). In addition, each of these distinct knowledge structures can be represented graphically by 'key visuals', e.g. classification using a tree diagram or sequence using a timeline (see Table 9.3). These visuals have no or lowered linguistic demands and can help the learner understand complex content even though their English ability may be limited.

	Classification	*Principles*	*Evaluation*
BK	Classification Generalization about descriptions Definition	Explanation Prediction Interpretation Hypothesis formation Generalizations Principles/Theories Causes/Effect Rules/Strategies Results/Ends/Means	Evaluation Judgement Criticism Justification Argumentation
AS	Description Comparison Contrast Quantification Spatial order	Sequence Chronological order Cycles Processes Narration	Personal opinion Refutation Problem/Solution
	Description	*Sequence*	*Choice*

BK = background knowledge   AS = action situation

Table 9.1 Mohan's knowledge structures

Graphics of this sort have proven useful to native-English speaking learners as well as ESL students. Key visuals have at least three major applications: (1) generative – to promote language generation (related to content); (2) representative or explanatory – to increase content understanding; and (3) evaluative – to evaluate content and language understanding. In summary, the framework acts as an integrator of content and language. After a topic has been broken down into the six boxes, it provides a starting point for developing student tasks which integrate the development of academic discourse and the comprehension of content. Key visuals can be used in tasks as links between language and content for the learner.

Classification	Principles	Evaluation
verbs of class membership: *to be*	cause: *is due to, is the result of*	describing emotions: *is satisfactory/ unsatisfactory like/dislike*
verbs of possession: *to have*	condition and contrast: *if ... then, unless*	stating preference: *prefer, would rather*
possessives: *his, her, your, their, my*	generalization: *in short, for example*	stating standards: *is good/bad, right/wrong*
generic nouns: *apples, animals, music*	words of general or inclusive meaning: *everything, most*	stating viewpoint: *That is the forestry company's opinion*
specific nouns: *kind, sort, class*	scale of amount: *all, none, every, always*	
nouns of measure: *ton, gallon, cup*	predicting: *must, ought to, should*	
	stating probability: *is likely, may be*	
NP + be + NP/Adj Prepositional phrases DP + be + NP Relative clauses Adjectives Demonstratives Articles Possessives Adverbs of comparison	Prepositions and prepositional phrases of time, cause and purpose Clauses of time, condition and reason Sentence time relators: *first, next, earlier, later* Tenses Reported speech Imperatives	Modals: *can, will, may, must, ought, should, would In my opinion ... I think that ... I choose ...*
Description	*Sequence*	*Choice*

Table 9.2 Samples of language related to each knowledge structure

Classification	Principles	Evaluation
Web Tables Tree Graph Database	Line graph Tables Venn diagram Cycles	Table Grid Mark book Rating chart
Diagram Map Picture/Slide Plans/Drawing Table	Action strip Timeline Flow chart Cycle Table with numbered steps	Flow chart Decision tree
Description	Sequence	Choice

Table 9.3 A selction of key visuals for each knowledge structure

For the past several years the Vancouver School Board has supported the development of instructional strategies using the Knowledge Framework approach described above to assist ESL learners to cope with the language demands of topics and subject areas. This unit of study was designed using this same approach. It also provides ESL and classroom teachers with a means for drawing on their respective areas of expertise around language and content. The knowledge structures dealt with in Part II of this unit are shown in Table 9.4.

Outline of the Lessons

The seven lessons originally planned for Part II of this unit were designed to span approximately four weeks (with three 40 minute periods per week). The unit ended up taking almost three months. A summary of the seven lessons follows, including a description of the lessons as they were planned, a summary of what actually happened in the classroom (how tasks and activities built on one another) and commentary on the integration of biology content and academic discourse.

Classification	*Principles*	*Evaluation*
living things | animals plants protists | vertebrate non-vertebrate | mammals birds reptiles amphibians fish		
Name: *common name* **Class:** *mammal, bird, amphibian,* *reptile or fish* **Body temperature:** *warm-blooded or* *cold-blooded* **Respiratory system:** *lungs or gills* **Skin covering:** *smooth, hair, fur or scaly* **Reproduction:** *born alive or eggs* **Appendages:** *limbs, legs, wings, fins, none* **Habitat:** *land or water* **Hibernation:** *yes or no* **Locomotion:** *walk, swim, fly, slither* **Migration:** *yes, no, partial* **Diet:** *carniverous, herbivorous or* *omniverous*		
Description	*Sequence*	*Choice*

Table 9.4 The classification of living things

The major objective behind this unit was for the students to understand how vertebrates are grouped into five classes; mammals, birds, amphibians, reptiles and fish. To understand this classification scheme, it was necessary for the students to build their concepts of each class. Lessons 1–4 were planned to meet this objective where the students wrote their own definitions of each class. In lessons 5–7 the students used the definitions they had developed to perform other tasks related to the classification of vertebrates. Each lesson provided opportunities for English language development and each one built on the other.

Lesson 1

The aim of lesson 1 is to review for the students the groups by which living things are classified (living things can be divided into animals, plants and protists as in Part I) and in particular to introduce the students to the classification of vertebrates. Up to this point the students had studied the differences and similarities of animals, plants and protists. The students were exposed to an increasingly detailed examination of living things. They had studied protists in some detail in Part I of the unit, but they had not, at this point, studied the classification of plants or animals to any degree. We decided to examine the animal kingdom in more detail. As a way of introducing the topic the students were presented with an unlabelled key visual: a classification tree, showing what groups living things are divided into (see Figure 9.1). (This graphic also serves as an advance organizer which reflects an overview of the entire unit.) The students filled out the names of the three groups of living things: plants, animals and protists.

The teachers then had the students brainstorm names of animals. As names were called out the teachers put the animals into one of two groups, the titles of which were concealed from the students (vertebrate or invertebrate). When a suitable number of animals were listed, the students were asked how the two groups were different. Eventually, with the teacher's guidance, the students were able to conclude that one group had backbones but the other one did not. The teachers supplied the students with the correct biological terms, vertebrates and invertebrates, and placed them above the appropriate group. Following this the students added more animals to each group. Of the two groups, the vertebrates were investigated in more detail. The students generated the names of the classes of the vertebrates they knew and the teachers filled in the rest. They then added a few examples of each class.

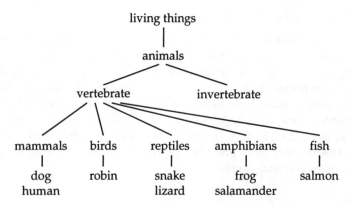

Figure 9.1 Key visual for classification of living things

To sum up the lesson, the students received an oral description of Figure 9.1. There are three major groups of living things; animals, plants and protists. The animal kingdom can be divided into two large groups, the vertebrates and the invertebrates. The vertebrates can be classified into five classes: mammals, birds, amphibians, reptiles and fish.

This lesson sets the context for the introduction of the descriptors in lesson 2.

Lesson 2

The aim in lesson 2 was for the students to examine features or descriptors that each of the classes have in common. The content in this unit has to do with a definition of a vertebrate. They also had to make judgements about which descriptors might be more powerful in separating the vertebrates into groups.The descriptors were focused on to set the stage for introducing vertebrate examples in lesson 3 which would be the basis for writing definitions in lesson 4.

The first step in this direction asks the student to suggest characteristics vertebrates have in common, e.g. skin covering, locomotion, diet and so on. This was the first of two lessons which focused on the makeup of a definition. Then the students were given a partially filled-in chart (see Figure 9.2) with the descriptors on the left and examples of how these descriptors would be manifested amongst the vertebrates on the right. In some cases the examples were limited definitions of the descriptors, e.g. descriptor: habitat, example: land or water. In others the examples described the occurrence of some phenomena, e.g. descriptor: migration, example: yes, no, or partial. While the descriptors served to show the similarities amongst vertebrates, the examples of the same descriptors were being used to show the differences amongst the classes.

The students then ordered the descriptors from most significant to least according to their ability to show differences amongst the vertebrates. For example body temperature was considered significant because it separated the vertebrates into two large groups: those that are warm blooded and those that are cold blooded. Again this component of a definition was focused on in order to give the students input when it came time for them to write definitions of the vertebrate classes in subsequent lessons. The model for the definition was not made explicit to the students at this time. Had it been it would have resembled this:

A _____ *is a vertebrate which* _____
    (class)   (unique features)

A. Instructions: Read this exercise carefully and with your partner supply the missing information. You may have to use a dictionary.

DESCRIPTORS	EXAMPLES
(1) _____	*cold/warm blooded*
(2) respiratory system	_____, _____
(3) skin covering	_____, _____, _____, _____
(4) _____	*born alive, eggs*
(5) appendages	*legs,* _____, _____
(6) habitat	_____, _____
(7) hibernation	_____, _____
(8) locomotion	_____, _____, _____, _____
(9) migration	_____, _____
(10) diet	_____, _____

B. Order the descriptors from the most significant to the least significant in showing the differences among the five classes of vertebrates.

1.	4.	7.	10.
2.	5.	8.	
3.	6.	9.	

Figure 9.2 Student exercises on descriptors

In Part A above the students drew on their own background knowledge and used dictionaries to do this task. It took the students longer to do this task than was expected. The vocabulary for many of the students was new and it was difficult for some. In Part B half of the students had a difficult time understanding the assignment, especially the ESL students. More time was given to the students to do the task. The students seemed to have a difficult time because they were still grappling with the meaning of the descriptors. This would clearly have some bearing on their ability to order the terms.

Each descriptor was considered a vocabulary item. The students had to know the words in order later, in lesson 4, to write definitions incorporating them. Part of learning the meanings of the words also entailed making judgements about which of them would be more useful in separating the vertebrates into classes. These activities were done to give the students some input as to how definitions are structured in order to prepare them for lesson 4

Lesson 3

The aim for lesson 3 was for the students to become familiar with key visuals which were used to display information on vertebrate classes. The students selected two animals from each class; mammal, bird, amphibian, reptile and fish, and filled in their descriptors in a chart. The students read descriptions of several animals and discussed which ones to include in their classification chart. The students had 15 animals in each class to choose from, as shown in Figure 9.3. Following this an example of a completed shortened chart is shown in Figure 9.4.

Mammals	*Birds*	*Amphibians*
duck-billed platypus	ostrich	toad
wallaby	king penguin	arrow-poison frog
shrew	flamingo	firebelly
horseshoe bat	mallard	mud puppy
orangutan	swan	newt
pangolin	cuckoo	axolotl
prairie dog	owl	brown spelerpes
musk-rat	kingfisher	alpine newt
dingo	woodpecker	greater siren
cheetah	cockatoo	olm
wolverine	vulture	amphiuma
grizzly bear	eagle	bull frog
beluga whale	kiwi	marsh frog
african elephant	stork	tiger salamander
three-toed sloth	secretary bird	caecilian

Reptiles	Fish
alligator	bluefin tuna
tuatara	lungfish
box turtle	great white shark
terrapin	sea lamprey
crocodile	swordfish
adder	sardine
komodo dragon	goldfish
iguana	piranha
indian cobra	flying fish
chameleon	dragonfish
anaconda	goby
boa constrictor	electric eel
gecko	atlantic salmon
moluccan skink	seahorse
viviparous lizard	sea-perch

Figure 9.3 75 vertebrates: key visual descriptions

Name	Class	Body temp	Respiratory system	Covering	Reproduction	Appendages	Habitat	Hibernation	Locomotion	Migration	Diet
wallaby	mamm	warm	lungs	fur	born alive	limbs	land	no	walk	no	herbiv
kiwi	bird	warm	lungs	feather	eggs	wings	land	no	walk	no	omniv
olm	amphib	cold	gills	scales	eggs	legs	land	no	walk	no	carniv
komodo dragon	reptile	cold	lungs	scales	eggs	legs	land	no	walk	no	carniv
dragon fish	fish	cold	gills	scales	eggs	fins	water	no	swim	no	carniv

Figure 9.4 Completed chart

Lesson 4

Here the aim was for the students to generalize from (think about and talk about) their specific examples of each class and write definitions for them (as shown in the previous figure). Before the students began writing their definitions they worked through a series of short tasks on what made a good definition. Initially the students were presented with a definition of a definition. They were then shown definitions which were very vague. For example: *a mammal is a vertebrate which has appendages*. The students were asked what was wrong with the definitions. The underlying aim was to show the students how important it was to include features that were unique to a particular class in a definition.

The students were asked, when generating their definitions, to make them precise and capable of sorting animals into the appropriate classes. This meant selecting the examples of the descriptors which were unique to a class and using this information to write definitions for each of the five classes, e.g. *A mammal is a warm blooded vertebrate which bears its young alive and* .... This involved the students in comparing and contrasting the characteristics of each class from their charts, then listing the descriptors that were unique to each class and finally using this information to write their definition.

I have included here two examples of the discussions that took place between the students that lead to their written definitions.

Example: Thai (ESL) and Dawn (First Nations)

T: A mammal is ... let's see ... umm a mammal is an animal that is got reproduction and ...

D: has..a mammal has reproduction ... they're born alive

D: locomotion

T: yeah

D: walk

T: a mammal is uh ... is a animal that is born alive

D: and is warm blooded

T: mmm yes

D: has fur

T: yeah, has fur

D: ...animal that is born alive is ...born ...alive ...er born alive ...should we use born alive or reproduction, well it's the same thing but ...yes, born alive ...alive ...is warm blooded ...or ...

The following is a first draft of Thai and Dawn's definition of a mammal: *A mammal is an animal that is born alive and breathes with lungs and lives on land.*

Example: Scott (NS) and Jenny (NS)

The dialogue concerning a definition of a bird below is based on the chart Jenny and Scott filled out above:

S: Kay, birds ...um, lay eggs ...um, what's the most important thing here?

J: I would say feathers

S: cause they're the only group that has feathers?

J: yeah, that's right

S: so it'll say ... a bird is an animal that is covered with feathers and is warm blooded with lungs

J: yeah, also laying eggs is really important

S: yeah

J: well, what we could, what we could do ...a bird is a egg-laying animal with feathers and is warm blooded

S: yeah

J: cause like, a lot of them have lungs

S: yeah, but that's not that important

J: OK, so we said a bird is an egg-laying animal with feathers and is warm blooded. OK (writing definition) a bird is an ...

S: ...egg-laying ...animal ...

S&J: ...with feathers and is warm blooded

The following is a first draft of Scott and Jenny's definition of a bird: *A bird is an egg laying animal with feathers and is warm blooded.*

Following are some examples of the students' first attempts at writing their definitions of mammals, birds, amphibians, reptiles and fish:

David (NS) and Pat (ESL)

A mammal is a warm blooded animal it has lungs and fur and it also born alive and their diet is omnivorous.

Stuart (NS) and Lucy (ESL)

A mammal is an animal that is warm blooded. Most breathe through lungs.

A bird is an animal that is warm blooded. It has lungs. They are born as eggs. They live on land. They have feathers. Most fly.

An amphibian is an animal that has smooth skin (most). They are born as eggs. Most have legs. all amphibians live in water and land. Most swim.

A reptile is an animal that is cold-blooded. They have lungs and scales. They are born as eggs. They are carnivorous.

A fish is an animal that is cold blooded. fish breathe through the gill. They have gills. they have scales. All fish are born as eggs. Most fish have fins. All fish live in water. All fish swim.

Once the definitions were completed the plan was to have the students begin classifying other animals in the list using their definitions to help them. However, the two periods that had been planned for the students to write the definitions in proved to be too little time. After examining the rough drafts of the definitions we decided to spend more time helping the students develop their definitions. This was not seen as being a negative experience but one that would provide positive opportunities for language development.

The ESL specialist suggested that the pairs of students be combined to form two groups. Each group was then responsible to write a 'group' definition for each of the vertebrate classes. The process followed in the task was identical to how the students had done their first drafts of the definitions. The students' goal was to include features in the definitions that demonstrated the uniqueness of each class. Each teacher acted as facilitator to help the groups along. Students took turns offering features they thought should be in the definition of the mammal. This discussion provided a venue for students to share the background knowledge they had on vertebrates on their charts. The sharing of this knowledge necessitated making changes in the definition as is captured in the following dialogue which occurred in one group:

Tara: I think it should be: mammals are born alive.

Jenny: But there's this animal the duck-billed platypus its a mammal and it has eggs (one of the animals in the mammal class the students had in their examples).

The teacher asked how Tara's phrase might be changed to account for this fact. Students suggested using words like 'almost all' or 'most'. The Grade 7 teacher pointed out that adding words like these (qualifiers) made the definition more accurate.

In several instances the students offered information that was at odds with the current draft definitions. This often meant restructuring the definition. The students were eager to make their definitions precise. The teachers were able to introduce the students to language structures which made their definitions more accurate. At one point the students wanted to know how more effectively to connect sections of their definitions. We introduced the students to relative clauses using the definitions.

Ten days later the students were still working on their definitions not only in science but in any spare time that could be found. The ESL specialist felt that the unit had really taken flight at this time. The Grade 7 teacher was amazed at the students' sustained interest in discussing and writing accurate definitions. Even when the students had to go on to the next lesson in the unit, that of classifying animals on a database, the content teacher, now two weeks later, was still working on the language and content accuracy of the students' definitions.

The main purpose of this lesson was for the students to think about, talk about and then write their definitions for the five vertebrate classes. This is the culmination of the last three lessons

Lessons 5, 6 and 7

Lessons 5, 6 and 7 were designed to provide the students with opportunities to use their newly created definitions. In lesson 5 the students were presented with a chart where the names and classes of the animals had been omitted. The students' task was to classify each vertebrate as a mammal, bird, amphibian, reptile or fish. The students had to use their definitions to justify their classification, e.g. 'It must be a (certain class) because it has (these features)'.

	Name of Animal	Class	Why you think it belongs to this class
1.	cat	mammal	warm-blooded, has fur
2.			
3.			
4.			
5. (etc.)			

This list includes only the characteristics of the animals. The class has been left out. Read over the characteristics of the animal and then refer to your definitions. Fill out the chart below indicating name, class (mammal, bird, amphibian, reptile, fish) and why you think it belongs to this class.

Figure 9.5 Classification exercise

In lesson 6 each pair of students was given a form with the descriptors laid out as they had earlier in the unit. This was used to retrieve information from the library resource centre on five other vertebrates.

---

(1) Prepare five index cards as follows:

Name:

Class:

Body Temp.:

Covering:

Resp. System:

etc.

(2) Select five animals, one from each class. Do not use the animals on the chart. Show your list to the teacher. At the library, research each animal and fill out an index card.

Figure 9.6 Library research

As an example of the students drawing on their background knowledge of vertebrates to do this task, one of the students commented, 'Some of the descriptors could be filled out automatically because you knew that class had certain things true all the time, like mammals are always warm-blooded.' This lesson was accomplished in one period. The Grade 7 teacher observed that the students were able to accomplish this task in one period.

In lesson 7 the students grouped the vertebrates in many ways. They grouped the animals using the descriptors. For example they asked the question, 'Which of the vertebrates are carnivorous?'

Comments and Conclusions

This unit of study was viewed by the Grade 7 teacher, the ESL specialist and myself as a success for the students involved. I have included some observations on the effectiveness of the unit and how it might be improved.

Language and content accuracy

Having examined the rough drafts of the definitions it is clear why so much time was spent developing them further. To develop language and content accuracy there seem to be at least five major areas that required attention. They included morphological and syntactical errors, rules for writing definitions and changing language to reflect content reality. Some common morphological errors were taking words like 'locomotion' and using them this way; '..its locomotion is fly or walk.' Syntactical errors were made with sentence word order and ordering adjectives, to name a few examples. The next area had to do with how definitions are structured, that there is a pattern for how information is ordered in a definition and also that definitions have a purpose. Further then, the content of the definition must be accurate and if it is not, changes must be made in the language of the definition to make it so. This was illustrated above with the duck-billed platypus example.

Finally, that there are some general patterns or rules which are brought to bear when writing a definition. These five areas were quite evident in the students' draft versions of their mammal definitions.

Integrating language and content instruction: the teachable moment

In lesson 4 the students were composing definitions of vertebrates. If one student suggested some information on a particular vertebrate which did not agree with its respective definition, the students then looked for ways to include the information in their definitions. This often meant restructuring the definition. The students were eager to make their definitions precise. The teachers were able to introduce the students to language structures which made their definitions more accurate. For example, instead of introducing the students to relative clauses in a language arts class unrelated to a content area, the biology content provided a context in which the students wanted to know what language input they needed in order to improve their definitions (thereby increasing the students' language awareness). At this point learning about relative clauses was relevant to the students.

Descriptors

It appears that the descriptors as they have been used in this unit of study have made a significant difference in how the students have learned throughout the unit. The descriptors were used in lessons 2–7 for several different tasks. By the time the students reached lesson 6 where they researched other vertebrates using the descriptors on a retrieval sheet, they were very familiar with the descriptors. The Grade 7 teacher reported that the students were able to collect information on vertebrates accurately and efficiently and had improved in their ability to do this kind of task. When comparing Parts I and II of the unit the ESL specialist said that in her experience the unit really took off when the descriptors were focused on in lesson 2. I observed students using the descriptors in the retrieval sheet not as a simple fill-in-the-blank exercise but one that appeared cognitively demanding. For example, library reference materials did not always mention if certain mammals were warm-blooded or cold-blooded. However, the students knew that mammals were warm-blooded so they were able to fill this in based on their background knowledge.

While I think the descriptors played a pivotal role in the unit, it did take some time for the students to really understand them, which meant that the unit did not proceed as well for some students. In order to improve this situation Peter suggested some preparatory work be done which would involve the students observing shore creatures, describing them, developing their own descriptors, designing a database, entering their information in the database and finally performing classificatory tasks using the database. The students would then be in a better position to understand the function of the descriptors in the vertebrate database.

Teacher planning and organization of a unit of study

Three issues were particularly relevant:

(1) *Teacher-fronted lessons versus teacher-guided lessons.*
    In this unit, out of 20 lessons, approximately two were teacher fronted and the rest were orchestrated in such a way that the students worked in pairs or in small groups. The teachers acted as guides and facilitators. The students were active participants in their learning. It appeared that there was a positive affect on the students' learning.

(2) *The science and language specialist teachers were partners in planning and teaching this unit.*
    This partnership was beneficial to the teachers and the students. Traditionally English Language Centre (ELC) teachers withdrew ESL students from their content classes in order to teach them language. In this unit of work the ELC teacher joined the content teacher in teaching the science unit. Rather than spending time with a few students who were drawn out of class the ELC teacher worked with the entire class on language issues related to science content. The teachers were able to work collaboratively, each bringing their own strengths to bear on the planning and teaching of the unit. Not only ESL students but also native-English speaking students benefited from this collaborative effort.

(3) *Suggestions for improving the resources used for this unit.*
    This unit provided learners with resources to write and apply definitions for the vertebrate classes. While the data served well as

sources of information on vertebrates and were used to develop English they were not without faults. For example, as the information exists there are very few physical descriptors, which would make it difficult for anyone to assemble a mental image of the animal. This might be rectified by adding descriptors such as size, weight and color.

A second improvement would be to use visuals of the vertebrates. I think this would make the descriptors more meaningful to the student when they can see an example of what they are reading about.

Thirdly, by adding descriptors which divide the vertebrate classes by genus and species, the number of different task design possibilities would be increased.

Last words

A combination of intentional teaching and student centred learning seems critical to integrating language and content. The teachers involved were conscious of the language and content learning outcomes for their students. The framework acted as a means to coordinate the activities the students were involved in.

These ideas have been applied with younger and older students and across subject areas with a great deal of success. These principles are offered to others who may be considering the value of organizing the language and content gains for their students.

References

Mohan, B.A. (1986) *Language and Content*. Reading, MA: Addison-Wesley.
Smith, H.A. (1977) *Exploring Living Things*. Toronto: Doubleday.

Endpiece

JOHN CLEGG

One thing which these accounts show is that there is more than one route to the same goal. In this domain, as in education generally, it is not useful to be dogmatic. Contexts are infinitely variable and a school needs to find a response which fits it. Students are also infinitely variable and need to be offered multiple pathways to mainstream education. In any one school, there may be mainstream classrooms into which some ESL students will fit easily without explicit language support. There will be other classrooms where language support can provide an ESL-friendly environment; and there may be yet others where a mainstream teacher needs to do a lot of work before ESL students will feel comfortable. In addition, the school may wish to maintain a separate capacity for reception or specific ESL needs where withdrawal is called for.

The classrooms described here also show variability in teaching style. This is also appropriate, simply because teachers tend to do things in different ways. There are many reasons for this variation. One is clearly the external factor of numbers: when ESL learners are in the majority there is pressure to allow language issues to determine both higher- and lower-order planning and teaching decisions; when they are a minority, language support can be more easily provided at the point of need. But other influences are also powerful. Pedagogical tradition, for instance, dies hard. This is especially true of the child-centred primary classroom, with its topic-driven planning and enquiry-orientated tasks. It is fortunate that this pedagogical style, adjusted in the ways this book illustrates, often coincides considerably with the style which ESL learners need. Adjustments to secondary traditions are often more painful. Finally, teachers have personal styles which must be respected. For this reason in particular, as long as teachers know what the chief needs of ESL learners are, they must be allowed to find their own ways of meeting them.

One aspect of mainstreamed ESL which the book may be accused of glossing over is the downside. As Cressida Jupp succinctly points out, things are lost in mainstream support, and things can go wrong. We are talking here mainly of matters such as contact, control, and cooperation. Contact with ESL children may be less, and ESL expertise may be more thinly spread; teachers may not be able to focus on their ESL children's needs as much as they might wish. An ESL teacher in a mainstream classroom, however equitable her team-teaching relationship, may lament the loss of control which she might have had in a withdrawal context. She may simply find it more appealing to be in charge of her own class. And cooperating with another teacher is never easy, and sometimes difficult, for both personal and logistical reasons. There is nothing to be gained by under-estimating these potential problems. What we have to do is to foresee them and use our professional skills to find ways of either avoiding them or coming to terms with them.

The abiding message of the book is that ESL is ultimately an educational enterprise, not merely a linguistic one. We may often deal in linguistic means, but we should keep our eyes firmly on educational outcomes; and we should describe these in the same terms as we describe the academic goals of children who are fluent in the medium of instruction. As long as we see ourselves simply as language-teachers, then language is all our students will get from us.

At the same time, however, mainstream education is being urged to give proper value to the role of language in learning; and over the last 30 or so years powerful schools of educational thinking have been pushing teachers in this direction (Britton, 1970; Wertsch, 1985; Wells, 1986). Such 'constructivist' views of learning in the tradition of Vygotsky (1978) and Bruner (1986) see language as the chief means wherewith the child builds knowledge. Many teachers work in ways which reflect – and indeed stimulate – these ideas, but 'language across the curriculum' (DES, 1975) as a movement has not taken widespread root in any of our four countries. New initiatives are needed to take this project forward.

Against this background ESL, with its goals redefined in academic terms, begins to look particularly interesting; not only because it shows ESL teachers how to link language to content, but also because it shows mainstream teachers how content can be informed by language. Of all the bodies of expertise available to subject teachers who want to acknowledge the role of language in their practice, ESL has probably the most user-friendly classroom achievements to its credit. As we see in the work of the authors of this book, ESL teachers have developed ways of analysing the language demands of the curriculum, of revealing relations between discourse structures and knowledge structures, and of teaching subjects in

a language-informed way. From this point of view, the potential contribution of ESL to the development of cross-curricular language development
as a whole might in the long run be just as significant as its current
second-language focus. Over the next few years, new developments in
mainstream language support will no doubt take ESL even further in the
direction of exploring how teachers teach school subjects and of making
more accessible the linguistic and cognitive processes which children
engage in when they learn them. These insights will undoubtedly meet
needs which are common to both ESL and English-fluent students.
Mainstreaming, if we get it right, can provide a critical stumulus to our
perspective on the role of language in education. It is an exciting prospect.

References

Britton, J. (1970) *Language and Learning*. London: Allen Lane.
Bruner, J.S. (1986) *Actual Minds, Possible Worlds*. Cambridge, MA: Harvard
  University Press.
DES (Department of Education and Science) (1975) *A Language for Life (The Bullock
  Report)*. London: HMSO.
Wells, G. (1986) *The Meaning Makers*. London: Hodder & Stoughton.
Wertsch, J.V. (1985) *Culture, Communication and Cognition: Vygotskian Perspectives*.
  Cambridge, MA: Cambridge University Press.
Vygotsky, L.S. (1978) *Mind in Society*. Cambridge, MA: Harvard University Press